War Made Easy

War Made Easy

How Presidents and Pundits Keep Spinning Us to Death

NORMAN SOLOMON

WILEY

John Wiley & Sons, Inc.

Published by John Wiley & Sons, Inc., Hoboken, New Jersey
Published simultaneously in Canada

Song lyrics from "I-Feel-Like-I'm-Fixin'-To-Die Rag" words and music by Joe McDonald © 1965 Alkatraz Corner Music Co., BMI, and from "An Untitled Protest" words and music by Joe McDonald © 1968 Joyful Wisdom Music Co., BMI. Used by permission.

Design and composition by Navta Associates, Inc.

For general information about our other products and services, please contact our Customer Care Department within the United States at (800) 762-2974, outside the United States at (317) 572-3993 or fax (317) 572-4002.

Wiley also publishes its books in a variety of electronic formats. Some content that appears in print may not be available in electronic books. For more information about Wiley products, visit our web site at www.wiley.com.

Library of Congress Cataloging-in-Publication Data:

Solomon, Norman, date.
   War made easy : how presidents and pundits keep spinning us to death / Norman Solomon.
      p. cm.
   Includes bibliographical references and index.
   ISBN-13 978-0-471-69479-3 (cloth)
   ISBN-10 0-471-69479-7 (cloth)
   1. War—Press coverage—United States. 2. Press and politics—United States.
3. Government and the press—United States. 4. United States—Foreign relations—20th century. I. Title.
PN4784.W37S65 2005
070.4'4935502—dc22   2004023477

Printed in the United States of America

10 9 8 7 6 5 4 3 2 1

Contents

Prologue

Building Agendas for War

Sometimes a war begins suddenly, filling the national horizon with a huge insistent flash. At other times, over a period of months or years, a low distant rumble gradually turns into a roar. But in any event, the democratic role of citizens is not simply to observe and obey the exigencies of war. In the United States, what we think is supposed to matter. And for practical reasons, top officials in Washington don't want to seem too far out of step with voters. Looking toward military action overseas, the president initiates a siege of public opinion on the home front—a battleground where media spin is the main weapon, and support for war is the victory. From the outset, the quest is for an image of virtual consensus behind the commander in chief. A media campaign for hearts and minds at home means going all out to persuade us that the next war is as good as a war can be—necessary, justified, righteous, and worth any sorrows to be left in its wake.

For three decades the Dominican Republic suffered under the rapacious dictatorship of Rafael Trujillo, until his assassination in 1961 opened up new possibilities for the Caribbean nation. Free elections came in December 1962, and Juan Bosch received almost two-thirds of the ballots cast. After seven months of the Bosch presidency, a military coup swept him out of office.

In late April 1965 a popular uprising gained momentum until it seemed to be on the verge of restoring Bosch to power. But President Lyndon Johnson quickly sent in Marines and went on television to explain that military action was necessary to rescue Americans.[1] Other justifications soon followed.

Nearly forty years later, one of Johnson's assistants recalled what went on behind the scenes. "With our troops already in the air,"

Richard Goodwin wrote, "Johnson called a White House meeting to explain the decision he had already made. Gathered in the Cabinet Room, we were told by William Raborn, the incoming head of the CIA, that Communists had infiltrated, perhaps even dominated, the Bosch insurgency. That belief, not any supposed bloodshed, was of course the real reason for Johnson's intervention. After the meeting, Bill Moyers, also a Johnson aide, and I met privately with some CIA staff members. 'Who were these Communists,' we asked, 'and how do we know?' We were given incredibly flimsy evidence, such as that one Bosch confederate had been seen in an apartment building suspected of housing a Communist cell. It proved nothing. Yet 20,000 Marines had been sent to forestall this enemy whose very existence was suspect."[2]

White House phone tapes from that era, released in 2001, provide insights into President Johnson's decision to launch an invasion of the Dominican Republic. The tapes are especially helpful to researchers because he made prodigious use of the telephone. "Johnson chose to commit troops despite what he knew to be a lack of solid evidence of communist danger," wrote Alan McPherson, a scholar who assessed the recordings. The president "was perhaps more concerned with the domestic political fallout from the fear of 'another Cuba' in the Western Hemisphere than he was with the reality itself of a communist takeover."[3] On the morning of April 26, 1965, with the pro-Bosch revolt gaining ground, Johnson spoke to Thomas Mann, an assistant secretary of state.

Johnson: "We're going to have to really set up that government down there and run it and stabilize it some way or other. This Bosch is no good. . . ."

Mann: "He's no good at all. . . . If we don't get a decent government in there, Mr. President, we get another Bosch. It's just going to be another sinkhole."

Johnson: "Well that's what you ought to do. That's your problem. You better figure it out."

Mann: ". . . The man to get back, I think, is Balaguer. He's the one that ran way ahead in the polls."

Johnson: "Well, try to do it, try to do it."[4]

The day after that conversation, the Dominican uprising surged through Santo Domingo.[5] Back in Washington, news of the advance spiked up the alarm among policymakers. The White House had been more than rooting against the rebellion—it actively sided with the Dominican army's move to smash it, approving bombardment of the city along with a major tank attack by infantry forces. The U.S. embassy cabled that it had okayed the assault "even though it could mean more bloodshed" because "it is the only way to forestall a left-ist takeover."[6] But the attack failed, and President Johnson opted for an invasion.

To present the U.S. public with an anti-Communist explanation, researcher McPherson notes, "Johnson had to make two qualitative leaps in his logic. The first was that leftist rebels were trained in Cuba, and the second was that those trained in Cuba were led by Castro. There was apparently scant evidence for the first and none for the second, but Johnson made both leaps with ease. In so doing, he could justify the intervention on the grounds that the United States prevented an international communist aggression."[7]

Johnson gradually fed that justification to the public. During a televised speech on April 28, announcing that some Marines had gone ashore in Santo Domingo, he held back from claiming that the action was to counter communism. Instead, the initial emphasis was on safeguarding U.S. citizens in the country. (Decades later, newspaper columnist Jan Glidewell, who had participated in the invasion as a young Marine, remarked: "Johnson said we were being sent in to 'protect American lives.' Nobody I spoke to ever saw an American who wasn't either wearing a military uniform or a Red Cross armband."[8])

New waves of U.S. troops were reaching Santo Domingo. On April 30, during a second speech on television, Johnson mentioned "signs that people trained outside the Dominican Republic are seeking to gain control."[9] Two days later, LBJ pulled out the rhetorical stops, telling a national TV audience that "what began as a popular democratic revolution, committed to democracy and social justice, very shortly moved and was taken over and really seized and placed into the hands of a band of Communist conspirators."[10] As a practical political matter, the decision to blame Communists was a way of throwing down a gauntlet about the invasion.

"It seems that Johnson made the statement not because he had new evidence," McPherson points out, "but because a key liberal, John Bartlow Martin, had returned from Santo Domingo that afternoon and had made the same assertion in a press conference."[11] Martin was a former U.S. ambassador to the Dominican Republic with a reputation as a judicious diplomat; when he told reporters that in recent days a revolt by Bosch's Partido Revolucionario Dominicano had fallen under "the domination of Castro/Communists and other violent extremists," President Johnson was elated.[12] That same afternoon, Johnson expressed fervent appreciation to Martin during a phone conversation, saying "I'm very, very proud of you and what you have done." The commander in chief assured the diplomat that "there's no gunboat stuff about this" and then underscored Martin's special value at that moment of crisis: "I think you ought to tell about your sympathies and your feelings and how you are opposed to dictatorship. . . . Maybe you, as a man that's not responsible for this operation, could talk better than somebody else."[13]

It was a classic moment. With new U.S. military action in the spotlight, the president valued the political cover being provided by someone known for restraint and democratic principles. In connection with the quickly launched invasion of the Dominican Republic, the helpful fig leaf was provided by John Bartlow Martin. Almost forty years later, during the drawn-out preliminaries before the invasion of Iraq, similar services—on a much grander scale—were to be provided by Colin Powell.

Whatever dangers may have loomed for American citizens inside the Dominican Republic, they were gone in a jiffy. "At the time, there were nearly 2,000 U.S. citizens in the Dominican Republic," international law professor John Quigley has written. "Of these, one thousand lived in Santo Domingo, the only scene of hostilities. On April 27, the day preceding the intervention, 1,172 of them were evacuated by ship and helicopter by the U.S. Navy, without the landing of troops. On April 28, but before the Marines arrived, another 684 were evacuated by the same means. In all, then, 1,856 Americans had already been evacuated before the intervention."[14] But in the days that followed, U.S. Marines and army soldiers kept landing.

Soon after Pentagon troops stormed the beaches by the thousands, President Johnson declared that "99 percent of our reason for going in there was to try to provide protection for these American lives and the lives of other nationals."[15] The pretext was so thin that, as *Washington Post* diplomatic reporter Murrey Marder noted in an article a couple of decades later, "the actual request for American intervention did not even mention saving lives when it first came from the military junta ruling the Dominican Republic."[16] At a closed session of the Senate Foreign Relations Committee, 2½ months after the invasion, Assistant Secretary of State Mann testified that the U.S. government had asked its ambassador in Santo Domingo to see if the Dominican military's head man would "be willing to give us an additional message which places the request squarely on the need to save American lives." In testimony that remained secret for many years, Mann told senators on the committee: "All we requested was whether he would be willing to change the basis for this from one of fighting communism to one of protecting American lives."[17]

The invasion had some domestic critics, including Senator Robert Kennedy and print outlets such as the *New York Times* and the *New Yorker* magazine. But the White House's sales job was quite successful at home—overcoming the scattered qualms about dubious rationales for the war or its death toll, variously reported at between twenty-six and thirty-one invading soldiers and about three thousand Dominicans, many of them civilians. Along the way, reassurance materialized from the Organization of American States.

Under enormous U.S. pressure, the OAS stepped into line, retroactively endorsing the invasion and providing soldiers a few weeks later to help patrol the Dominican Republic. Most of those troops—1,129 of them—came from Brazil, where a repressive dictatorship had recently begun when a military coup toppled a democratically elected government with U.S. help.[18] Some of the other soldiers in the "Inter-American Peace Force" were supplied by such odious regimes as fascistic Paraguay and Anastasio Somoza's Nicaragua. "The multinational force justified what many considered a precipitous act on the part of the United States," according to writer Juleyka Lantigua, who was born and raised in the Dominican Republic. "Ironically, the unified effort violated the OAS charter which, in Article 15, stipulated that no member state had 'the right to intervene in the internal or external affairs of any other member.'"[19]

Like numerous other Latin American diplomats, Clara Nieto—part of Colombia's U.N. delegation at the time—saw the invasion of the Dominican Republic as "nothing short of a scandal." She has described the reaction this way: "Though both citizens and outsiders condemned the invasion, public opinion polls indicated that the immense majority in the United States supported their president, satisfied with the way in which he crushed this new upsurge in revolutionary activity." Nieto added: "A messianic and interventionist fever gripped the majorities in the United States Congress. In September 1965, by a vote of 312 to 54, the House of Representatives approved a resolution authorizing the government to intervene in the affairs of other nations, including armed intervention, where there was a risk of Communist subversion, thus legitimizing the Johnson Doctrine."[20]

The U.S. government needed a new leader for the Dominican Republic, and Joaquin Balaguer fit the bill. He'd been appointed vice president by Trujillo in 1956 and became a figurehead president in 1960 before losing his job. But in the late spring of 1965, with U.S. soldiers in full control weeks after the invasion, that special someone was prepared to take power. "With imperial arrogance," Nieto writes, "Johnson kept the troops and special advisers in place and intervened in the country's affairs at his whim, including placing former president Joaquin Balaguer once again in the presidency; living in exile in New York, Balaguer had served as an adviser to Johnson during the invasion."[21] For the next few decades, in and out of office, Balaguer thrived while Dominican society as a whole sank farther into dire poverty.[22]

Twenty years after the invasion, an illuminating *New York Times* story drew on a week of interviews. "One point on which there is little controversy among Dominicans . . . is that the reasons Mr. Johnson gave publicly for intervening seem to have no basis in fact," the newspaper found. "Nearly all those interviewed said they believed the danger to the several hundred Americans then in the capital was minimal and that the smattering of virtually leaderless Dominican Communists posed no serious threat to anyone." Even a key military leader against the efforts to reinstate Juan Bosch to the presidency in 1965 disparaged the merits of Washington's case, the *Times* reported: "General Elias Wessin y Wessin, retired, one of the most prominent troop commanders opposing Mr. Bosch, said he never believed that American civilians were in danger or that there was a possibility of the Dominican Republic becoming a second Cuba."[23]

Late April has sometimes been a time of upheaval in the Dominican Republic. On the thirty-second anniversary of the uprising that precipitated the invasion, demonstrations in the capital turned into clashes between students and soldiers. The Autonomous University of Santo Domingo suspended classes "to avoid further unrest," the Associated Press reported. "The Dominican flag was lowered to half-staff at the university as a symbol of mourning over the invasion."[24] A dean of social sciences at the University of Calgary, Stephen J. Randall, calling the invasion "the first direct military intervention by the United States in Latin America since the late 1920s," commented that "the direct result was the establishment of a repressive political regime under Balaguer and the repression of Partido Revolucionario Dominicano activists."[25]

Several decades later, the impacts on the Dominican Republic were ongoing. "After the invasion, Balaguer stayed in power for many of the next 28 years, winning one tainted election after another," writer Lantigua recounted in 2000. "And the legacy of 1965 lives on. Dominican leaders still rule on behalf of a privileged social class and foreign powers. Presidents still arrive at the National Palace on the shoulders of mighty backroom political pacts with Balaguer and his strongmen. And corruption is rampant. Thirty-five years ago, the Marines prevented the people of the Dominican Republic from determining their political fate. This is not an anniversary that many people in my country are celebrating."[26]

When a former president of the country, Leonel Fernandez, won the election in 2004 to regain the top job after four years out of office, he draped himself in Juan Bosch's mantle, leading a victory rally to the cemetery where Bosch was buried and calling Bosch his "spiritual guide." Yet Fernandez was a former protégé of Balaguer, and—more significantly, as the Associated Press noted—"his current conservative economic policies bear little resemblance to Bosch's original ideas of land reform and bold moves to aid the poor."[27] Forty years after the invasion, the Dominican Republic was still impoverished and policymakers in Washington would not view its president as "no good."

In retrospect, the 1965 invasion of the Dominican Republic foreshadowed a series of U.S. military actions in the Western Hemisphere and beyond. While covert intervention by the CIA in Latin America was as constant as the seasons, the overwhelming arrival of so many U.S. troops in the small country was a kind of political and media prototype for a pair of lightning-strike invasions in the 1980s— Grenada and Panama—as well as, in more complicated ways, the relatively limited U.S. military interventions in Haiti during the Clinton and George W. Bush administrations. In each case, the man living in the White House found ways to set the media agenda for public approval to affirm the kind of desire expressed by Lyndon Johnson to Assistant Secretary of State Mann: "We're going to have to really set up that government down there and run it and stabilize it some way or other."[28]

Since the 1960s, the USA's favorite wars have been quick and—for most people back home, anyway—"successful" at generating some sense of national accomplishment.[29] With the clear exceptions of Vietnam and the aftermath of the Iraq invasion, modern wars have not been terribly divisive in the U.S. political arena. As matters of popular perceptions, we nicely took care of the Dominican Republic, Grenada, and Panama in the hemisphere; likewise, farther away, the Gulf War, Yugoslavia, and Afghanistan. Smaller and more fleeting interventions—the bombing of Libya in 1986, the firing of missiles into Sudan and Afghanistan in 1998, or the ill-fated expeditions to Lebanon in 1983 and Somalia in 1993—are praised as missions accomplished, denigrated as inadequate actions, or ruefully written off as experiments with bad results. Unless the president bites off more than the Pentagon can effectively chew, most Americans have found Uncle Sam's military ventures to be suitable for acceptance, if only in the form of passivity. Unhappiness festers and grows when the war cannot be wrapped up in weeks or months—with the commanders in Washington finding that they cannot "win the peace" without prolonged and difficult involvement of U.S. troops, while the justifications for the war become increasingly suspect to the public—when, in short, might hasn't made everything seem right.

The tragic invasion of the Dominican Republic highlights some chronic elements of how the people of the United States have been sold a succession of wars, in their names and with their tax dollars, time after time. Whatever the pace of agenda-building—whether the rationales for a war suddenly burst into news media or gradually percolate into daily coverage—the executive branch policy players, their congressional supporters, and varied media enablers come to insist that military action is necessary to prevent all manner of calamities, such as the killing of American citizens, the further triumph of tyrants, or the development of weapons of mass destruction in the wrong hands. Any number of mainstream journalists seem willing to take the administration's word for it when "intelligence" is in the air. Skepticism and harsh judgments, if they come at all, tend to emerge quite a bit later: after bombs have fallen and after soldiers have marched into battle, some never to return, many more to go home with wounds to body and spirit. As for the people at the other end of America's cutting-edge weaponry, their lives, too—in far greater numbers—are also shattered.

Intense public controversy may precede the onset of warfare, but the modern historical record is clear: No matter what the Constitution says, in actual practice the president has the whip hand when it comes to military deployments—and if a president really wants a war, he'll get one. That can hardly be said about congressional passage of land-mark domestic legislation. (A comprehensive overhaul of the nation's health-care system, for instance, is likely to be more elusive than another war.) In matters of war and peace, the White House is much less constrained by other branches of government.

When the president of the United States is determined to go to war, a vast array of leverage and public-relations acumen can and will be brought to bear. Consent of the governed takes form as deference, active or tacit, gained at least long enough for the war to proceed. What comes to the surface later—including evidence of prewar decep-tions and wartime distortions—may cause us to feel that we live in a society with freedoms sufficient to make sure the truth will shine through, sooner or later. But war happens in the interim—after widely told lies are widely believed and before the emergence of some clarity in the mass media. The information that comes out later does not come out soon enough to prevent the unspeakable. No matter how much we follow the news, we rarely know more than little of the human consequences.

A quarter of a century after the Marines landed in Santo Domingo, a different set of U.S. troops went into action nine hundred miles south-west of the Dominican Republic. The new invasion was a rousing success.[30] And plenty of breathlessly reported details reinforced the understanding that forces of evil had been suitably vanquished.

With a Panama dateline the day after Christmas 1989, one *New York Times* story led off this way:

> The United States military headquarters here, which has por-trayed General Manuel Antonio Noriega as an erratic, cocaine-

snorting dictator who prays to voodoo gods, announced today that the deposed leader wore red underwear and availed himself of prostitutes.

Furthermore, the American command, headed by General Maxwell Thurman, asserted in a two-and-a-half-page report to the press, that when the United States invasion took place last week, "Noriega's first action was not to call his wife, but rather his mistress" and her family.

"According to our sources," the statement continued, "he never attempted to call his wife."[31]

The Pentagon's news release concluded: "The story of this truly evil man continues to unfold with bizarre evidence of his incredible life style. We will keep you updated on other details as they become available."[32]

In passing, the *New York Times* account described Noriega as "a longtime intelligence officer and onetime collaborator with the Central Intelligence Agency." In fact, the period of collaboration included Noriega's theft of the 1984 election in Panama for his chosen presidential candidate, Nicolas Ardito Barletta, with Secretary of State George Shultz attending the inauguration. During his visit, Shultz lauded the country's "democratization." But after a falling-out later in the decade, few drops of ink were available to dwell on the U.S. government's prior embrace of the "truly evil man." (It was a pattern to be repeated less than a year after the invasion of Panama, as top U.S. officials and journalists worked overtime to belatedly decry the evilness of another erstwhile Washington pal, Saddam Hussein, when Iraqi troops moved into Kuwait.) The Panamanian dictator's willingness to cross Washington made him no longer an asset. Noriega's transgressions included a halt to his cooperation with Uncle Sam's policies fueling war in Nicaragua.[33]

Front and center in Washington's 1989 denunciations was evidence of Noriega's involvement in drug trafficking. Yet such evidence had been well known in Washington for years while the Reagan administration made nice with Noriega. As Norman Bailey, a member of the National Security Council during the Reagan presidency, was to testify at a congressional hearing, by the early 1980s there was "not a 'smoking gun' but rather a 21-gun barrage of evidence" of Noriega's drug trafficking.[34] No problem—the joint work between Washington and Noriega persisted with winks and nods. In May 1986 a letter to Panama's dictator from the administrator of the U.S. Drug Enforcement Agency, John C. Lawn, was quite complimentary: "I would like to take this opportunity to reiterate my deep appreciation for the vigorous anti-drug policy that you have adopted."[35]

New derogatory information about Noriega leaked into the U.S. press when the summer of 1986 got under way, but the White House praised him, as the Associated Press reported: "The Reagan administration told Congress Thursday that Panama is providing useful cooperation against drug trafficking and money laundering and sought to disassociate itself from a published report alleging personal involvement by the chief of Panamanian armed forces [Noriega] in such activities."[36] At the same time, not coincidentally, top officials in Washington still viewed Noriega as an ally against the Sandinistas. The *Los Angeles Times* cited accounts from congressional sources that, in the newspaper's words, "Noriega is believed to have a connection to U.S.-backed rebels fighting the Sandinista government of Nicaragua."[37]

While he played ball with Washington, the strongman was a good man. But later in 1986 and in 1987, signs increased that Noriega was no longer a reliable helper.[38] Noriega's noncooperation and even interference with the Contra war led to a falling-out.[39] "Noriega was a means to an end," columnist Haynes Johnson recounted a couple of days after the invasion began. "In this decade, the desired end has been to provide secret help to U.S.-backed Nicaraguan Contra forces. For years, Noriega had been a Central Intelligence Agency 'asset.' In the Reagan era, he established a personal relationship with William J. Casey, the late director of central intelligence. What Casey wanted, and received, from Noriega was his assistance in facilitating arms shipments to the Contras. Through his control of Panama's security apparatus, Noriega could arrange Panamanian 'end user' certificates that legitimized arms shipments to Panama. Once the arms had arrived there, Noriega was able to sell them to the highest bidder, legally and with no questions asked."[40] Johnson's column appeared not in an obscure publication, but in the *Washington Post*. Yet its observations weren't the sort to reverberate in the national media echo chamber—and anyway, by the time that column reached print, the intervention horse was already out of the barn and galloping down a bloody trail.

The invasion of Panama followed a series of White House moves on economic, military, and media fronts after Noriega had fallen off the CIA payroll and out of favor. By early 1988, a U.S. campaign of economic sanctions was causing severe hardships among Panama's poor. In May 1989, authorities in the Noriega government voided the results of a nationwide election that he lost. In the United States, television footage vividly showed pro-Noriega goons beating up opposition partisans on Panama City streets. In typical coverage, ABC *Nightline* correspondent Judd Rose narrated—with a sardonic reference to "democracy, Panamanian style"—footage of a journalist struggling for breath after being attacked by some of Noriega's thugs.[41] (Two months earlier, when the U.S.-backed military in El Salvador had murdered three journalists during Salvadoran elections, ABC and the other networks were not nearly so energetic about scrutinizing or condemning the antidemocratic violence.) President George H. W. Bush responded by urging the Panamanian military to overthrow the general's regime and ordering two thousand more Pentagon troops into the U.S. zone in Panama. Relaying the spin, a United Press International dispatch on May 15 said the deployment aimed "to protect Americans based in the Panama Canal Zone." The UPI story added: "The administration has indicated that it was not interested in military intervention but was concerned for the safety of U.S. citizens."[42]

By late summer 1989, Panama was provoking high-level comparisons to the Third Reich. Officials in Washington denounced Noriega for remaining in power. And they pointed to his indictment by federal grand juries in Florida the previous year for drug trafficking. "That is aggression as surely as Adolf Hitler's invasion of Poland 50 years ago was aggression," Deputy Secretary of State Lawrence Eagleburger declared at a meeting of the Organization of American States. "It is aggression against us all, and some day it must be brought to an end."[43] At the same time that an OAS report criticized Noriega's government for human rights abuses, the organization also faulted the United States for recent military exercises that could increase political tensions in Panama; naturally, Washington heralded only the criticism of Noriega. Signals abounded that U.S. military maneuvers were just getting started. An unnamed State Department official told the press: "Clearly, the multilateral approach didn't work with Noriega, and so we are now looking at other options for acting alone. At this point, I wouldn't rule anything out."[44]

While violently authoritarian, Noriega's reign was mild compared to the murderous U.S.-backed regimes that were entrenched in El Salvador and Guatemala. But on the whole, news coverage in the United States took cues from the Bush-Quayle administration, increasingly targeting Noriega as an intolerable blight on the hemisphere. The main drumbeat encouraged the White House to get tough with the Panamanian "strongman," although there were some caveats. The *Boston Globe* editorialized that the Bush team "has made matters worse in recent weeks by ratcheting up a dangerous game of military chicken"—"repeatedly sending forces out of the Panama Canal Zone and into contact with Noriega's troops. . . . The maneuvers are justified as asserting the rights the U.S. has under the Panama Canal treaties. Yet how essential are 'hostage-rescue' exercises that involve sudden troop deployments and low-altitude buzzing of Panamanian government buildings with assault helicopters?" Prophetically, the editorial warned: "The saber-rattling could get someone shot."[45]

But when it came to U.S. policy toward Panama, the main critical theme revolved around the notion that Bush wasn't getting tough enough fast enough. A failed coup attempt in early autumn 1989 set off alarm bells in the U.S. media echo chamber. On Capitol Hill, members of both parties were caustic, sometimes appearing to cast aspersions on the president's nationalistic virility. One GOP member, Representative Dan Burton, complained that the president's "accommodating approach" to Congress "is giving Bush a weak-kneed image in foreign affairs."[46] Many Democrats joined in, huffing and puffing. "And for the United States, with all of our strength and force and all of our belief in democracy, to stand by—two miles away as the crow flies—and do nothing, and allow these people to fail, personally I think is wrong," said David Boren, the Democrat chairing the Senate Intelligence Committee.[47] Many conservative outlets took to goading the Republican president in a spirit recapped by a *Washington Times* editorial that bemoaned the U.S. failure to remove Noriega: "When October's coup against him foundered and the U.S. national security establishment found 50 plausible reasons not to help rebellious troops kick the tyrant into the canal, he read President Bush's lips—and realized the president had nothing to tell him."[48]

Tensions escalated, and U.S. enthusiasts for military intervention got a break when Panama's National Assembly seemed to engage in some *Mouse That Roared* posturing with a declaration that Panama was in a "state of war" with the United States. But as author John Quigley has noted in *The Ruses for War*, "Since we had 12,000 troops stationed in Panama at the time, it would have been foolhardy for Panama to start anything." So why the "state of war" resolution? "In all likelihood," Quigley wrote, "the motive was to rally the population behind General Noriega by showing the United States trying to bring him down through military pressure and financial sanctions." The resolution also conferred on Noriega the names "chief of government" and "maximum leader of national liberation"—a fact that Quigley saw as significant: "The pronouncement about a state of war was a basis for giving General Noriega these new titles. The Bush administration kept close enough watch on Panamanian politics for it to understand that this was the import of the December 15 resolution. While the administration knew that the resolution was not a formal declaration of war, it seized on the opportunity to take the phrase 'state of war' out of context, in order to find a pretext to invade."[49]

Predictable incidents swiftly provided fodder to the likes of the *Washington Times*: Its December 19 editorial told readers that "the general's praetorians, egged on by a mob, fired on unarmed U.S. Army officers, killing one [actually, a Marine] and drawing blood from another. Around the same time, PDF [Panamanian Defense Forces] hoodlums seized a U.S. Navy officer and his wife and brutalized them. The officer was repeatedly kicked in the groin and beaten, while his wife was slammed against a wall and made to stand with her arms over her head until she collapsed, then threatened with sexual assault."[50]

An invasion of Panama began promptly before dawn on December 20, with about twenty-four thousand U.S. troops in action. Thanks to a Washington-run media pool system, the TV networks weren't getting much of the bang-bang footage they craved, but that didn't stop the fusillades of rapid-fire spin. "Well, there are many reasons why Panama's a problem for the United States," anchor Peter Jennings told ABC evening news viewers half a day after the invasion began. "It's been a base for narcotics trafficking, a center for money laundering, a transit point for arms shipments to anti-American guerrilla forces elsewhere in the hemisphere and, according to a study done by the National Security Council, a major center of illegal technology transfers to the Soviet Union. All of the above with the approval, often the direct involvement, of one man, who tonight has a million-dollar price on his head: Manuel Noriega."[51]

Not to put all the president's rationales in one basket, the White House quickly provided four reasons for the invasion. The war's supporters could take their pick. Even if some of the reasons didn't seem to pan out, others would. News accounts could neatly summarize the objectives—in the words of one newspaper, "to protect the lives of Americans in Panama, to restore the democratic process there, to preserve the Panama Canal treaties and to apprehend Noriega."[52] Overall, the news media were in no mood to poke holes in the list.

Yet there was scant indication that American lives were in danger (before the invasion, anyway); the cited incidents appeared to be spontaneous rather than preplanned by any Panamanian authorities. As for the "democratic process," it had been throttled in Panama for many years while Washington worked well with Noriega. And there was no basis for claiming a threat to the canal treaties or the canal—in fact, the U.S. invasion itself had just forced closure of the Panama Canal for the first time in its seventy-five-year history. "There is no evidence that might prove that Noriega or his forces had any intention of attacking the installations of the waterway," the Madrid newspaper *El Pais* reported.[53] "Even after the invasion began," John Quigley noted, "our forces showed no concern that the canal might be sabotaged, and while they took no precautions to protect the canal, the PDF made no moves against it." Quigley concluded: "Of the long list of reasons Bush gave for invading Panama, none withstood scrutiny."[54]

Enthusiasm for the invasion was overwhelming on Capitol Hill, as bipartisanship clicked its heels and saluted the commander in chief. "We had no other choice," said Democratic congressman Bill Richardson of New Mexico. "Noriega was like a cancer. He was making us a laughingstock. He was baiting us. He was threatening American lives and I believe that the action was justified."[55] In his role as Senate majority leader, George Mitchell recited customary lines: "I support the president's decision. It was made necessary by the reckless actions of General Noriega."[56] And there were the usual vague, almost mystical references to special information available only to in-the-know officials. Nicholas Mavroules, a Democrat on the House Armed Services Committee, had this to say after a White House briefing: "I believe that intelligence reports must have indicated Mr. Noriega really had a chip on his shoulder and was taking control. The president must have felt he had to move to protect our citizens."[57]

There was little media space for voices like House member Ron

Dellums, who provided some context scarcely noted in news accounts: "Manuel Noriega is a direct creation—and consequence—of our hemispheric militarism. A CIA 'asset' for almost 20 years, he was one of the 'tools' employed by the Reagan administration to help destabilize another foreign nation—despite the fact that he was a known drug thug who plays a central role in international drug trafficking."[58] On a similar note, Representative Don Edwards described the invasion as "a trigger-happy act of gunboat diplomacy that continues our mindless, 100-year abuse of small Central American nations."[59]

Such dissent was threshed as political hay by the president's party. Edward Rollins, cochair of the National Republican Congressional Committee, sent out individualized news releases to media in the home districts of five antiwar congressmen. The "first instinct" of the dissenting House member, Rollins charged, "was to blame President Bush and sympathize with General Noriega." The message to Oregon media declared: "While American soldiers are fighting and dying on the beaches and streets of Panama, Peter DeFazio is sitting in the cozy confines of Eugene, Oregon, criticizing them. Congressman DeFazio's apologist attitude is inexcusable."[60] It was boilerplate demagoguery, equating opposition to U.S. policy with support for a foreign dictator and conflating a critique of the president's orders with criticism of U.S. troops.

During the first day of warfare, the Pentagon said, 21 U.S. soldiers had been killed and 208 wounded. In passing, a typical news account added: "Over 100 Panamanian civilians and 58 members of the Panamanian Defense Forces have also been reported killed."[61] After Noriega "thanked his supporters in a 52-second radio broadcast," U.S. forces quickly "blew up the station's transmission tower."[62]

The next day, as fighting raged in Panama, the president told a White House news conference how he might make the situation clear to Soviet president Mikhail Gorbachev, who'd been critical of the invasion. Not only was it "real bad" for an American serviceman to be killed,[63] Bush said, but "if they threaten and brutalize the wife of an American citizen, sexually threatening the lieutenant's wife while kicking him in the groin over and over again, then Mr. Gorbachev, please understand this president is going to do something about it."[64] The reprised morality play went over big with U.S. media.[65]

Two and a half days into the invasion, the Pentagon airlifted two thousand more troops into Panama, which the Associated Press described as "still chaotic."[66] Hemispheric opinion could be gauged by the votes of delegates to the Organization of American States. While six countries abstained, twenty voted to deplore the invasion and urged the U.S. government to immediately withdraw its troops. The only vote against the resolution came from the United States. It was, the *Washington Post* reported, "the first time since the hemispheric body's founding 42 years ago that it has formally criticized the United States."[67] But the Yankee delegation did win a linguistic skirmish over the resolution: while the Spanish version said OAS members "deeply deplore [*deplorar profundamente*] the military intervention in Panama," the English text was softened to "deeply regret."[68] That was helpful for spin, as when AP reported that a "State Department official, who spoke on condition of anonymity, noted that the language of the resolution was to 'regret' rather than condemn."[69]

President Bush said the U.S. servicemen would remain in Panama "to do what is necessary."[70] Meanwhile, a U.S. military spokesperson told about the discovery of a 50-pound supply of cocaine in one of Noriega's private locations. The head of the U.S. Southern Command, General Thurman, upped it to 120 pounds.

The Pentagon was busily dribbling out juicy stories to pools of reporters, who funneled the salacious tales to colleagues and the waiting world. Seventy-two hours after the battles had begun, a *Washington Post* article led with the kind of fixation that was by then a media obsession: While searching for Noriega during the first hours of the invasion, U.S. troops had found at a suspected Noriega residence, "among other things, a vat of blood, animal entrails and other evidence of dabbling in the widespread Caribbean voodoo-like cult of santeria."[71]

Colonel Mike Snell, of the Task Force Bayonet Command, said: "General Noriega kept his Brazilian witches here. This was the brewery for the witches, if you will."[72] Another *Post* article the same day included an indication that on Capitol Hill, fascination with the occult—or at least with Noriega's reported occultist leanings—was substantial. A pair of Southern gentlemen in the world's oldest deliberative body conveyed some relevant intelligence. The chairman of the Senate Armed Services Committee, Sam Nunn, and fellow senator John Warner "said they were told there was evidence of witchcraft at one Noriega hideaway. And defense officials here and in Panama made the same assertion."[73] High-ranking military men were quick to elucidate. General Thurman informed reporters that "voodoo practitioners . . . practiced rituals for Noriega's protection."[74] The tone of much of the coverage gave new meaning to the term *witch hunt*. One article reported: "The Army apparently just missed capturing four Brazilian witchcraft specialists, said Lieutenant Curtis Vinyard."[75]

A front-page story in the *St. Louis Post-Dispatch* added such intelligence as: "In a bedroom were left gold-colored high heels, pantyhose, face cream and women's garments."[76] Like many others, the article emphasized opulence, as though it somehow underscored the extent of Noriega's depravity: "Signs of luxury, including Noriega's Mercedes-Benz, were everywhere. At his headquarters was a 30-foot French-style marble dining room."[77] At Noriega's Fort Amador facilities in Panama City, the invaders encountered jewelry, art, a movie theater, and antique guns—causing the operations director for the Joint Chiefs of Staff to tell reporters in Washington that the GIs were "stunned. . . . They saw opulence unlike anything they've ever seen before."[78] Numerous accounts referred to finding pornographic movies.

Many stories told about the discovery of a framed photo or poster of Hitler on a bunker wall. A wire service picture appeared in newspapers on Christmas Day with this caption: "Pfc. Michael McCann of Texas looks over a portrait of Hitler in the office of General Manuel Noriega in the Panamanian Defense Forces headquarters in Panama City."[79] Few news stories mentioned that photos of the Israeli general Moshe Dayan and Mother Teresa had also made Noriega's cut to be hung on his walls. Perhaps more unfortunate was the scarcity of mention in the U.S. press that, as the *Jerusalem Post* reported, "[S]everal prominent Panamanian Jews . . . served in high positions under deposed dictator Manuel Noriega." The Hitler spin about Noriega was new to Moises Mizrachi, chairman of the Anti-Defamation League of B'Nai B'rith of Panama, who said that the story about Nazi paraphernalia in Noriega's lair was a "big surprise . . . because Noriega was always so friendly to Israel."[80]

The situation on the ground in Panama was not turning out to be as forecast from Washington. Problems went well beyond Noriega's initial success at eluding capture. Under the headline "Invasion That Became a Nightmare," the *Times* of London published a grim news account:

Three days after Bush pronounced Operation Just Cause "pretty well wrapped up," U.S. officials admitted that American troops could be involved in urban warfare for weeks or months.

A usually optimistic American military commander had to concede that things had not worked out quite as planned. . . . Another weary commander added: "Cities eat up manpower very quickly, and in Panama City everyone has a gun."

The scene in Panama City is one of unrelenting anarchy. Heavy fighting broke out for the third day running as armed mobs roamed the streets. . . .

The invasion has destroyed the last vestige of civilization in a city which once considered itself the Paris of Latin America. . . .

The death toll among civilians is unknown, but bodies litter the streets. Ambulances trying to pick up the injured have been shot at. Local hospitals have confirmed 51 civilian fatalities, but the final total will be much higher. Heavily armed mobs are roaming the city center, looting, terrorizing civilians and taking potshots at U.S. patrols. Whole sections of the city are no-go areas. . . .

Down by the harbor, the wooden shanty town around Noriega's military headquarters is just brown ashes, having caught fire in the initial American attack. Its occupants are a couple of miles away in the football stadium at Balboa high school, where about 7,000 refugees have gathered. Many have only what they managed to grab when the American attack started and many have lost family members. One screaming woman said she didn't know which side had shot her husband, only that he was dead.[81]

Hours after that story appeared, Noriega turned up on the doorstep of the Catholic nuncio building in Panama City, seeking asylum. From Washington, longtime Associated Press correspondent Walter Mears summarized the view that George H. W. Bush's administration, in tandem with mainstream media, had been able to project about the Panamanian general for the U.S. public: "Noriega's pockmarked face, brandished machete and defiance of his own countrymen when they voted for his opponents all add to the image of the prototype dictator. U.S. officials say there is evidence he meant to attack unarmed

American civilians, that he was involved in voodoo or Satanism, that he admired Adolf Hitler, that he plotted a terrorist takeover of the Panama Canal."[82]

Such images filled the media screen, conveying certainty that the invasion had been justified and successful. But some results, disturbing rather than soothing, got short media shrift. As Alexander Cockburn wrote at the time in an against-the-grain piece on the editorial page of the *Wall Street Journal*, "One has to read the dispatches long and hard to find the news that some 25,000 Panamanians are now homeless, shanties destroyed in the U.S. bombardment of Noriega's headquarters."[83] The U.S. press showed little interest in the civilian death toll, but journalists who bothered to dig were apt to come up with numbers much higher than what was on the official handouts. After investigating on the ground in Panama, *Toronto Globe & Mail* correspondent Linda Hossie reported: "Virtually all the Panamanians interviewed agreed that the vast majority of the dead are civilians."[84] The *Christian Science Monitor* sought records at medical facilities and funeral homes in Panama City as well as informed estimates from the countryside. The newspaper found that three-fifths of the deaths had occurred in the city, and overall the available data indicated that the invasion caused about 1,000 civilian deaths.[85]

But some stories were everywhere in the U.S. news media. The druggie aspect got especially big play. Two days into the invasion, Colonel Snell announced that the United States had an airtight case against Noriega in the form of the big stash of white powder, telling journalists that although it had yet to be analyzed, "we're sure it's cocaine."[86] The *Boston Globe* was among the media outlets that dispensed with any preliminaries, reporting flatly that the U.S. soldiers "found the cocaine, worth well over $1 million."[87] The news that so much cocaine had been seized in Noriega's personal quarters swiftly became a symbol of his character—and further verification that the invasion had toppled a truly evil man.

The Noriega cocaine story had plenty of time to become part of journalistic history. Thirty-two days passed after the "we're sure it's cocaine" statement set off countless media reports—until the news broke that it was a lie. The sensational yarn had been front-page news, but the correction was much less newsworthy. The Pentagon "retracted claims made during the Panama invasion that U.S. soldiers had found a large cache of cocaine in a guest house used by General

Manuel Antonio Noriega," the Associated Press reported on January 23. The supposed cocaine was actually tamales wrapped in banana leaves. A Pentagon spokesman said: "It was not cocaine."[88] But it was a heck of a good story that served a useful purpose.

"American virtue and innocence in an ugly world has been the sustaining narrative of the Panama invasion," the *Nation* magazine commented, "and it is now used as a defense in the tamale episode. 'The guys who first saw the stuff did not know what cocaine was,' the Pentagon says. But the issue is less the naivete of our cornfed boy soldiers than the gullibility of our more worldly reporters, who swallow all this nonsense with never a word of protest and then show no greater skepticism when the Pentagon repackages its clash between good and evil—Noriega is now said to have used the tamales for unspeakable acts of witchcraft and voodoo."[89]

When Ronald Reagan died in June 2004, the retrospective coverage by the *New York Times* told readers that he "sent American forces to Grenada in a mission to rescue American students in medical school there and to evict a Grenadian government that he called 'a brutal group of leftist thugs.'"[90] Ever since the invasion of the tiny Caribbean island began on October 25, 1983, the motivation of saving American lives has been central to the official story.

From the outset the tale benefited from the fact that throughout the intervention's first few days, the White House barred reporters from Grenada, imposing (in the words of the *New York Times*) "extraordinary restrictions on news coverage of the military invasion."[91] Two days into it, the *Times* reported, "The only pictures of the fighting in Grenada so far have been made by Defense Department photographers with the invasion force"—and the department had not yet decided "which pictures will be released."[92] The managing editor of the *Washington Post*, Howard Simons, commented: "I think a secret war, like secret government, is antithetical to an open society. It's absolutely outrageous."[93] It was also absolutely helpful in reducing the chances that news reports from Grenada would undercut President Reagan's invasion-day claim that the factor "of overriding importance" was the need to protect "innocent lives, including up to a thousand Americans, whose personal safety is, of course, my paramount concern."[94]

The president launched the invasion of Grenada just two days after a truck bomb killed 241 Americans at the U.S. Marine headquarters in Beirut. The invasion quickly pushed the Lebanon disaster out of the media spotlight. Opinion polling showed a net gain of several points for Reagan's favorable numbers. The military triumph in Grenada served as rapid-fire successor to mortifying loss.[95]

The imperative of saving American lives has been a durable theme. The commander of U.S. forces during the Dominican Republic invasion, General Bruce Palmer Jr., remarked in his book *Intervention in the Caribbean*: "it is interesting to note that the initial problem faced by the United States in the Dominican Republic in 1965, Grenada in 1983, and Panama in 1989 was the protection of U.S. citizens who were endangered. The protection of a state's own nationals in a foreign land has long been recognized as a legitimate, humanitarian act under international law."[96] Such vague uses of passive voice—"has long been recognized"—often facilitate the pretense that a dubious assertion is beyond reasonable dispute.

Actually, in each of the three examples cited by General Palmer, the saving-American-lives rationale for invasion doesn't stand up to scrutiny, as legal scholar John Quigley has documented:

- *Dominican Republic, 1965*: "U.S. citizens wanting to get out had been evacuated *prior* to American military intervention." After the shooting stopped, "Secretary of State Dean Rusk declared that overall we had evacuated 1,800 U.S. citizens from the Dominican Republic, counting those evacuated both before and after the intervention. But with 1,856 evacuated prior to the intervention, that left none to be evacuated by the time the Marines arrived. Even more remarkably, President Johnson claimed on May 2 that 1,500 of our citizens in the Dominican Republic were still desperate to be saved, thus giving him the excuse to send in more Marines. Even if there were American citizens in the Dominican Republic desiring to leave after April 28 [when the 1,856 had already been evacuated], they could have been evacuated without a military intervention and occupation. Residential areas occupied by Americans in Santo Domingo were free of hostilities, and all the major Dominican factions had agreed to facilitate the evacuation of any foreigners who wanted to leave."[97]

- *Grenada, 1983*: Attention focused on the medical students who comprised most of the U.S. citizens on the island. "These students had not, however, come to any harm, nor had they been threatened. . . . James Budeit, one of several State Department officials sent to Grenada two days before the invasion to talk to Grenadian officials and to the medical students, found no reason to believe that the Grenada government would harm the students. . . . The [Reagan] administration could not present a logical explanation why the Grenadian government might take hostages; indeed, that government had good reasons to treat the students well." On October 22 and 23, according to Budeit and the medical school's vice chancellor, "only 100 to 150 students wanted to leave, and their fear was prompted by the threat of a U.S. attack." Five hundred of the students' parents "sent President Reagan a telegram on October 24, asking him not to invade Grenada, because they did not want their children endangered. . . . There were no hostilities, and the Grenadian government was not preventing the students from leaving. . . . The State Department had been purposely avoiding options for a peaceful evacuation. . . . The medical students, in fact, were part of the administration's plan for invading Grenada. It needed the appearance of their being in danger as a pretext to remove Grenada's government. . . . While there was little reason to expect harm from the Grenadian government, a full-scale military invasion with one thousand United States civilians in the line of fire was extremely hazardous. . . . Reporters understood that the administration had invented facts to justify the Grenada landing. The *New York Times* [November 6, 1983] wrote that the administration put out 'deliberate distortions and knowingly false statements of fact.' *Time* magazine [November 7, 1983] called the administration 'disingenuous in its public explanations,' and said that 'American aims' went 'well beyond those stated.' Most media coverage, however, accepted the administration statements at face value. The television networks broadcast and rebroadcast scenes of the medical students kissing the ground at U.S. airports after their return flights, giving the impression that our forces had saved them from certain danger."[98]

- *Panama, 1989*: In mid-December a confrontation at a Panama Defense Force checkpoint involving four lost U.S. officers left one dead and another wounded, not far from where (according to the Pentagon) some Panamanian soldiers beat up a U.S. navy officer and threatened his wife. "But the circumstances indicated that the incident was not part of any overall plan to attack Americans in Panama, even if the U.S. version were accurate. Since the four American officers drove up to the checkpoint unannounced, the attack could not have been planned in advance. As for the treatment of the navy officer and his wife, the Defense Department conceded that the PDF soldiers responsible were intoxicated, which strongly suggests that the incident was not part of a general plan. Although President Bush insisted that the invasion was prompted by the [National Assembly's rhetorical] 'declaration of war' and the checkpoint incident, he had been planning it for months. Military officers posing as tourists had spread through Panama to reconnoiter locations they planned to attack. Fred Hoffman, a former Pentagon official, referring to classified planning documents for the invasion, said the administration 'had a plan' and was 'just waiting for an excuse to use it.'"[99]

Thirteen months before the invasion of Iraq began, a former arms control director for President Reagan wrote an op-ed article that appeared in the *Washington Post*. "I believe demolishing Hussein's military power and liberating Iraq would be a cakewalk," Ken Adelman declared. "Let me give simple, responsible reasons: (1) It was a cakewalk last time; (2) they've become much weaker; (3) we've become much stronger; and (4) now we're playing for keeps."[100] Fourteen months later, just a few days after the fall of Baghdad, he was on the same page with a follow-up essay headlined "'Cakewalk' Revisited," reminding readers of his foresightedness and rejoicing in the victory. Adelman praised some high-level administration hawks by name and proclaimed that "now is an occasion for pride, and for thanks to our fighting men and women."[101]

A lot of Americans may be bothered by war reportage, but the day-to-day news is not awfully uncomfortable for most of us, even when U.S. military forces are directly involved.[102] Messages that underscore the normality of an ongoing war tend to blend with the customary media landscape. Citing analysis by theorist Jacques Ellul, the writer Nancy Snow has emphasized that "propaganda is most effective when it is least noticeable." A former cultural affairs specialist at the U.S. Information Agency, she comments: "In an open society, such as the United States, the hidden and integrated nature of the propaganda best convinces people that they are not being manipulated."[103]

The most effective agenda-building for war is apt to seem like the logical unfolding of events at a time of crisis. The dynamic is akin to an approach that the legendary advertising wizard David Ogilvy described several decades ago: "[A] good advertisement is one which sells the product *without drawing attention to itself*. It should rivet the reader's attention on the product. Instead of saying, 'What a clever advertisement,' the reader says, 'I never knew *that* before. I must try this product.' It is the professional duty of the advertising agent to conceal his artifice." (Emphasis in original.) Ogilvy added: "When Aeschines spoke, they said, 'How well he speaks.' But when Demosthenes spoke, they said, 'Let us march against Philip.' I'm for Demosthenes."[104]

A media-propelled march to war has many parallels with an advertising campaign. And such campaigns are more constant than episodic. From hard-sell messages to subtle product placement, plugs are unceasingly part of the media terrain; the process of generating acceptance is 24/7.

Among the most acclaimed practitioners of advertising, Charlotte Beers—with her résumé including the top jobs at both the J. Walter Thompson and the Ogilvy & Mather advertising agencies—was a standout. She seemed a perfect fit when the Bush administration hired her in early autumn 2001. With the formal title "undersecretary of state for public diplomacy," her path had come to an intersection of Madison Avenue and Pennsylvania Avenue. Tipping his diplomatic hat, Secretary of State Colin Powell told an NBC interviewer in early November: "She got me to buy Uncle Ben's rice. So there is nothing wrong with getting somebody who knows how to sell something."[105] Beers went beyond voicing enthusiasm for her new post. "It is almost as though we have to redefine what America is," she said, adding: "This is the most sophisticated brand assignment I have ever had."[106]

The propagandist "strives for simplicity and vividness coupled with speed and broad impact," wrote sociologist Alfred McClung Lee in his book *How to Understand Propaganda*. The effort "stimulates popular emotional drives in existing grooves which are most likely to forward his objectives. In so doing, he must for the most part bypass factual discussion and debate of an adequate sort."[107] Yet at the time, the opposite might appear to be the case. The lead-in to the invasion of Iraq, for instance, involved a deluge of prewar media coverage that spanned eight months. In the process, American media consumers may have believed they were drowning in facts and debates. But much of the discourse amounted to the field testing and fine-tuning of a successful public-relations juggernaut that ended up—as usual—carrying the nation into war. The oft-repeated "facts" were often not factual; the standard debates were exceedingly narrow. Oceans of ink and thousands of airtime hours concentrated on disputes over how and when to go to war. Whether you're selling food from McDonald's or cars from General Motors or a war from the government, repetition is crucial for making propaganda stick.

In a democratic society, persistent agenda-building is necessary to gain and retain public support for war. The previous pages have described some cases in point. Now this book shifts to focusing on specific types of prowar spin. The following chapters probe and scrutinize key "perception management" techniques that have played huge roles in the promotion of American wars during recent decades. The better we understand those ongoing techniques, the more clearly we'll be able to see wars coming and understand what's really behind them. Hopefully, *War Made Easy* will help to blow away the fog of media war and enhance possibilities for democratic participation in decisions that are truly matters of life and death.

1

America Is a Fair and Noble Superpower

News outlets may feature arguments about the wisdom of going to war in a particular place at a specific time, but these are usually differences over tactics and priorities. While the administration's upper echelons might be fiercely criticized as ideologues, bunglers, myopic policy wonks, or dissembling politicians, the media assumption largely remains that Washington has laudable motivations. Unlike certain countries that object to U.S. military actions, Uncle Sam does not march to the beat of crass ulterior motives, or so the conventional wisdom goes; the grave matters of foreign policy and war are not mainly about American self-interest, much less about corporate interests. While there are enormous geopolitical advantages to be gained and massive profits to be made as consequences of exercising Pentagon muscle, the media discourse customarily excludes drawing attention to such dynamics as major factors in deployment of the country's armed forces.

The nation's biggest newsmagazine closed 1999 with a forward-looking headline on its back page: "A Second American Century?" Providing some answers was *Time* columnist Charles Krauthammer. "The world at the turn of the 21st century is not multipolar but unipolar," he wrote. "America bestrides the world like a colossus." Readers were encouraged to perceive that as a very good situation. "The main reason for the absence of a serious challenge to American hegemony is that it is so benign," Krauthammer went on. "It does not extract tribute. It does not seek military occupation. It is not interested in acquiring territory." Krauthammer certainly recognized that foreign rivals were restless. ("The world is stirring.") Yet the outlook was favorable: "None have the power to challenge America now. The unipolar moment will surely last for at least a generation."[1]

Many other media outlets were also buoyant. "There's every reason to think the upcoming 100 years will prove to be yet another American century," according to *Fortune* magazine.[2] On 1999's last telecast of the CBS program *Sunday Morning*, a confident pronouncement came from Harold Evans, editor of *U.S. News & World Report* as well as the *New York Daily News*: "I would be prepared to say it will be another American century."[3] The preparations were far more than just rhetorical. In 1997 some prominent superhawks—including Dick Cheney, Donald Rumsfeld, and Paul Wolfowitz—had founded an organization they chose to call the Project for a New American Century. The subsequent foreign policy of President George W. Bush proved to be a global breakthrough for the project.

While assertions of American benevolence have been never-ending, the first years of the twenty-first century brought some variations in the mantra depicting the U.S. government as beloved the world over (except for some malcontents). One of the punditocracy's leading hawks with intellectual plumage, Charles Krauthammer, reiterated in late spring 2001: "We run a uniquely benign imperium. This is not mere self-congratulation; it is a fact manifest in the way others welcome our power."[4] But the results of global surveys rendered such claims increasingly laughable. A year after the invasion of Iraq, "discontent with America and its policies has intensified rather than diminished," said an international study released in March 2004 by the Pew Research Center, which reported that "perceptions of American unilateralism remain widespread in European and Muslim nations, and the war in Iraq has undermined America's credibility abroad."[5] The very war that had been promoted, in part, as necessary for maintaining American "credibility" was, in fact, severely damaging it.

But belief in the capacity of U.S. military might to bring salvation to benighted portions of the world was a type of patriotic faith—so intense and so deeply held that it could be understood as a form of religiosity. To its adherents, the doubters were the rough political equivalents of heathens, no matter how much the ranks of the unfaithful continued to swell. Extreme gaps in perceptions between people in the United States and the rest of the world were markers for the ease with which the American public was apt to accept rationales for going to war that were widely rejected elsewhere on the planet. Gauging attitudes in the United States and three historically allied nations (Britain, France, and Germany) as well as in Jordan, Morocco, Pakistan, Russia, and Turkey, the study by the Pew Research Center found "there is broad agreement in nearly all of the countries surveyed—the U.S. being a notable exception—that the war in Iraq hurt, rather than helped, the war on terrorism." The disparities of outlooks foreshadowed any number of scenarios when the United States, with its window on the world tinted red-white-and-blue, could engage in warfare that the vast majority of the world renounced.[6]

In American media and political arenas, it is routine to ascribe lofty motivations to U.S. foreign policy, a mind-set that tends to limit outcries even when White House policies are undergoing harsh criticism. In contrast, the Pew research findings were clear: "Publics in the surveyed countries other than the United States express considerable skepticism of America's motives in its global struggle against terrorism. Solid majorities in France and Germany believe the U.S. is conducting the war on terrorism in order to control Mideast oil and dominate the world. People in Muslim nations who doubt the sincerity of American anti-terror efforts see a wider range of ulterior motives, including helping Israel and targeting unfriendly Muslim governments and groups."[7]

But to a pundit like Krauthammer, the sincerity of American power is inherent and necessarily unapologetic. Four months after George W. Bush became president, Krauthammer's lengthy essay "The Bush Doctrine" had been effusive in the *Weekly Standard*: "Today, the United States remains the preeminent economic, military, diplomatic, and cultural power on a scale not seen since the fall of the Roman Empire. . . . At the dawn of the 21st century, the task of the new administration is to develop a military and foreign policy appropriate to our position of overwhelming dominance. . . . By position and nature, we are essentially a status quo power. We have no particular desire to remake human nature, to conquer for the extraction of natural resources, or to rule for the simple pleasure of domination. We could not wait to get out of Haiti, and we would get out of Kosovo and Bosnia today if we could. Our principal aim is to maintain the stability and relative tranquility of the current international system by enforcing, maintaining, and extending the current peace." Celebrating such a pose of simultaneous humility and grandeur, Krauthammer rejoiced that the George W. Bush administration had embraced "the premise that overwhelming American power is good not just for the United States but for the world."[8]

Tactical setbacks and propaganda disasters can be jarring, but the assurances of moral virtue and military capability seem to carry the day. Whatever the question or circumstance, American power remains the potential answer—sometimes utilized, sometimes withheld, always an option. War scenarios can get swift traction on a track paved with the assumption that "overwhelming American power is good not just for the United States but for the world." And this kind of feel-good talk about an American empire is hardly peculiar to neo-conservative pundits. Many other commentators with big media megaphones, across a mainstream political spectrum, took it up during the first few years of the twenty-first century.

A frequent writer for the *New York Times Magazine*, Michael Ignatieff at Harvard's Kennedy School of Government, had this to say in its first edition of 2003: "America's empire is not like empires of times past, built on colonies, conquest and the white man's burden. We are no longer in the era of the United Fruit Company, when American corporations needed the Marines to secure their investments overseas. The 21st century imperium is a new invention in the annals of political science, an empire lite, a global hegemony whose grace notes are free markets, human rights and democracy, enforced by the most awesome military power the world has ever known. It is the imperialism of a people who remember that their country secured its independence by revolt against an empire, and who like to think of themselves as the friend of freedom everywhere. It is an empire without consciousness of itself as such, constantly shocked that its good intentions arouse resentment abroad."[9]

How pleasant and appealing this "empire lite" is apt to sound, with the lilts of "free markets, human rights and democracy," so that any wars involved are very likely to merit full support! Commenting on Ignatieff's assertion, the historian Howard Zinn wrote: "Only someone blind to the history of the United States, its obsessive drive for control of oil, its endless expansion of military bases around the world, its domination of other countries through its enormous economic power, its violations of the human rights of millions of people, whether directly or through proxy governments, could make that statement."[10]

. . .

While striving to portray a foreign regime as an unambiguous source of evil, the president insists that our side is close to saintly. The White House usually has good reason to be satisfied that U.S. media coverage does not dwell on information running counter to such neat divisions of labor. So, when there's news that American spying operations have undermined possibilities for peace, the shelf life of the story is apt to be fleeting.

During 1998, Clinton administration officials and U.S. news media kept insisting that the U.N. weapons inspectors in Iraq weren't spies and had to be given full access to all sites in the country. For several nights in December 1998, the United States and Britain fired hundreds of cruise missiles at Iraq—with the rationale that the regime in Baghdad hadn't cooperated enough with the inspectors.

Weeks later, the news broke that some of those inspectors had been conducting espionage. "U.S. Spied on Iraq Under U.N. Cover, Officials Now Say," a front-page *New York Times* headline announced on January 7, 1999. The article was unequivocal: "United States officials said today that American spies had worked undercover on teams of United Nations arms inspectors ferreting out secret Iraqi weapons programs. . . . By being part of the team, the Americans gained a first-hand knowledge of the investigation and a protected presence inside Baghdad." A follow-up *Times* story pointed out: "Reports that the United States used the United Nations weapons inspectors in Iraq as cover for spying on Saddam Hussein are dimming any chances that the inspection system will survive."[11]

A brief flurry of critical analysis occurred in a few media outlets. "That American spies have operations in Iraq should be no surprise," a *Hartford Courant* editorial said on January 10. "That the spies are using the United Nations as a cover is deplorable." While noting "Saddam Hussein's numerous complaints that U.N. inspection teams included American spies were apparently not imaginary," the newspaper mentioned that the espionage operatives "planted eavesdropping devices in hopes of monitoring forces that guarded Mr. Hussein as well as searching for hidden arms stockpiles." But such concerns quickly evaporated in U.S. news media, with the Washington press corps engaged in selective attention deficit disorder.

Fast forward: The media buildup for an invasion of Iraq benefited

from routine omissions of facts about the use of the U.N. inspection
teams for espionage. Such information, forthrightly presented, would
have been relevant in news reports during 2002 and early 2003 to
explain some of the earlier tensions as well as some current Iraqi
concerns.[12] The virtual disappearance of the early 1999 story about
U.S. spying via the U.N. inspections made it easy for President Bush to
slip this righteous line into his March 17, 2003, speech just before the
invasion: "Over the years, U.N. weapons inspectors have been threatened by Iraqi officials, electronically bugged and systematically
deceived."

Journalists working for the London-based *Observer* revealed other
threads of a spying tapestry that showed the U.S. government to be
persistently engaged in espionage to smooth the way for war. In early
March 2003, a few days after that British newspaper revealed a secret
memo about U.S. spying on U.N. Security Council delegations, I
asked Daniel Ellsberg to assess the importance of the story. "This
leak," he replied, "is more timely and potentially more important than
the Pentagon Papers." The key word was "timely." Publication of the
top-secret Pentagon Papers in 1971, made possible by Ellsberg's
heroic decision to leak those documents, came after the Vietnam War
had been under way for many years. But with an invasion of Iraq still
in the future, the leak about spying at the United Nations might erode
the Bush administration's already slim chances of getting a war resolution through the Security Council.

"As part of its battle to win votes in favor of war against Iraq," the
Observer had reported on March 2, 2003, the U.S. government developed an "aggressive surveillance operation, which involves intercep-
tion of the home and office telephones and the e-mails of U.N.
delegates." The smoking gun was "a memorandum written by a top
official at the National Security Agency—the U.S. body which intercepts communications around the world—and circulated to both senior agents in his organization and to a friendly foreign intelligence
agency." The *Observer* added: "The leaked memorandum makes clear
that the target of the heightened surveillance efforts are the delegations from Angola, Cameroon, Chile, Mexico, Guinea and Pakistan at
the U.N. headquarters in New York—the so-called 'Middle Six' delegations whose votes are being fought over by the pro-war party, led by
the U.S. and Britain, and the party arguing for more time for U.N.
inspections, led by France, China and Russia."

The NSA memo, dated January 31, 2003, outlined the wide scope of the surveillance activities, seeking any information useful to push a war resolution through the Security Council—"the whole gamut of information that could give U.S. policymakers an edge in obtaining results favorable to U.S. goals or to head off surprises." The *Times* of London, noting that the Bush administration "finds itself isolated" in its zeal for war on Iraq, called the leak of the memo an "embarrassing disclosure."[13] And the embarrassment was nearly worldwide. From Russia to France to Chile to Japan to Australia, the story was big mainstream news. But not in the United States.

Several days after the "embarrassing disclosure," not a word about it had appeared in America's supposed paper of record. The *New York Times*—the single most influential news outlet in the United States— still had not printed anything about the story. How could that be? "Well, it's not that we haven't been interested," *Times* deputy foreign editor Alison Smale said on the evening of March 5, nearly ninety-six hours after the *Observer* broke the story. But "we could get no confirmation or comment" on the memo from U.S. officials. Smale told me: "We would normally expect to do our own intelligence reporting." Whatever the rationale, the *New York Times* opted not to cover the story at all. And the sparse U.S. coverage that did take place mostly downplayed the significance of the *Observer*'s revelations.[14]

2

Our Leaders Will Do Everything They Can to Avoid War

While revving up the nation's war machinery, presidents are at pains to proclaim that they despise war. On April 10, 1965, early into a fateful spring that dramatically escalated the U.S. military role in Vietnam, President Johnson told the American people: "We love peace. We hate war. But our course is charted always by the compass of honor." Such peace-loving refrains from top officials in Washington are routine. Vice President George H. W. Bush, during his successful presidential campaign, offered this assurance in mid-August 1988: "I hate war. I love peace. We have peace. And I am not going to let anyone take it away from us."[1] Sixteen months later, he was ordering the invasion of Panama.

When a president stresses that deployment of U.S. troops is "defensive," his attack plans are often in high gear. "America does not seek conflict, nor do we seek to chart the destiny of other nations," Bush said on August 8, 1990. "But America will stand by her friends. The mission of our troops is wholly defensive."[2] Even some customary peace advocates were, at least initially, fooled by the spin. On August 3, 1990—the day after Iraqi troops invaded Kuwait—Jesse Jackson said that Saddam Hussein "must know he has pushed us over the line and that his insistence on the occupation of Kuwait and the threat against Saudi Arabia is an extreme act of provocation that would be met with force."[3]

By the second week of September, the White House claimed that at least 250,000 Iraqi troops and 1,500 tanks were in Kuwait and poised to keep moving. Much of the initial public rationale for a U.S. military buildup in the Persian Gulf that fall was based on the argument that those Iraqi soldiers represented an imminent threat to invade Saudi Arabia (at a time when more than 100,000 U.S. soldiers were already stationed in that country). The claim that additional U.S. troops being sent to the gulf were on a mission to defend Saudi borders came in handy for numerous media venues. In mid-October, on ABC's *Nightline*, a former U.S. commander in Vietnam, General William Westmoreland, asserted: "Our troops are there to deter any further aggression by Iraq. . . . [T]hey'll be used if Saddam Hussein attacks Saudi Arabia. . . . They're on the battlefield, but they haven't been committed to combat."[4]

After purchasing photos of the region from a Soviet commercial satellite agency, the *St. Petersburg Times* in Florida published a front-page article on January 6, 1991—more than a week before the Gulf War began—reporting that "Soviet satellite photos of Kuwait taken five weeks after the Iraqi invasion suggest the Bush administration might have exaggerated the scope of Iraq's military threat to Saudi Arabia at the time." (Similar information had gotten almost no media attention in autumn 1990.) Analysis of the photos indicated that the actual Iraqi troop strength in Kuwait was perhaps 25 percent of the figure that the White House had trumpeted while building its war agenda. However, the *St. Petersburg Times* reporting on the satellite photos got little play in the national media.

Overall, that autumn and winter felt a lot like 1964 to the man who'd given the Pentagon Papers to the press. "I was just appalled," Daniel Ellsberg said. "The American newspapers seemed as willing to collaborate in this hoax—this approach to war being carried on covertly—as they had been 25 years earlier, when I was in the Pentagon making plans for the bombing of North Vietnam."[5]

In general, the more a president persists with making war, the more he touts his commitment to peace.

After the Tonkin Gulf Resolution, the Johnson administration—eager to reassure Congress and the public—filled every year with fervent homilies to peace while heightening the carnage in Vietnam. A few samples:

1964

"Our one desire—our one determination—is that the people of Southeast Asia be left in peace to work out their own destinies in their own way."[6]

—President Johnson

1965

"Our commitment to strengthening the peace has not weakened."[7]

—Vice President Humphrey

1966

"I do not genuinely believe that there's any single person any-where in the world that wants peace as much as I want it."[8]

—President Johnson

1967

"There is no quick and easy way to peace—it must and will be built out of the cumulative acts of men and women who dedi-cate their lives to the service of their fellow men—and therefore to the service of God."[9]

—Vice President Humphrey

1968

"But our goal is peace—and peace at the earliest possible moment. . . . I wish—with all of my heart—that the expendi-tures that are necessary to build and to protect our power could all be devoted to the programs of peace. But until world condi-tions permit, and until peace is assured, America's might—and America's bravest sons who wear our Nation's uniform—must continue to stand guard for all of us—as they gallantly do tonight in Vietnam and other places in the world."[10]

—President Johnson

A change of administrations brings a new wave of pledges for the pursuit of peace.

At their inaugurals, I. F. Stone wrote a few days after Richard Nixon moved into the White House, presidents "make us the dupes of our hopes."[11] Flowery phrases from the inauguration were in the air. ("We can build a great cathedral of the spirit—each of us raising it one stone at a time, as he reaches out to his neighbor, helping, caring, doing.") In his inaugural speech, the incoming president fore-shadowed several more years of mass slaughter under the guise of diplomatic efforts to end the war in Vietnam: "I know that peace does not come through wishing for it—that there is no substitute for days and even years of patient and prolonged diplomacy." Stone observed days after Nixon's inauguration, "It's easier to make war when you talk peace."[12]

As a practical propagandistic matter, Americans' desires for peace frequently become hostages to war. "I pledged in my campaign for the presidency to end the war in a way that we could win the peace," Nixon said a year after he won the election that made him president. "I have initiated a plan of action which will enable me to keep that pledge. The more support I can have from the American people, the sooner that pledge can be redeemed."[13]

At the White House, policymakers rely on trust in presidential judgment to override any skepticism. That's one of the main reasons that the unauthorized release of the Pentagon Papers caused alarm at the pinnacle of the government, even though the documents covered a span of years that did not include the presidency of the incumbent. Oval Office tapes have revealed that the day after the *New York Times* began to publish the Pentagon Papers in mid-June 1971, top aide H. R. Haldeman told President Nixon: "To the ordinary guy, all this is a bunch of gobbledygook. But out of the gobbledygook comes a very clear thing: you can't trust the government; you can't believe what they say; and you can't rely on their judgment. And the implicit infallibility of presidents, which has been an accepted thing in America, is badly hurt by this, because it shows that people do things the president wants to do even though it's wrong, and the president can be wrong."[14]

Although the gist of that message from the Pentagon Papers was widely heard by Americans in the summer of 1971, many had trouble believing that the present-day president was engaging in similar decep-tions. It was as if, for most people, a default assumption of trustwor-thiness—in effect, "that was then, this is now"—conferred special benefits of doubts on the current occupant of the Oval Office. Presi-dent Nixon strived to maximize trust in his leadership while continu-ing the war with a shift toward more technological killing.

Nixon "was increasing deceptively labeled 'protective reaction strikes' against the North to a level that amounted to the resumption of Johnson's bombing," Daniel Ellsberg has written. "Starting the day after Christmas 1971 [six months after the Pentagon Papers came out], he launched a thousand U.S. bombers during five days of bombing against North Vietnam, in the heaviest raids since 1968. . . . Most Americans in truth had wanted out of the war long before the [Pentagon] papers were published; a majority had even come to regard it as immoral. . . . In the face of that majority sentiment, the president had kept the war going by reducing ground troops, while he increased the bombing, and by recurrently convincing the public that he was on the verge of a settlement. He did that again in the next few months, unveiling in January 1972 the secret talks and a deceptively 'generous' offer that he knew was unacceptable to Hanoi."[15]

In public, using tones that must have reassured millions of Americans, the president spoke with gravity about the war and his heartfelt yearning for peace. In private, top-level discussions were something else. The disconnect went to extremes that most citizens would find unimaginable.

On April 25, 1972, for instance, the White House taping system recorded this noontime dialogue among President Nixon, White House press secretary Ron Ziegler, and Henry Kissinger:

President: "How many did we kill in Laos?"

Ziegler: "Maybe ten thousand—fifteen?"

Kissinger: "In the Laotian thing, we killed about ten, fifteen. . . ."

President: "See, the attack in the North that we have in mind . . . power plants, whatever's left—POL [petroleum], the docks. . . . And I still think we ought to take the dikes out now. Will that drown people?"

Kissinger: "About two hundred thousand people."

President: "No, no, no . . . I'd rather use the nuclear bomb. Have you got that, Henry?"

Kissinger: "That, I think, would just be too much."

President: "The nuclear bomb, does that bother you? . . . I just want you to think big, Henry, for Christsakes."[16]

Nine days later, while conferring with Kissinger, Al Haig, and John Connally, the president said: "I'll see that the United States does not lose. I'm putting it quite bluntly. I'll be quite precise. South Vietnam may lose. But the United States *cannot* lose. Which means, basically, I have made the decision. Whatever happens to South Vietnam, we are going to *cream* North Vietnam. . . . For once, we've got to use the maximum power of this country . . . against this *shit-ass* little country: to win the war. We can't use the word 'win.' But others can."[17]

The commander in chief is a civilian, but often speaks in wartime as if mere civilians should not hope to be part of the decision-making process. The message to the public, niceties aside, is apt to be rather unsubtle: butt out. "I have not, and do not, intend to announce the timetable for our program, and there are obvious reasons for this decision which I'm sure you will understand," President Nixon told the nation in a November 1969 speech. "As I've indicated on several occasions, the rate of withdrawal [from Vietnam] will depend on developments." Nixon, of course, reassured the public that he was among the warmakers perennially in pursuit of peace and justice everlasting. "I have initiated a plan which will end this war in a way that will bring us closer to that great goal to which Woodrow Wilson and every American president in our history has been dedicated—the goal of a just and lasting peace."[18]

The same phrase, "lasting peace," was in Nixon's second inaugural address. Moments after being sworn in again, Nixon was spinning for the history books and more immediately for public opinion. "Because of America's bold initiatives," he said, "1972 will be long remembered as the year of the greatest progress since the end of World War II toward a lasting peace in the world."

In late November—two months before Nixon spoke those words— "Kissinger and Le Duc Tho, the North Vietnamese negotiator, held four days of talks, which failed," *Los Angeles Times* reporter Jacques Leslie was to write in a memoir. "They met over a 10-day period in December [1972] and failed again. Then the Americans tried another gambit: in return for [South Vietnamese premier] Thieu's signature on the ceasefire pact, they pounded North Vietnam. They unloosed the biggest bombing campaign in the history of warfare, striking canals, highways, factories, air and sea ports, and three days before Christmas they leveled a Hanoi hospital; in case the bombing was perceived as unbecoming, they imposed a blackout on all news related to it."[19] Daniel Ellsberg describes the U.S. government's late December bombing spree this way: "President Nixon sent B-52s over Hanoi for the first time ever. In the next 11 days and nights—with Christmas off—American planes dropped on North Vietnam 20,000 tons of bombs," amounting to "the explosive equivalent of the Nagasaki A-bomb."[20]

In the first hours of 1973, Nixon halted the attacks. Later in January came an agreement between the American and North Vietnamese governments. The document—which "the North Vietnamese clearly had been prepared to sign all along"—"instructed the Vietnamese parties to negotiate a final settlement but offered no incentive to do so," Leslie wrote. "Instead, the U.S. was already busy rearming the ARVN [South Vietnam's army], while the North Vietnamese kept their troops in the south as part of the agreement. The accord's major achievement was in providing for the two sides to slug it out alone, while the United States, together with its POWs, finally went home. This was Nixon's 'peace with honor.'"[21] American media reported that the war was ending at last.[22]

On January 20, 1973, just weeks after the massive Christmastime bombing of North Vietnam's capital, Nixon said in his second inaugural address: "Today, I ask your prayers that in the years ahead I may have God's help in making decisions that are right for America." He laid claim to the mantle of peacemaker: "Let us be proud that by our bold, new initiatives, and by our steadfastness for peace with honor, we have made a breakthrough toward creating in the world what the world has not known before—a structure of peace that can last, not merely for our time, but for generations to come."

On the first day of May 2003, under a "Mission Accomplished" banner, President George W. Bush used his elaborate photo-op aboard the aircraft carrier USS *Abraham Lincoln* near San Diego to proclaim the end of major hostilities in Iraq. But the occupation proved to be perfectly compatible with a lot more killing of fighters as well as civilians who happened to be in the wrong place at the wrong time.[23]

As for peace, the Prussian general Karl von Clausewitz remarked two centuries ago: "A conqueror is always a lover of peace."[24] On his own terms, of course.

In early 1999, reporting about prospects of a U.S.-led NATO war on Yugoslavia, the American media glided past a key aspect of negotiations taking place at Rambouillet in France. The U.S. government

kept insisting on a provision—rejected by the Serb president, Slobodan Milosevic, before the bombing began in late March—that
allowed for NATO troops to occupy all of Yugoslavia. It was the kind
of demand that no sovereign nation would accept without a fight. But
the major U.S. news outlets were silent about this provision, failing to
inform the public about appendix B of the Rambouillet text, which
stated: "NATO personnel shall enjoy, together with their vehicles,
vessels, aircraft, and equipment, free and unrestricted passage and
unimpeded access throughout the FRY [Federal Republic of
Yugoslavia] including associated air space and territorial waters. This
shall include, but not be limited to, the right of bivouac, maneuver,
billet, and utilization of any areas or facilities as required for support,
training, and operations."[25]

Appendix B also insisted:

- "NATO personnel shall be immune from any form of arrest,
  investigation, or detention by the authorities in the FRY."

- "NATO is granted the use of airports, roads, rails and ports
  without payment."

- "[NATO shall have] the right to use all of the electromagnetic
  spectrum."[26]

Later, after more than two months of war, the *Washington
Post* mentioned some of those terms at the end of a June 10 news
story, on page A-24. The article noted that "a provision of the
U.S.-drafted peace agreement that Belgrade rejected in February as
especially unpalatable has been dropped from the new military
agreement." The story went on to say that appendix B "would have
limited the peacekeeping force to troops from NATO countries"—
and "would have allowed the peacekeepers to go wherever they
wanted and do whatever they wanted throughout Yugoslavia, not just
in Kosovo." The article described it as a "little-noticed appendix to
that peace plan."

The appendix had been "little noticed" because the Clinton
administration, after slipping it into the Rambouillet proposal as a
poison pill, had no desire to highlight it. And the U.S. news media,
while reporting on the Rambouillet talks as part of extensive prewar
coverage of diplomatic maneuvers and saber-rattling, had not
informed the American people that their government was, in effect,
insisting on a far-fetched provision: so war would seem like the only

wise option after Washington's supposedly good-faith negotiation efforts failed to culminate with an agreement. It would be a mistake to blame only government officials. The big U.S. media outlets did not cover appendix B—before *or* during the war.

Appendix B was no secret. And information about it continued to reach newsrooms, before and after the war began. For instance, on April 16, fully eight weeks before the *Post* described the appendix B provisions as "little noticed," my colleagues at the Institute for Public Accuracy put out a news release under the headline "Troubling Questions About Rambouillet," which went to well over a thousand U.S. reporters, editors, and producers via fax and e-mail. "The Clinton administration has repeatedly claimed that bombing is necessary because Milosevic would not agree to negotiations, citing his refusal to accept the Rambouillet text," the news release said. "But did Rambouillet represent real negotiations or an ultimatum?" The release pointed out: "The Rambouillet text of February 23 [1999], a month before NATO began bombing, contains provisions that seem to have provided for NATO to occupy the entire Federal Republic of Yugoslavia, not just Kosovo."[27]

Why does such crucial information become footnotes to history rather than high-profile news that can inform public debate *before* a war starts? The habitual American media reliance on official U.S. sources predisposes most coverage to remain in sync with what is coming out of high places in Washington. Time after time, during military and public-relations buildups before a war begins, the press corps keeps relaying the points that the administration wishes to emphasize. What's downplayed or left out—omissions such as the "little noticed" matter of appendix B—can make a profound difference.

While the intensive bombing of Yugoslavia proceeded, not all American journalists deferred to the guidance of U.S. officials by ignoring the fine print of Rambouillet. At the annual Overseas Press Club awards dinner in April 1999, two recipients of honors demanded that the event's guest speaker, special U.S. envoy Richard Holbrooke—who had personally delivered the ultimatum to Belgrade hours before the bombs started falling—account for the little-known stipulations in the Rambouillet text. Amy Goodman and Jeremy Scahill, progressive journalists with the Pacifica Radio–affiliated program *Democracy Now*, confronted him with a question that America's mainstream media had failed to ask. But, aided by awards presenter Tom Brokaw, the esteemed diplomat slipped away without answering. Nor did the assembled editors, reporters, and producers support Goodman and Scahill in their quest for a full explanation. In a banquet room filled with hundreds of American journalists, the ambassador was among friends. Their lack of curiosity about the Rambouillet text spoke volumes.[28]

Rather than being a means to avoid war, "diplomacy" is sometimes a way of laying the propaganda groundwork *for* war. Along that line, Washington's maneuvers at the United Nations have been integral to public-relations efforts for domestic and foreign consumption.[29] In practice, one of the key steps toward starting a war is to go through the motions of exploring alternatives to war. Such pantomimes of diplomacy help to make war possible.

So Fareed Zakaria, a former managing editor of the elite-flavored journal *Foreign Affairs*, recommended PR prudence in the quest for a confrontation that could facilitate an invasion of Iraq. "Even if the inspections do not produce the perfect crisis," Zakaria wrote in late summer 2002, "Washington will still be better off for having tried because it would be seen to have made every effort to avoid war."[30]

Policymakers in Washington are often eager to "be seen" as "having tried" to "avoid war." And to that end, they're often willing to give the United Nations a chance to be relevant. Many pundits are also happy at the prospect that the United Nations might redeem itself for past inadequacies—as far as the U.S. government is concerned. "In the world of a single, dominant superpower, the U.N. Security Council becomes even more important, not less," Thomas Friedman wrote on November 13, 2002. The *New York Times* columnist was greatly enamored of the evident potential of the world body: "The Bush team discovered that the best way to legitimize its overwhelming might—in a war of choice—was not by simply imposing it, but by channeling it through the U.N."

For many American journalists, recalcitrant allies are sometimes tantamount to betrayers. Three weeks into 2003, the *Washington Post* reported on its front page that the French government signaled plans to "wage a major diplomatic fight, including possible use of its veto power" on the Security Council to prevent a resolution authorizing war on Iraq. The news story informed readers that France and other balking countries had just engaged in "a diplomatic version of an ambush"—a description attributed to no one. The same article closed with a quote from Secretary of State Colin Powell: "If the United Nations is going to be relevant, it has to take a firm stand."[31]

When Colin Powell made his dramatic presentation to the U.N. Security Council in early February 2003, he fudged, exaggerated, and concocted.[32] Along the way, Powell played fast and loose with translations of phone intercepts to make them seem more incriminating. And, as researchers at the media watch group FAIR (where I'm an associate) pointed out, "Powell relied heavily on the disclosure of Iraq's pre-war unconventional weapons programs by defector Hussein Kamel, without noting that Kamel had also said that all those weapons had been destroyed."[33] But the secretary of state wowed U.S. journalists.

Thirty-eight and a half years earlier, another high-drama presentation by a U.S. official to the Security Council had come from Ambassador Adlai Stevenson in early August 1964, when he depicted Tonkin Gulf events of recent days in no uncertain terms. "Without any shadow of doubt," Stevenson said, the North Vietnamese government had been guilty of "planned deliberate military aggression against vessels lawfully present in international waters."[34] Like Powell's stellar performance, Stevenson's presentation—also based on lies—helped to lay the pseudo-diplomatic groundwork for an aggressive U.S. war to come.

Powell's televised speech at the United Nations on February 5, 2003, exuded great confidence and authoritative judgment. But he owed much of his touted credibility to the fact that he had long functioned inside a media bubble shielding him from direct challenge.[35] It might puzzle an American to read, in a book later compiled by Britain's *Guardian* newspaper, that Powell's much-ballyhooed speech that day went over like a lead balloon. "The presentation was long on assertion and muffled taped phone calls, but short on killer facts," the book said. "It fell flat."[36]

Fell flat? Well, it did in Britain, where a portion of the mainstream press immediately set about engaging in vigorous journalism that ripped apart many of Powell's assertions within days. But not on the western side of the Atlantic, where Powell's star turn at the United Nations elicited an outpouring of media adulation. In the process of deference to Powell, many liberals were among the swooners.

In her *Washington Post* column the morning after Powell spoke,

Mary McGrory proclaimed that "he persuaded me." She wrote: "The cumulative effect was stunning." And McGrory, a seasoned and dovish political observer, concluded: "I'm not ready for war yet. But Colin Powell has convinced me that it might be the only way to stop a fiend, and that if we do go, there is reason."[37] In the same edition, *Post* columnist Richard Cohen shared his insight that Powell was utterly convincing: "The evidence he presented to the United Nations—some of it circumstantial, some of it absolutely bone-chilling in its detail—had to prove to anyone that Iraq not only hasn't accounted for its weapons of mass destruction but without a doubt still retains them. Only a fool—or possibly a Frenchman—could conclude otherwise."[38] Inches away, *Post* readers found Jim Hoagland's column with this lead: "Colin Powell did more than present the world with a convincing and detailed X-ray of Iraq's secret weapons and terrorism programs yesterday. He also exposed the enduring bad faith of several key members of the U.N. Security Council when it comes to Iraq and its 'web of lies,' in Powell's phrase." Hoagland's closing words sought to banish doubt: "To continue to say that the Bush administration has not made its case, you must now believe that Colin Powell lied in the most serious statement he will ever make, or was taken in by manufactured evidence. I don't believe that. Today, neither should you."[39]

On the opposite page the morning after Powell's momentous U.N. speech, a *Washington Post* editorial was figuratively on the same page as the *Post* columnists. Under the headline "Irrefutable," the newspaper laid down its line for rationality: "After Secretary of State Colin L. Powell's presentation to the United Nations Security Council yesterday, it is hard to imagine how anyone could doubt that Iraq possesses weapons of mass destruction."[40]

Also smitten was the editorial board of the most influential U.S. newspaper leaning against the push for war. Hours after Powell finished his U.N. snow job, the *New York Times* published an editorial with a mollified tone—declaring that he "presented the United Nations and a global television audience yesterday with the most powerful case to date that Saddam Hussein stands in defiance of Security Council resolutions and has no intention of revealing or surrendering whatever unconventional weapons he may have." By sending Powell to address the Security Council, the *Times* claimed, President Bush "showed a wise concern for international opinion."

And the paper contended that "Mr. Powell's presentation was all the more convincing because he dispensed with apocalyptic invocations of a struggle of good and evil and focused on shaping a sober, factual case against Mr. Hussein's regime."[41]

What happened in early 2003 occurs time and again: American envoys are shuttling to foreign capitals. Dramatic speeches underscore U.S. efforts to galvanize international support. The White House warns that the United Nations, at this historic juncture, must decide whether to take responsibility or risk irrelevance. Washington stresses that the U.S. government does not need permission to act decisively on behalf of freedom and security. As war appears more likely, media coverage grows more intense. Tearful loved ones say good-bye at ports, army bases, and airports. Poignant interviews with soldiers, pilots, and sailors remind us how young and brave they are. More American flags are on TV screens. Feature stories elaborate on the capabilities of the Pentagon's latest weaponry. The president offers assurances that innocents have nothing to fear from us. While leaders of some other countries express opposition to the probable attack, the White House explains that *not* going to war is now the worst option.

In mid-November 1998, when Saddam Hussein's pledge of full cooperation with U.N. weapons inspectors led President Bill Clinton to cancel air attacks at the last minute, a strong wave of frustration swept through American news media. Quite a few pundits sounded very disappointed. The pattern was all too familiar, the refrain went— yet again, after a tense confrontation, the U.S. government did not let the missiles fly. Many commentators griped about the cost of mobilizing and then not attacking. Each time the United States sent a fleet to the Persian Gulf, the tab for the buildup amounted to another $1 billion or so. What good is repeated deployment of enormous firepower if it isn't used?

President Clinton proclaimed that "Iraq has backed down."[42] But two days later, the *Washington Post* filled its opinion page with caustic reactions from three prominent syndicated columnists across the mainstream political spectrum:

- Clinton again proved his international impotence, George Will observed from the front lines of his keyboard, warning against restraint: "U.S. forces should quickly destroy any site, such as a presidential compound, that inspectors are prevented from examining."

- Charles Krauthammer wrote that "Clinton was given an extraordinary opportunity to strike a massive blow against Saddam. He flinched." Krauthammer briefly noted that "the military's estimate of casualties from an initial strike" was "10,000 Iraqi dead"—but who cared? Uncle Sam should strive to "disarm, disrupt and destroy Saddam's regime. A relentless air campaign had a good chance of doing that."

- Richard Cohen was not to be outdone in the blood-thirst department. "Both countries backed down—one the world's only superpower, the other a Third World country, short of everything but gall," he declared. "Something is out of balance here. The Clinton administration waited too long to act. It needed to punch out Iraq's lights, and it did not do so."[43]

In the aftermath of that standoff, the media concerns were often framed in macho terms. News coverage focused on a question that led off a front-page *New York Times* article: "Who blinked?"[44] Many American journalists lamented that Clinton did not entirely stare down Saddam Hussein. With such coverage, news consumers could easily slip into spectator mode—vicarious and detached—while euphemisms were wrapped around playground posturing.

Will, Krauthammer, Cohen, and other pundits had to cope with their disappointment, but not for too long. After the false start that had subjected the Clinton administration to withering media criticism in November 1998, the year culminated with bombardment of Iraq for several days.

When the next president was planning an invasion of Iraq, the publicized arguments included claims that being credible meant going ahead with war. In July 2002 a top Pentagon adviser, James R. Schlesinger, rang the bell: "My view is that given all we have said as a leading world power about the necessity of regime change in Iraq means that our credibility would be badly damaged if that regime change did not take place."[45] Such fixations on "credibility" are setups for self-justification. Painting himself into a corner with other people's blood, a president makes a virtue out of a disastrous course.[46]

. . .

During the summer of 2002, elected officials and high-level appointees were resolute. It was no time for the U.S. government to risk taking "yes" for an answer from Iraq. The administration of the second President Bush moved the goal posts, quickly pounding them into the ground. In early August, before Iraq agreed to let U.N. weapons inspectors back into the country, a State Department undersecretary swung a heavy mallet. "Let there be no mistake," said John Bolton. "While we also insist on the reintroduction of the weapons inspectors, our policy at the same time insists on regime change in Baghdad—and that policy will not be altered, whether inspectors go in or not."[47] Meanwhile, rationales for launching an attack were floating across op-ed pages. A *Wall Street Journal* essay by a pair of ex-Justice Department attorneys maintained that the United States would be "fully within its rights" to attack Iraq and overthrow the regime—based on "the customary international law doctrine of anticipatory self-defense."[48] Of course, if such claims as "anticipatory self-defense" were valid reasons for starting a war, then the same excuse could have been used by the Iraqi government to justify an attack on the United States.

A cloud briefly fell over the sunny skies for war when the U.S. Congress got an invitation in midsummer. A letter from an Iraqi official said "congressional visitors and weapons experts of their choice could visit any site in Iraq alleged to be used for development of chemical, biological or nuclear weapons," *USA Today* reported, while the *New York Times* noted that "the letter said members of Congress could bring arms experts and should plan to stay three weeks."[49] The news had potential to impede the acceleration toward war. But U.S. media treatment matched the bipartisan refusal by leaders in Congress to do anything but scorn the offer. Summing up the diplomatic overture, the front page of the *New York Times* informed readers that the letter "was apparently trying to pit legislators against the Bush administration"—a pithy phrase that spurned the invitation as nothing more than mischievous.[50] The first words of *USA Today*'s news coverage called it "the latest Iraqi bid to complicate U.S. invasion plans."[51]

The last things administration officials wanted were complications before the war could get under way. Congress was a flimsy obstacle that could easily be overcome. The leadership of both parties had quibbles at times—but did not question the fundamentals. In August

2002, when the Senate Foreign Relations Committee held hearings about the wisdom of making war on Iraq, the arguments were overwhelmingly about military tactics and realpolitik strategies. Scott Ritter, a former U.N. weapons inspector with long experience in Iraq, was perceptive when he charged that chairman Joseph Biden and most of the congressional hierarchy "have pre-ordained a conclusion that seeks to remove Saddam Hussein from power regardless of the facts and are using these hearings to provide political cover for a massive military attack on Iraq."[52] Naturally, given his attitude, Ritter was excluded from the witness list. "To date," he said, "the Bush administration has been unable—or unwilling—to back up its rhetoric concerning the Iraqi threat with any substantive facts."[53]

Among those testifying at the Senate committee's hearing on Iraq was Richard Butler, the head of the U.N. weapons inspection program in Iraq several years earlier (at a time when some of the team's members were, as later admitted, spying for Washington). At the Senate hearing, Butler suggested that perhaps the Russian government could be induced to tell Baghdad: "You will do serious arms control or you're toast."[54] Like numerous other notables treated with great deference by the national press corps, Butler tried to seem suave and clever as he talked of launching a high-tech attack.

In Britain, some of the press was less welcoming of the war to come—and more candid about key circumstances leading up to it. On August 4, in the *Observer*, foreign affairs editor Peter Beaumont wrote: "The question now appears to be not whether there will be a war, but when. The answer is that in war, as other matters, timing is all. For President George W. Bush that timing will be dictated by the demands of a domestic political agenda." The late summer was just a mild prelude to an autumn PR onslaught. As the White House chief of staff, Andrew Card, confided in a rare burst of public candor, "You don't introduce new products in August."[55]

As usual, during the prewar agenda-setting, reliance on official sources dominated news coverage. Centers of power in the executive branch were overwhelming. The Tyndall Report, a media research outfit, crunched the numbers for ABC, CBS, and NBC—the three largest broadcast networks—between September 2002 and February 2003. During that six-month period, just before the war began, more than 90 percent of the 414 stories about Iraq had originated at the State Department, the Pentagon, or the White House.[56]

Media appearances were apt to be deceiving. Objections to launching a war seemed to loom large during the late summer and fall of 2002; weeks or months later, the bulk of the establishment's objectors would collapse into silence or voice support. Few of the most widely publicized skeptics were willing to stand up to presidential insistence; caveats from the likes of loyal Republicans Dick Armey, Chuck Hagel, and Brent Scowcroft—along with Senator Dianne Feinstein and many other Democrats—were inclined to disintegrate.

Likewise, history gave the president ample reasons to believe that most hand-wringing punditry would turn into applause at the first launch of missiles. In fact, many of the arguments marshaled in the mainstream media against a precipitous attack on Iraq already accepted the need for the U.S. government to impose massive violence on that country. Whether the venues were Capitol Hill or media outlets, most of the criticism was largely concerned with style, timing, and tactics. And quite a bit of the flak came from prowar commentators who wanted the president to get his militaristic act together. The editor of the *Atlantic* magazine, Michael Kelly, used his August 21, 2002, column in the *Washington Post* to lament "the president's refusal to wage a coherent campaign to win public—and, let's force the issue, congressional—approval for the war."

While President Bush huddled with hawks at the top of the pecking order at his ranch in Crawford, Texas, war enthusiasts went on the offensive across the nation's media landscape. Their efforts added to a sustained volume of news coverage as the midterm congressional elections neared. The more that Iraq dominated front pages, magazine covers, news broadcasts, and cable channels, the less space there was for such matters as the nation's overall economic woes, the intensifying retirement worries of many Americans, the Wall Street scandals, and specific stories about entanglements that linked Bush or Dick Cheney with malodorous corporate firms including Enron, Harken, and Halliburton. Bush's advisers had every reason to want a similar pattern through Election Day.[57]

Old hands in prior administrations weighed in. Some made cautionary statements. But a typical assist came just after Labor Day from George Shultz, who wrote a long piece in the *Washington Post* that was as emphatic as it was deceptive, beginning with a flourish to indicate that continued absence of war would be a tragedy of Shakespearean dimensions: "Are we to be the Hamlet of nations, debating

endlessly over when and how to act?" From there, the former secretary of state was off to the polemical races.

Saddam Hussein "has relentlessly amassed weapons of mass
destruction and continues their development," Shultz wrote. He
asserted: "A strong foundation exists for immediate military action
against Hussein and for a multilateral effort to rebuild Iraq after he is
gone. . . . The failure to take military action against Hussein after his
flagrant violation in 1998 has given him nearly four years to continue
unencumbered in his development and accumulation of weapons of
mass destruction. . . . Military force against Hussein is both necessary
and authorized to rid Iraq of weapons of mass destruction. . . . The
evidence is clear that Hussein continues to amass weapons of mass
destruction. . . . By now, the risks of inaction clearly outweigh the
risks of action. If there is a rattlesnake in the yard, you don't wait for
it to strike before you take action in self-defense. The danger is immediate. The making of weapons of mass destruction grows increasingly
difficult to counter with each passing day." And Shultz insisted: "No
longer can anyone plausibly claim that Iraq's weapons of mass
destruction can be eliminated by an inspection program."[58]

In late autumn, large teams of U.N. weapons inspectors returned
to Iraq, where they scoured the country for several months. The White
House went through the motions of supporting the effort while simultaneously denigrating its ultimate utility. Many news outlets frequently made it known that the inspection regimen was bound to fail.
The media wisdom was that surely Saddam Hussein possessed large
arsenals of mass destruction.[59] (How did journalists know? Top
officials in Washington told them so.) When Saddam Hussein
denied having weapons of mass destruction, the response was
derisive. "If you believe that," a *Wall Street Journal* editorial declared,
"you are probably a Swedish weapons inspector."[60] Like many other
journalists, Christopher Hitchens grew very impatient with the inspections; they were delaying the necessary war. "Those who are calling
for more time in this process," he wrote, "should be aware that they
are calling for more time for Saddam's people to complete their
humiliation and subversion of the inspectors."[61]

Thirty-one years earlier, as a Vietnam veteran, John Kerry had
denounced the war in Southeast Asia. But on October 9, 2002, it was
no surprise when Senator Kerry announced that he would vote for the

Iraq war resolution. Kerry included this rhetorical question in his oratory on the Senate floor: "Why is Saddam Hussein attempting to develop nuclear weapons when most nations don't even try . . . ?" And, Kerry stressed, "according to intelligence, Iraq has chemical and biological weapons."

To help set the stage for his Senate war vote, Kerry appeared for an hour on MSNBC's *Hardball* program, live from The Citadel. An audience of young cadets provided a backdrop as the graying senator burnished his warrior persona. "Soldiers who love each other and really fight for each other as much as for anything else, I think that that's what we want to make certain is what happens if and when we go into Iraq," Kerry said. "I'm prepared to go. I think people understand that Saddam Hussein is a danger. But you want to go maximizing your capacity for victory, not beginning with deficits. That's one of the lessons of Vietnam."[62] Among politicians and journalists, the lessons often seemed ambiguous, contradictory, pliable: indeed, manipulable. In practice, the overlap of agreement was that wars were far better won than lost.[63]

In March 2003, days before the invasion of Iraq began, President Bush went on television from the White House and offered an explanation for why Americans need not feel the slightest drop of blood on their hands. "Should Saddam Hussein choose confrontation, the American people can know that every measure has been taken to avoid war," he said, "and every measure will be taken to win it."[64]

3

Our Leaders Would Never Tell Us Outright Lies

During an early stage of the Vietnam War buildup, Daniel Ellsberg worked as special assistant to John T. McNaughton, a key Pentagon official on Vietnam policies. "I often watched McNaughton with reporters, because he called me into his office whenever he had to give an interview," Ellsberg was to recall. As a new employee, Ellsberg "watched and marveled. John was great at this. As he got into areas where he had to be especially untruthful or elusive, his Pekin, Illinois, accent got broader till he sounded like someone discussing corn at a country fair or standing at the rail of a riverboat. You looked for hayseed in his cuffs. He simply didn't mind looking and sounding like a hick in the interests of dissimulation. My future boss in Vietnam, Edward Lansdale, had the same willingness to appear simpleminded when he wanted to be opaque, as he did with most outsiders. In both cases it was very effective. Reporters would tell me how 'open' my boss was, compared with others they ran into, this after I had listened to an hour of whoppers. It became clear to me that journalists had no idea, no clue, even the best of them, just how often and how egregiously they were lied to."[1]

In late February 2002, news broke that the mission of the Pentagon's oddly named Office of Strategic Influence included trying to deceive the international media. After nearly a week of negative coverage, President Bush proclaimed zero tolerance for lies from U.S. officials. "We'll tell the American people the truth," he vowed.[2] The next day, the controversial office became history when a somber defense secretary Donald Rumsfeld announced: "It is being closed down." He took the opportunity to offer assurances that the Defense Department would not ever try to deceive journalists: "This is something the Pentagon has not done, is not doing and would not condone."[3]

And so the Office of Strategic Influence went from obscurity to infamy to oblivion during a spin cycle that lasted just seven days. The bad publicity was embarrassing—but the inky cloud had a silver lining. The scuttling of the project was an occasion to explicitly affirm the trustworthy character of Washington's official sources on military matters. "I'm absolutely convinced that in no way would top officials of the administration ever have approved lying to the media," said a retired air force general, Donald Shepperd, wearing his media hat as a CNN military analyst.[4] With considerably more candor, *Newsday* columnist Ellis Henican wrote: "But don't worry, Rumsfeld's people were whispering yesterday around the Pentagon. They'll keep on spreading whatever stories they think they have to—to foreigners especially. Call it the free flow of misinformation. Who needs a formal office for that?"[5]

Some of the media attacks on the Office of Strategic Influence actually reinforced the notion that the U.S. government had no rational motive for hiding truth, since its real endeavors could proudly stand the light of day. It was an easy misconception that would hardly displease the propagandists who concocted the Office of Strategic Influence in the first place. None of them should have minded the message near the end of a tough *New York Times* column, headlined "Office of Strategic Mendacity," with Maureen Dowd applying an oily salve to PR wounds she'd just inflicted. "Our cause is just," she concluded. "So why not just tell the truth?"[6] With the Office of Strategic Influence declared to be null and void, the public-relations dividends were quickly noticeable. The *Chicago Tribune* quoted Lucy Dalglish, executive director of the Reporters Committee for Freedom of the Press, generously praising officials at the Pentagon: "This is good news for the public. Now we can have more confidence that what they're telling us is true."[7]

But such confidence was misplaced. During the year that followed, the Pentagon put out a profuse supply of bogus stories based on "intelligence"—about Iraq's weapons of mass destruction and purported links to Al Qaeda—with the goal of promoting an invasion of Iraq. Lieutenant Colonel Karen Kwiatkowski saw the disinformation process unfold, working at the Pentagon's Near East and South Asia bureau and observing the defense secretary's beloved Office of Special Plans, which provided talking points to top-level administration officials. "You could find bits and pieces of fact throughout," she later told documentary filmmakers. "But framed, articulated, crafted to convince someone of what—well, of things that weren't true." She looked back ruefully: "I worked in a place where they concentrated on preparing this story line and selling it to everyone that they could possibly sell it to."[8]

Anyone would be ill advised to assume truthfulness of Pentagon pronouncements—or to trust that officials weren't cloaking essential facts with the simple strategy of withholding information. As a Pentagon official remarked to a *Newsday* reporter at the time of the Gulf War, "We lie by not telling you things."[9]

Our leaders never lie to us—unless you mean lying by omission, lying with statistics, lying via unsupported claims, or lying with purposeful obfuscation, misleading statements, and successions of little white lies. Citizens make decisions based on information from presidents, pundits, and their colleagues in government and the news media. Often these esteemed public figures claim to have special knowledge. Our trust may be essential to their plans, but it is unwarranted.

Ninety-five days before the invasion of Iraq began, I sat in the ornate Baghdad office of the deputy prime minister as he talked about the U.N. weapons inspectors in his country. "They are doing their jobs freely, without any interruption," Tariq Aziz said. "And still the warmongering language in Washington is keeping on." The White House, according to Aziz, had written the latest U.N. Security Council resolution "in a way to be certainly refused." But, he added pointedly, "We surprised them by saying, 'OK, we can live with it. We'll be patient enough to live with it and prove to you and to the world that your allegations about weapons of mass destruction are not true.'"[10]

That night in mid-December 2002, Tariq Aziz—dressed in a well-cut business suit, witty and fluent in English—seemed to epitomize the urbanity of evil.[11] As a prominent servant of a murderous despot, he lied often.[12] But not that time.

On March 17, 2003, in a major address to the American people just days before the invasion began, President George W. Bush declared: "Intelligence gathered by this and other governments leaves no doubt that the Iraq regime continues to possess and conceal some of the most lethal weapons ever devised." Bush was able to make the claim stick with most Americans at the time because of media coverage that had accepted leaked U.S. "intelligence" reports as credible— even though extensive contrary information was readily available at the time.[13] Any "intelligence failure" was matched by a contemporaneous media failure.[14]

After devoting thousands of network hours and oceans of ink to stories about "weapons of mass destruction" in Iraq, major U.S. news outlets did little but yawn when *Newsweek* published an exclusive report on the subject in late February 2003—a piece headlined "The Defector's Secrets."

It was hard to imagine how any journalist on the prewar beat could read the article's lead without doing a double take: "Hussein Kamel, the highest-ranking Iraqi official ever to defect from Saddam Hussein's inner circle, told CIA and British intelligence officers and U.N. inspectors in the summer of 1995 that after the Gulf War, Iraq destroyed all its chemical and biological weapons stocks and the missiles to deliver them." The article was written by *Newsweek* national security correspondent John Barry, who had been with the magazine since 1985. After following the Iraq weapons story for a dozen years, he drew on in-depth knowledge—in stark contrast to journalists who simply relayed the pronouncements coming out of Washington and the United Nations. "I think the whole issue of Iraq's weaponry has become steadily more impacted and complicated over the years," Barry told me in an interview two days after his article appeared. People often had trouble making sense out of the "twists and turns of the arguments." And, Barry added, what was being reported as "fact" provided by the U.S. government or the U.N. in many cases amounted to mere "supposition."[15]

Barry's potentially explosive story noted that "Kamel was Saddam Hussein's son-in-law and had direct knowledge of what he claimed: for 10 years he had run Iraq's nuclear, chemical, biological and missile programs." Making use of written documentation that *Newsweek* had verified as authentic, the article reported: "Kamel's revelations about the destruction of Iraq's WMD stocks were hushed up by the U.N. inspectors, sources say, for two reasons. Saddam did not know how much Kamel had revealed, and the inspectors hoped to bluff Saddam into disclosing still more. And Iraq has never shown the documentation to support Kamel's story. Still, the defector's tale raises questions about whether the WMD stockpiles attributed to Iraq still exist."[16]

The *Newsweek* story came off the press on Sunday, February 23. The next day, a would-be authoritative source—the Central Intelligence Agency—explained that it just wasn't so. "It is incorrect, bogus, wrong, untrue," declared CIA spokesman Bill Harlow. For good measure, Reuters quoted an unnamed "British government source" eager to contradict *Newsweek*'s documented account of what Kamel had said. "We've checked back and he didn't say this," the source contended. "He said just the opposite, that the WMD program was alive and kicking."[17] Under the unwritten rules of American media coverage, such denials tend to end the matter—especially when the president and Congress have already decided that war is necessary.

It wasn't as if Kamel ranked as a nobody in media circles. Journalists and U.S. officials were fond of recounting that Saddam Hussein made sure he was quickly killed after the defector returned to Iraq following six months of voluntary exile. "Until now, Kamel has best been known for exposing Iraq's deceptions about how far its pre–Gulf War biological weapons programs had advanced," media analyst Seth Ackerman pointed out. He added that *Newsweek*'s story "is particularly noteworthy because hawks in the Bush administration have frequently referred to the Kamel episode as evidence that U.N. inspectors are incapable of disarming Iraq on their own."[18] Ackerman cited a speech Dick Cheney had made in August 2002, when the vice president said that what occurred with Kamel "should serve as a reminder to all that we often learned more as the result of defections than we learned from the inspection regime itself."[19] Accounts of Kamel's debriefing as a defector and his subsequent demise often served to illustrate the dishonesty and brutality of Iraq's government. But when other information emerged about what he had to say, the fellow suddenly became much less newsworthy.

American journalists assumed that Iraqi officials were lying about weapons of mass destruction—and also assumed that officials such as George W. Bush, Donald Rumsfeld, and especially Colin Powell were being truthful.[20] Overall, the news media helped to create a great market for war. And an author who soared in that bullish marketplace was Kenneth Pollack, the former CIA analyst whose 2002 book *The Threatening Storm: The Case for Invading Iraq* was a media-driven smash. A frequent presence on national television, Pollack eagerly promoted a book and a war at the same time. He called for a "massive invasion" of Iraq.[21]

Later, after the invasion occurred, Pollack was to write a long essay with a somewhat regretful tone, declaring in the *Atlantic* magazine's first issue of 2004: "What we have learned about Iraq's WMD programs since the fall of Baghdad leads me to conclude that the case for war with Iraq was considerably weaker than I believed beforehand. . . . I had been convinced that Iraq was only years away from having a nuclear weapon—probably only four or five years. . . . That estimate was clearly off, possibly by quite a bit."

On May 26, 2004—long after publishing front-page articles about Iraqi WMDs that boosted the momentum toward an invasion of Iraq—the *New York Times* printed a fourteen-paragraph "From the Editors" note that finally acknowledged there was something wrong with the coverage. But the unusual new article, appearing under the headline "The *Times* and Iraq," indicated that top editors at the newspaper were still refusing to face up to its pivotal role in the prewar era. The *Times* semiapology was more self-justifying than self-critical. Assessing a page-one December 2001 article that promulgated a bogus tale about biological, chemical, and nuclear weapons facilities in Iraq, the editors' note said that "in this case it looks as if we, along with the administration, were taken in." The same tone echoed through an internal memo to the *Times* newsroom from the paper's executive editor, Bill Keller, on the same day: "The purpose of the [published] note is to acknowledge that we, like many of our competitors and many officials in Washington, were misled on a number of stories by Iraqi informants dealing in misinformation."[22] But the *Times* editors and Bush administration officials had chosen to trumpet what they were told by certain dubious sources. For the readers of the *Times*, disinformation—on behalf of a war agenda—was served up on the front page, time after time, in the guise of journalism.

Unnamed in the *Times* editors' note was star reporter Judith Miller, who wrote or cowrote four of the six articles singled out as flawed. Keller's internal memo explained that the editors' public article "is not an attempt to find a scapegoat or to blame reporters for not knowing then what we know now."[23] The phrasing was seriously evasive. A comment from the media watchdog organization FAIR pointed out: "If Keller thinks the problem with Judith Miller's reporting was her lack of clairvoyance rather than her failure to exercise basic journalistic skepticism, then it's clear that he didn't learn much from this fiasco. He describes the publication of the editors' note as 'a point of journalistic pride'—as if a publication should be proud of acknowledging egregious errors that other people have been pointing out for more than a year."[24]

Miller had routinely avoided letting her readers know that she was relying on the Pentagon's pet Iraqi exile, Ahmad Chalabi.[25] The belated semi-mea-culpa article by the *Times* editors—while failing to provide any forthright explanation of Chalabi's role as a chronic source for Miller's prewar stories—appeared a week after the U.S. government turned definitively and publicly against its ally Chalabi, giving the nod for a raid on his Baghdad headquarters and widely leaking the accusation that he'd passed classified information to the Iranian government. Only then did the top *New York Times* editors turn definitively and publicly against key stories spun by the Chalabi-Miller duo. Yet ample evidence had been readily available for years that Chalabi was a stellar con man and confabulator.[26]

More revealing than they evidently intended, the editors' article repeatedly lumped together two institutions—the *New York Times* and the U.S. government—as though they were somehow in comparable situations during the lead-up to the war. The excuses for both were sounding remarkably similar. So the *Times* editors insinuated that they, along with top officials in Washington, were victims rather than perpetrators: "Administration officials now acknowledge that they sometimes fell for misinformation from these exile sources. So did many news organizations—in particular, this one."[27] While the "From the Editors" article took a step toward setting the record straight, it did so while sidestepping responsibility. A terrible truth went unacknowledged by the *New York Times*: The most influential newspaper in America did not "fall for misinformation" as much as eagerly jump for it. The paper helped the administration tell lies. And no amount of self-examination, genuine or otherwise, could make up for the carnage in Iraq that the *Times* facilitated.

4
—

This Guy Is a Modern-Day Hitler

Evil that warrants the large-scale killing of war needs a face. But that face cannot belong to some amorphous mass of an enemy population; in fact, it's a ritual for the president to offer assurances that civilians who may be caught in the crossfire are not among the Pentagon's targets. The bull's-eye must be painted on someone who links the nascent war to an indisputably justified one of the past. For this purpose, Hitler's name has been pressed into service, intermittently, for decades. Pointed mentions of Nazi Germany and the Holocaust open floodgates of emotion, connecting a present-day foe with a regime that slaughtered millions of people near the fulcrum of the twentieth century. What helps to do the trick is the message that while horrors of the past cannot be changed, they can be prevented in the near future.

At a press conference on July 28, 1965, when President Lyndon B. Johnson spoke about the need to escalate the Vietnam War, he used a historical analogy. "We did not choose to be the guardians at the gate, but there is no one else," he said. "Nor would surrender in Vietnam bring peace, because we learned from Hitler at Munich that success only feeds the appetite of aggression. The battle would be renewed in one country and then another country, bringing with it perhaps even larger and crueler conflict, as we have learned from the lessons of history." And Johnson declared: "We just cannot now dishonor our word."[1]

A beauty of the Munich analogy, as several of LBJ's successors found, was that it could seem irrefutable on its own terms. The comparison might be very useful for likening a certain government to a Hitlerian menace.

Since the Vietnam era, various leaders—most famously Manuel Noriega, Slobodan Milosevic, and Saddam Hussein—have been promoted as sufficiently evil to necessitate U.S. military action. Singling out a particular villain (while winking at, or even cooperating with, a range of other tyrants) is vital to laying the rhetorical groundwork for war. To demonize—and that's just about a prerequisite for war—requires picking and choosing. With dozens of governments engaging in torture and political repression every day, sometimes accompanied by systematic military atrocities, targeting a specific regime is a matter of White House policy priorities.

During the 1980s those priorities involved so much hostility toward the leftist Sandinista government in Nicaragua that the momentum of Washington's rhetoric carried it to absurd comparisons with the Third Reich. At a World Affairs Council session in Boston on February 15, 1984, Secretary of State George Shultz said: "I've had good friends who experienced Germany in the 1930s go there and come back and say, 'I've visited many communist countries, but Nicaragua doesn't feel like that. It feels like Nazi Germany.'" Two weeks later, Boston University president John Silber, a member of the Bipartisan Commission on Central America appointed by President Ronald Reagan, likened Nicaragua's "overt violence" to Nazi Germany, without a mention that the U.S. government was subsidizing most of the violence in Nicaragua with aid to the Contra guerrilla army.[2]

When Iraq's invasion of Kuwait on August 2, 1990, abruptly soured the cordial relations between Washington and Baghdad, the White House suddenly propagated analogies between the Baathist and Nazi regimes. "A half century ago, our nation and the world paid dearly for appeasing an aggressor who should, and could, have been stopped," President George H. W. Bush said. "We are not going to make the same mistake again."[3] Some commentators warned against the facile comparison. Syndicated columnist William Pfaff, based in Paris, wrote in mid-August that "Saddam Hussein is not Hitler, and to describe him as Hitler feeds hysteria and confusion."[4] But for war planners in Washington, some hysteria and confusion were already proving to be quite helpful. Polls showed three-quarters of the American public in support of the large U.S. military deployment already under way to the Middle East.[5] And, as a news story noted when September began, "Support for President Bush climbed from 58 percent to 76 percent in the three weeks after Iraq seized the small oil-rich country of

Kuwait."[6] The Saddam-as-Hitler motif rapidly became a familiar pattern on the media wallpaper. "When he wasn't going after Congress, President Bush had a few choice words for Saddam Hussein," CBS newsman Charles Osgood intoned. "In a speech yesterday, Mr. Bush characterized the Iraqi leader's behavior as Hitler revisited."[7]

With the November congressional elections nearing, the president was hardly inclined to give the Adolf Hussein theme a rest. "I'm reading a book and it's a book of history—great, big, thick history about World War II," he told a Republican fund-raising breakfast in Vermont. "And there's a parallel between what Hitler did to Poland and what Saddam Hussein has done to Kuwait. Hitler rolled his tanks and troops into Poland." Bush added: "And do you know what followed the troops? It was the Death's Head regiment. Do you know what the Death's Head regiments of the SS were? They were the ones that went in and lined up the kids that were passing out leaflets. Do you know what happened in Kuwait the other day? Two young kids, mid-teens, passing out leaflets—Iraqi soldiers came, got their parents out and watched as they killed them."[8]

During that campaign swing, the president described Hussein as "a little Hitler."[9] Meanwhile, the same analogy came from retired general William Westmoreland, former commander of U.S. forces in Vietnam, who spoke up as a guest on ABC's *Nightline* program: "You know, here in the 1990s, Saddam Hussein is the Hitler of the Middle East. And if we're going to give him a free rein and not stand up to him and not have the troops available to resist him, the Middle East is going to be in turmoil."[10]

All in all, the LexisNexis media database shows, major American news outlets printed and aired comparisons between Saddam and Hitler at an average rate of several times each day during the 5½ months that led up to the Gulf War in mid-January 1991. But Saddam Hussein had long been a horrendous dictator: before, during, and after the Iran-Iraq war, which spanned most of the 1980s. Washington tilted toward Baghdad with tangible assistance in that conflict. Year after year, Saddam remained on good terms with the U.S. government, while negative press notices were sparse in the United States.

When the Iraqi invasion of Kuwait drastically changed Washington's view of Hussein, the mainstream American media had an epiphany about his unnerving resemblance to Hitler. Three years after the *New Republic* called for boosting U.S. military aid to Saddam in 1987, the influential magazine altered a cover photo of the Iraqi dictator to make his mustache look more like Hitler's.[11] Overnight, the doors in Washington had slammed shut for Saddam. As the *Washington Post* columnist Mary McGrory put it: "Iraq enjoyed special trade status up to the moment it invaded Kuwait and Saddam Hussein began to remind Bush of Hitler."[12]

Some congressional Republicans and certain normally hawkish pundits voiced opposition to the spring 1999 bombing of Yugoslavia, perhaps in part because it was being spearheaded by a loathed Democrat in the White House. But they could do little to impede the kind of war momentum that they were accustomed to enhancing and applauding. When the air war began, the usual media forms of bombing euphoria kicked in, along with further extensive publicity about the suffering of ethnic Albanians in Kosovo.

Clinton administration officials and many journalists had cranked up appreciable spin machinery over the winter. Slobodan Milosevic was "the closest thing to Hitler Europe has confronted in the last half-century," wrote liberal *Boston Globe* columnist David Nyhan three weeks into 1999. Nyhan was among many pundits drawn to the nobility of the upcoming war. (Typically, he wrote that the Yugoslav president "has taken the audacious steps of countenancing the massacre of Albanian civilians in Kosovo, refusing access to the U.N.'s war crimes prosecutor, and has expelled an American diplomat who blamed the massacre on Serb authorities."[13]) Media database searches attest to how well top Clinton administration officials and like-minded advocates stayed on message about similarities between Hitler and Milosevic. Hundreds of times, major U.S. media pieces addressed the matter, often in the form of news stories that reported such comparisons by officials without offering a critical counterview. Some commentators disputed the analogy, but the widespread media likening of Milosevic's tyranny to Hitler's seemed to burnish the evil of the Serbian president into the public mind. Overlaid on such narratives was a story line that presented war as an extraordinarily selfless option for NATO, with the United States leading the way. Yet the Kosovo conflict was riddled with complexities.

Back in 1993, the insightful NPR correspondent Sylvia Poggioli had written about dynamics of news coverage of warfare in the Balkans: "Policy in Western capitals—or lack of it—has increasingly been based on news reports, and from my experience I have seen that many times the media have been better at pulling emotional strings than at analyzing facts. The use of good-guy and bad-guy stereotypes often obscured the complex origins of the conflict."[14] During the 1990s, regimes based in Belgrade, Zagreb, and Sarajevo could point to horrible massacres perpetrated by each other; every side insisted that its own barbaric actions did not really occur—or were justified in response to earlier monstrous offenses. "The tendency to justify atrocities by pointing to those committed by the opposing side will merely ensure that the pattern of reciprocal massacre remains unbroken," BBC correspondent Misha Glenny observed in his book *The Fall of Yugoslavia*.[15]

The decade's huge quantities of U.S. media coverage about the Balkans included scant mention of what happened in August 1995 when the Croatian government—with a bright green light from the White House—sent in troops to inflict grisly "ethnic cleansing" on large numbers of Serbs living in the Krajina region. The president of Croatia, Franjo Tudjman, ordered the assault. Dubbed Operation Storm, it quickly drove at least 150,000 Serbian people from their homes in the Krajina. Meanwhile, the American news media—taking a cue from the Oval Office—just shrugged. "The entire offensive was undertaken by the authorities in Zagreb with the support of the United States government," Glenny wrote. "President Clinton himself welcomed Operation Storm, suggesting that it may open the way to a solution of the Yugoslav conflict. The rest of the international community was visibly shocked by America's encouragement of Croatia."[16]

But the U.S. news media weren't shocked. After all, the White House said the slaughter and expulsion of Serbs from the Krajina was okay; nothing to be alarmed about; no big deal. At the time Carl Bildt, who was a mediator for the European Union and a former Swedish prime minister, made a statement that years later was chilling to read: "If we accept that it is all right for Tudjman to cleanse Croatia of its Serbs, then how on earth can we object if [Boris] Yeltsin cleanses Chechnya or if one day Milosevic sends his army to clean out the Albanians from Kosovo?"[17]

In early 1999 the White House scriptwriters cast Milosevic as the fuehrer and Serbs as Brown Shirts, period. The day before he ordered the start of the bombing, President Clinton gave a speech likening Slobodan to Adolf and drawing the kind of analogy that U.S. presidents bent on war have been unable to resist in modern times: "And so

I want to talk to you about Kosovo today but just remember this—it's about our values. What if someone had listened to Winston Churchill and stood up to Adolf Hitler earlier?"[18] The *Washington Post* reported that "the president compared Milosevic explicitly to Hitler." Hours into the missile strikes, Clinton "included such language as 'dictator' and 'genocide in the heart of Europe' to describe the Serbian nationalist's deeds." As the *Post* observed, "Clinton and his senior advisers harked repeatedly back to images of World War II and Nazism to give moral weight to the bombing."[19] The heavy political freight ran parallel with profuse media accolades about allied bombing that would prevent a smaller version of the Holocaust from playing out.

When the bombing of Yugoslavia got under way, the Clinton administration initially played catch-up to attain the usual favorable wartime media treatment; big boosts came from a blitz of TV appearances by the secretaries of state and defense in the hours and days after the bombing began. Marlin Fitzwater, who had spoken for the White House during the Gulf War eight years earlier, drew on his spin-cycle expertise and adjudged the new PR moves to be "effective in the short term." Yet he found fault with the agenda-building for the latest war. "The problem is they didn't start the communications until the bombs started falling," Fitzwater remarked, sounding a bit like a retired pro doing color commentary about the performances of the players on the field. "That's not enough time to convince the nation of a course of action. But it's helpful because it convinces people to give the government the benefit of the doubt."[20]

Looking back with pride, the loquacious Fitzwater recalled a slick public-relations campaign he'd helped to shape. He reminisced that a few days before the Gulf War started, ABC did a kitchen-table interview with some people in Kansas—and "every answer at that table reflected one of the reasons we had given for going in." Among the precepts Fitzwater mentioned was the idea that war is "easier for people to understand if there's a face to the enemy." In chronological order, he ticked off the names of "Hitler, Ho Chi Minh, Saddam Hussein, Milosevic."[21]

Doubts and controversies about rationales for the war on Yugoslavia were largely moot once the war train left the station. "The analogies that President Clinton offered last week to rally public support do not stand up under close inspection," *Washington Post* columnist Jim Hoagland wrote after the first few days of bombing.

"Failure to repulse Slobodan Milosevic in Kosovo would parallel appeasement at Munich, the prelude to World War II and to the Holocaust, Clinton argued. But Kosovo is not the Holocaust or Munich. Serb dictator Milosevic is no Hitler on the march." Hoagland added: "This is a local conflict over self-determination and a crumbling dictatorship."[22] Meanwhile, a *Newsday* editorial took issue with the key analogy that had served as a very big PR flagstone on the garden path to war: "Comparing Milosevic to Hitler is a rhetorical stretch. Milosevic is a brutal tyrant and a rabid nationalist intent on consolidating his hold on power, but he has no territorial ambitions beyond what's left of Yugoslavia. And Milosevic's ferocity against Kosovars is motivated as much by his need to put down an internal insurrection as it is by ethnic hatred."[23] But from the vantage point of powerful offices near the banks of the Potomac, a faraway "local conflict" over "self-determination" was apt to seem like an abstraction. Another Hitler, in contrast, was a hefty concept, sellable in TV moments.

While the bombing continued in the early spring, so did the Milosevic-Hitler comparisons. The administration in Washington squandered no opportunity to lock onto Milosevic as the new incontrovertible enemy and pull the polemical trigger. Only a couple of months earlier, Secretary of State Madeleine Albright had described Milosevic as a leader who "wants to, at some stage, re-enter the international community."[24] But as April 1999 began, the Associated Press noted the extreme image makeover: "Now she portrays him as 'cruel and evil,' and caring of nothing except staying in power." And now the verbal targeting was carefully personalized: "Where once she criticized 'the Serbs,' 'them,' or 'Belgrade authorities' for intransigence, she and other senior officials speak as if the whole conflict were about NATO vs. Milosevic. Vice President Al Gore called him 'one of these junior league Hitler types' even as officials have stopped just short of calling Milosevic's actions 'genocide.'"[25] Numerous members of Congress provided echoes.[26] And many pundits found the user-friendly comparisons with Nazism still too enticing to resist. "America is a strong country because it is good," Christopher Matthews wrote. "We cannot be a good country if we stand aside and let the Serbians commit genocide. . . . We've got a leader in Serbia who wants to cleanse his country of what Hitler called the 'under people.' With him it was Jews and gypsies and homosexuals. With Slobodan Milosevic, it's now ethnic Albanians."[27]

Ironically, by then some Serbs were referring to the president of the United States as "Bill Hitler."[28] After two weeks of intense NATO bombardment, with U.S. planes in the lead, a woman in Belgrade named Jovana Sultanovic told an American reporter: "Nobody thinks about Milosevic. He is the last thing on our mind. We are aware that Milosevic is not good. We don't want to say he is good, but he doesn't throw bombs on us."[29] *Chicago Tribune* columnist Clarence Page described an evening seminar he'd just attended at the White House, with Holocaust survivor Elie Wiesel expressing support for the current war: "Much was said about how the catastrophe in Kosovo illustrates the perils of indifference. Too little was said about the perils of action, specifically the actions taken by President Clinton and NATO that have made bad matters worse."[30]

Deadly attacks by Serbs against ethnic Albanians in Kosovo had actually spiked upward massively—and predictably—when the U.S./NATO bombing began; so had the surge of desperate refugees. After four weeks of cheering on the bombing, *Boston Globe* columnist Nyhan felt compelled to acknowledge the point, though he trotted out the timeworn Hitler analogy to try to deflect blame away from those who had launched the present-day war. "What has to be conceded," he wrote, "is that the NATO planners made a colossal blunder in underestimating Milosevic's willingness to employ the scorched earth tactics of Hitler and Stalin. By a Reuters estimate, some 960,000 Kosovars have fled or been driven from Kosovo in the last year, 590,000 since the bombing began." The fact that more than half of the refugees had so quickly fled *after* the U.S.-led bombing began did not seem to faze Nyhan much, even as he informed readers: "A refugee crisis of a scale not seen in Europe since the Nazi era complicates NATO's strategy."[31]

Analysis in the mainstream U.S. press included some sober reflections. *Chicago Tribune* readers could find Page's astute comment: "Nothing excuses Milosevic's bloody tyranny, but he is not the same sort of tyrant as Hitler. We make a mistake if we try to demonize Milosevic too much. Unlike Hitler, who wanted to wipe out the Jews, Milosevic's forced removal of ethnic Albanians has different roots. It grew, in part, out of his overreaction to the [Albanian] KLA's attacks against Serbs and even some fellow ethnic Albanians who were believed to be insufficiently committed to the KLA's cause."[32] A month later, with the bombing in its eighth week, the *Washington Post* published a similar assessment by staffer Michael Dobbs, who had recently reported from the Balkans. He wrote: "While the Milosevic-as-Hitler analogy favored by Clinton and Albright makes for good rhetoric, it makes a mockery of history. It is certainly true that Milosevic's policies (which were matched by other nationalist leaders, notably Croatia's Franjo Tudjman) helped destroy the former Yugoslavia. And it's also true that tens of thousands of people have been killed as a result of the wars unleashed by Milosevic in Croatia, Bosnia and now Kosovo. At the same time, however, any comparison between the rump, Serb-led Yugoslavia and Nazi Germany is laughable. Yugoslavia is so weak militarily and economically that it could never pose a serious threat to its neighbors except, as in the present case, as a source of refugees and political instability. There is all the difference in the world between an expansionist totalitarian power like Hitler's Germany and a bankrupt police state like Milosevic's Yugoslavia."[33]

But when summer began, the American media's thematic last word on Milosevic and the necessity of the seventy-eight-day bombing campaign was much closer to this pronouncement in a *New York Daily News* editorial: "With his blessing, Serb soldiers have drenched Kosovo with the blood of tens of thousands of Albanians and sent perhaps a million more fleeing in panic. Not since Hitler and Stalin has Europe witnessed such massive barbarism."[34]

When the second Bush administration returned Saddam Hussein to the center stage of U.S. foreign policy, it was time to reprise countless stories about his evilness, while again eliding the cozy relationship that Hussein had long enjoyed with Washington.[35] (When I accompanied former U.N. assistant secretary-general Denis Halliday to a private meeting in Baghdad with Iraqi deputy prime minister Tariq Aziz in late January 2003, Aziz glanced at the latest *Time* magazine, which Halliday had just given to him. Secretary of Defense Donald Rumsfeld was on the cover. "Rumsfeld has become quite a warmonger," Aziz said. "He did not seem so when he came and visited us in the 1980s.") The Iraqi dictator had not ordered an attack on another country since 1990, and his military capabilities had obviously diminished—but comparing him to Hitler fit like an old shoe.

One of many politicians eager to keep putting it on was "moderate Republican" Christopher Shays, who repeatedly invoked memories of the Third Reich to justify an invasion of Iraq. Days before

Congress passed the war resolution in October 2002, Shays went on MSNBC and used the Hitler analogy as part of a slick repertoire about Saddam. "The burden of proof rests on those to prove that he hasn't continued his programs of mass destruction," Shays said. "That's where the burden of proof is. I've been in no classified briefing that said he has stopped his program. In every instance, he's moving ahead with it. And it's not one bomb. It's many. And we're talking about—the only thing he's basically waiting for and trying to acquire is the enriched uranium or plutonium, the nuclear-grade material to make a bomb. It is about the size of a softball. You can touch it and it's not detectable. We will not allow Saddam Hussein to have nuclear weapons." A minute later, Shays executed another smooth shuffle: "We're not talking about a criminal act that we have to prove in court. We're talking about the logic of events. Someone said to me, 'Prove that he will use his nuclear weapons.' To me, that's like saying, 'Prove Hitler's Germany was going to go into Poland.' We knew he went into Czechoslovakia. We knew he went into Austria. We knew he was building up his armament. We knew what he was about. We could never have proved he was going into Poland."[36] An all-purpose formulation: *When nothing need be proven, then no war need be justified*, ahead of time or later on.[37]

After more than two decades of representing a San Francisco area district in Congress, Tom Lantos was the ranking Democrat on the House International Relations Committee by the time an invasion of Iraq was on the near horizon. He was not to be outdone at conflating Baathist Iraq with the Third Reich, as though Saddam's forces were somehow comparable to Germany's Wehrmacht. In early October 2002, Lantos pulled out all the stops on Capitol Hill as he proclaimed: "Had Hitler's regime been taken out in a timely fashion, the 51 million innocent people who lost their lives during the Second World War would have been able to finish their normal life cycles. Mr. Chairman, if we appease Saddam Hussein, we will stand humiliated before both humanity and history."[38]

Although spared such humiliation, avid supporters of the Iraq invasion were soon struggling to respond to a plethora of belated revelations and difficulties with the occupation. At that point, references to Hitler and other historic mass murderers still came in very handy. After a brief stint as the head of the U.S. government's "civilian operations" in Iraq during early days of the occupation, Jay Garner was ready when challenged while appearing before a House subcommittee in Washington. "In response to criticisms about the administration's handling of the Iraq war, Garner compared Saddam to Adolf Hitler and Cambodian leader Pol Pot," reported United Press International. "He related his own experience seeing children's bodies being pulled from the mass graves of Saddam's 'killing fields.' This sort of response has become central to the Bush administration's messages in reply to criticism following the invasion of Iraq and still unanswered questions about the state of Saddam's alleged weapons programs."[39]

During the same week as Jay Garner's testimony about bodies being exhumed from mass graves of Saddam's "killing fields," subscribers to the *New York Review of Books* were considering a new essay by Norman Mailer that served as a de facto retort. Acknowledging that "the most painful single ingredient at the moment is, of course, the discovery of the graves," Mailer did not stop there. He went on: "We have relieved the world of a monster who killed untold numbers, mega-numbers, of victims. Nowhere is any emphasis put upon the fact that many of the bodies were of the Shiites of southern Iraq who have been decimated repeatedly in the last 12 years for daring to rebel against Saddam in the immediate aftermath of the Gulf War. Of course, we were the ones who encouraged them to revolt in the first place, and then failed to help them. Why? There may have been an ongoing argument in the first Bush administration which was finally won by those who believed that a Shiite victory over Saddam could result in a host of Iraqi imams who might make common cause with the Iranian ayatollahs, Shiites joining with Shiites! Today, from the point of view of the remaining Iraqi Shiites, it would be hard for us to prove to them that they were not the victims of a double cross. So they may look upon the graves that we congratulate ourselves for having liberated as sepulchral voices calling out from their tombs—asking us to take a share of the blame. Which, of course, we will not."

Digging deeper into history, Mailer continued: "Yes, our guilt for a great part of those bodies remains a large subtext and Saddam was creating mass graves all through the 1970s and 1980s. He killed Communists en masse in the 1970s, which didn't bother us a bit. Then he slaughtered tens of thousands of Iraqis during the war with Iran—a time when we supported him. A horde of those newly discovered graves go back to that period. Of course, real killers never look back."[40]

5

This Is about Human Rights

A persuasive argument for going to war is often a clarion call for action on behalf of human rights. The specter of continued political imprisonment, torture, and killings may come to seem unacceptable—especially when we learn some of the details and a remedy appears to be at hand. If American leaders tell us that human-rights abuses and atrocities must cease, there may be acknowledgment that war will cause hardship, pain, and death—but at the end of the day, peace will come and freedom can flourish. That's the pitch from the White House, anyway. But behind the tableau of official principles are realities that rarely get onto the public stage. Away from the media spotlight and unmentioned by policy promoters in Washington, some terrible human-rights violations get scant criticism—or even receive behind-the-scenes support—from the U.S. government. Seen in narrow light, the president's posture for war is apt to appear noble; yet from a wider view, it is difficult to miss the hypocrisy and manipulation.

Many governments engage in serious violations of human rights. But the Pentagon only bombs a few of them.

High-minded rhetoric can be reassuring. Yet when Washington gets down to policy, some torture is deplorable, some is ignorable, and some is fundable. Generally, top U.S. officials are careful to downplay or bypass entirely the horrendous deeds of allies.

Inside the Beltway and in U.S. mass media, Kurdish people killed by Saddam Hussein's regime were of great human significance—but in contrast, viewed through the same media window, the Kurdish people killed across the border by the Turkish government (a member of NATO) merited no appreciable concern. You can search in vain for a record of Washington condemning its ally Turkey while, in the 1990s, Turks drove millions of Kurdish people from their homes, destroyed thousands of villages, killed many thousands of Kurds, and inflicted horrific torture.[1]

To take another example: The invasion of Iraq was praised for closing down Hussein's torture chambers. Meanwhile, billions of dollars in aid continued to flow from Washington to the government in Cairo, still operating torture chambers for political prisoners. One might think that an appropriate way to oppose torture would be to stop financing it.

During the first several years of the twenty-first century, the disconnects between Washington's idealistic language and its actual actions became even more extreme. Annual reports from human-rights groups cataloged superpower hypocrisy run amok. In 2003, Amnesty International condemned the American and British governments for engaging in a "war on terror" that was actually emboldening many regimes to engage in horrible abuses of human rights. Amnesty International's secretary-general, Irene Khan, said that "what would have been unacceptable on September 10, 2001, is now becoming almost the norm"—with Washington promoting "a new doctrine of human rights à la carte."[2] In 2004 the Amnesty International annual report described the invasion of Iraq, and other actions taken under the rubric of the war on terrorism, as part of a U.S. global agenda "bankrupt of vision and bereft of principle." Secretary-General Khan led off the report with a statement that stressed the damaging activities of the U.S. government: "Sacrificing human rights in the name of security at home, turning a blind eye to abuses abroad and using pre-emptive military force where and when it chooses have neither increased security nor ensured liberty."[3]

Whether or not the exact phrase is used, "human rights" can often be found at the core of Washington's most common rationales for initiating and continuing wars—directly or indirectly.

And so it was with Jimmy Carter, a president known for embracing human rights. "The world itself is now dominated by a new spirit," Carter said at his inauguration. "People more numerous and more politically aware are craving and now demanding their place in the sun—not just for the benefit of their own physical condition, but for basic human rights." The new president's verbal emphasis on human rights was soothing, and not without substance; the Carter administration sometimes exerted pressure on regimes to release political prisoners and halt abuses. But Carter's uplifting words contrasted with U.S. policies from Central America to Asia.

Thirteen months before Carter spoke of "basic human rights" at his inauguration, the Indonesian military had invaded East Timor and began a methodical slaughter of civilians. Carter used his new power as president to boost U.S. military aid to the Jakarta regime. "By 1977, Indonesia had actually begun to exhaust its military supplies in this war against a country of 700,000 people," Noam Chomsky has recounted, "so the Carter administration took some time off from its pieties and self-acclaim about its devotion to human rights—'the soul of our foreign policy'—to arrange a large-scale increase in the flow of arms to Indonesia, in the certain knowledge that they would be used to consummate a massacre that was approaching genocidal proportions."[4] The death toll in East Timor rose to an estimated 200,000 people by the end of 1979.

Carter's effusive talk about human rights greased the path for aiding and abetting the carnage in East Timor. Denial persisted long after the fact; neither he nor the U.S. news media seemed willing to acknowledge the American government's role. Avoidance of uncomfortable accuracy was echoed by the *New York Times*. A third of a century after the tyrannical Suharto had grabbed control of Indonesia in a coup that led to the murder of at least several hundred thousand people (aided by the CIA and applauded by the *Times* and other U.S. media outlets), the *Times* repeatedly put the best face possible on Suharto as prodemocracy forces challenged his grip on power in spring 1998. According to the newspaper, Suharto was a "profoundly spiritual man" and a "reforming autocrat."[5] The *Times* offered this rationale for the mass murderer: "It was not simply personal ambition that led Mr. Suharto to clamp down so hard for so long; it was a fear, shared by many in this country of 210 million people, of chaos."[6]

During the time of Suharto's downfall, dozens of *New York Times* articles detoured around inconvenient history. The front page referred to "mass killings of 32 years ago, when Mr. Suharto took power from the country's founding president, Sukarno. At that time, as many as half a million people died in an anti-Communist purge."[7] The next day, another prominent *Times* story recalled that "hundreds of thousands were killed in the turmoil of the last political transition, as

Mr. Suharto presided over a hunt for leftists around the country and consolidated his power."[8] Actually, the CIA and other accessories of American foreign policy played key roles in the killing spree that took the lives of half a million Indonesians during the "turmoil" of the mid-1960s. Along the way, the U.S. government supplied a list of five thousand leftists to Indonesia's military, fingering them for assassination. Washington also supported Suharto throughout his subsequent crimes, including the systematic atrocities in East Timor.

During his presidency, Carter proclaimed human rights to be "the soul of our foreign policy"[9] and many journalists promoted that image. Despotic allies—from Ferdinand Marcos of the Philippines to the shah of Iran—received support from President Carter. In Nicaragua, contrary to myth, Carter backed dictator Anastasio Somoza almost until the end of his reign. Bloodshed in Guatemala scarcely missed a beat during the Carter years; despite highly publicized symbolic moves to the contrary, military aid to the Guatemalan government was scarcely reduced, and the Pentagon kept its supportive relationship with the military in Guatemala as Mayan Indians and dissidents were tortured and murdered en masse. And in El Salvador, the Carter administration played a key role.

Early in 1980, Archbishop Oscar Romero pleaded with President Carter not to send military aid to the brutally repressive Salvadoran government. The assassination of Romero happened in March of that year—on orders of Roberto D'Aubuisson, a United States–trained military officer. Carter persisted with military and political support to the regime in El Salvador, where throughout the 1980s the government assassinated students, clergy, peasants, and union organizers. Most military commanders were involved in atrocities, and most were trained by the U.S. government. The gruesome war went on until 1991, when the United Nations helped negotiate a truce between the Salvadoran regime and the country's FMLN revolutionary movement. The U.N. Truth Commission later documented the murders of more than sixty thousand civilians by the Salvadoran government and its paramilitary allies. In effect, the long war that brought about those deaths in El Salvador was aided by a pattern of U.S. media coverage, which conformed more with Washington's narratives than with reports from human rights experts and journalists in the field.

In January 1982, *New York Times* journalist Ray Bonner reported on a massacre of hundreds of children, women, and men in El Mozote carried out by the elite Salvadoran, U.S.-trained Atlacatl Battalion. After Washington denied there had been a massacre and the Reagan administration launched a smear campaign against Bonner, the *Times* pulled him out of El Salvador. A *Wall Street Journal* editorial denounced the unduly hard-hitting journalism by slurring the offensively diligent reporter. The editorial complained that in Bonner's reporting "Communist sources were given greater credence than either the U.S. government or the government it was supporting."[10] A decade later, the U.N. Truth Commission totally vindicated Bonner's reports after it excavated mass graves.[11] But the damage had been done back in the early 1980s, when the removal of Bonner by *Times* executives sent a powerful message to mainstream U.S. journalists who stayed behind in El Salvador. Reporting difficult facts in conflict with Washington could harm careers.

In February 1988, *New York Times* correspondent James LeMoyne (who had taken over Bonner's old beat) wrote a vivid account of an El Salvador atrocity—the public execution of two peasants by FMLN guerrillas. But the event never occurred. It had been invented by a Salvadoran army propaganda officer and placed in a right-wing San Salvador newspaper—which LeMoyne read and reported as fact. It took six months of petitioning before the *Times* would even acknowledge the error.[12]

Throughout the 1980s, news reports in U.S. media regularly used euphemisms to describe El Salvador. The government was referred to as a "democracy" or a "fledgling democracy." Military leaders who assassinated priests were termed "moderates." Reporters spoke of "a civil war" that claimed seventy thousand lives—when they knew from briefings at the San Salvador archdiocese human rights office that more than 90 percent of the dead were not battle casualties but civilians killed by government forces and allied death squads. In deference to Washington, news accounts referred to "human rights abuses on both sides"—when evidence showed them running about thirty to one toward the U.S.-supported government.[13]

Offering assurances that actual U.S. policy in Nicaragua was not actual U.S. policy there, President Ronald Reagan said on April 27, 1983: "But let us be clear as to the American attitude toward the government of Nicaragua. We do not seek its overthrow." The next winter, speaking about Nicaraguan elections, Secretary of State George Shultz was taking a high democratic tone: "The important thing is that if there is to be an electoral process, it be observed not only at the moment when people vote, but in all the preliminary aspects that make an election meaningful."[14] Shultz did not apply similar precepts that same year, or later, to elections promoted by the U.S. government in neighboring Guatemala and El Salvador. But then again, in the latter two cases, the Reagan administration was supporting brutally repressive regimes where electoral democracy did not exist.

On a Sunday in the spring of 1996, a ceremony at Arlington National Cemetery unveiled a small memorial for twenty-one American soldiers who died in secret combat during the 1980s. Back then, the American public remained unaware that U.S. troops were fighting guerrillas in the countryside of El Salvador—where a total of several thousand American servicemen, fifty-five at a time, played key combat roles such as calling in deadly air strikes. For most media, the ceremony at Arlington was a time-warp curiosity. Even the better coverage was severely flawed. On CBS, *60 Minutes* aired a segment that lauded the honor of the U.S. soldiers who'd been deprived of combat ribbons—and ignored the Salvadoran people deprived of their lives.[15]

One of the intrepid journalists who managed to uncover Central American realities, Robert Parry, worked for the Associated Press and *Newsweek* as the 1980s unfolded. He recalled that "editors and bureau chiefs in Washington were far too easily seduced by slick government propagandists, too willing to accept the smear campaigns directed against honest reporters." Truth is the first casualty of war, but it need not be a fatality. "If the American people knew that their tax dollars were being used to arm brutal armies which were butchering political dissidents, killing children and raping young girls, then support for the Reagan-Bush policies would have evaporated." But, Parry added, "with a few notable exceptions, the Washington news media went merrily along with the lies."[16]

Often the smooth evasions are lubricated socially. "I don't believe that whom I was or wasn't friends with interfered with our reporting at any of our publications," *Washington Post/Newsweek* owner Katharine Graham wrote in her autobiography.[17] However, Parry—recalling his work as a Washington correspondent for *Newsweek* during the last three years of the 1980s—shed some light on the shadows of Graham's reassurances. In sharp contrast to the claims in her book, Parry witnessed "self-censorship because of the coziness between *Post/Newsweek* executives and senior national security figures." Among his examples: "On one occasion in 1987, I was told that my story about the CIA funneling anti-Sandinista money through Nicaragua's Catholic Church had been watered down because the story needed to be run past Mrs. Graham, and Henry Kissinger was her house guest that weekend. Apparently, there was fear among the top editors that the story as written might cause some consternation." (In 1996, the memoirs of former CIA director Robert Gates confirmed that Parry had it right all along.[18]) Overall, according to Parry, "the *Post/Newsweek* company is protective of the national security establishment."[19]

The American public tends to remain in the dark about such matters, though sometimes exposure results in acute embarrassment at the White House. The "arms for hostages" Iran-Contra scandal that erupted during President Reagan's second term received much more media attention for the Iran and hostage aspects than the Contra arms implications. Reagan and his supporters emphasized how much he cared about hostages in Lebanon and his hope that Iranian officials might help free them. "The reason we had to have a covert operation," Reagan said on November 28, 1987, "is we believed that the people who wanted to talk to us, their lives would be forfeited if the ayatollah ever found out they were doing this." Relatively little focus went to the fact that the effort was helping CIA-backed Contras to terrorize Nicaraguans, murdering thousands of them in the process.

The war that raged in Nicaragua was facilitated by journalists and officials in Washington who gave short shrift to the intentional killing of civilians. Even when mentioned, atrocities by the Contras—financed with largess from U.S. taxpayers—were generally downplayed. In November 1987, a front-page photo of a Contra soldier with an adoring child accompanied a fifty-paragraph *New York Times* article that hyped the popularity of the Contra guerrillas. Buried near the end of the article was a passing reference to a just-released Americas Watch report stating that "the Contras systematically engage in violent abuses . . . so prevalent that these may be said to be their principal means of waging war."[20] The Contra abuses included murdering hundreds of children.

President Reagan conferred the laudatory buzz phrase "freedom fighters" on the Nicaraguan Contras—and on other favored insurgent armies, no matter how cruel the actions or repressive the guiding ideology.[21] "The freedom fighters of Afghanistan would tell us as well that the threat of aggression has not receded from the world," Reagan said.[22] As the decade went on, U.S. aid to the mujahadeen forces in Afghanistan trained the ranks of such "freedom fighters" as Osama bin Laden.

"The general consensus is that we shouldn't lose the peace by walking away from a significant foreign-policy success," an unnamed official in President George H. W. Bush's administration told the Associated Press in June 1991, commenting on plans to keep sending covert U.S. aid to Angolan guerrillas in 1992 despite a new pact to end Angola's sixteen-year civil war.[23] Ostensibly reassuring, the statement of commitment from Washington that "we shouldn't lose the peace" actually meant more war.

For people in Angola—already the world's artificial-limb capital due to a profusion of land mines—the "success" trumpeted by the White House became even more macabre. Central to Washington's strategy to make sure it didn't "lose the peace" was the ongoing pipeline of substantial aid to the guerrilla army known as Unita, long backed by the U.S. government. Fifteen months after the benevolent-sounding statement quoted by AP, the Unita guerrillas lost an internationally supervised election to Angola's ruling party. Unita immediately launched a new military offensive.

Within a year and a half following the election, five hundred thousand more Angolans had died, the British magazine *New Statesman* reported in March 1994: "Inexorably, month after month since the elections in September 1992, Unita's reign of terror has worsened, outstripping in horror the familiar scenes of starvation and factional or ethnic killing in Somalia, Liberia, Sudan, or Burundi. Yet this is a war the international community had the power to prevent."[24]

With high praise that echoed through American news coverage, President Reagan and President George H. W. Bush had lionized Unita leader Jonas Savimbi as a "freedom fighter." From the Oval Office, sustaining the Angolan war was a piece of cake. It received a tiny fraction of the U.S. media attention devoted to Bosnia—there was much coverage of Sarajevo's ordeal, for instance, but virtually none about the horrible sieges of Angolan cities such as Cuito, Huambo, and Malange—while the number of deaths in Angola was much larger and American culpability was direct.

The U.S. government was the latest in a series of powers fueling Unita's insurgency. "First the Portuguese colonists, then the South Africans in pursuit of regional dominance, then the U.S. in the name of anti-communism created and nourished Savimbi and his Unita," journalist Victoria Brittain wrote in the *New Statesman*. With U.S. encouragement, the United Nations had cooperated in appeasing Savimbi during the previous two years. Brittain concluded: "Angola has been destroyed by Unita leader Jonas Savimbi's determination to take by force the power successive United States administrations promised him, but which the Angolan people denied him in the polls."

Officials in Washington had made no secret of their zeal to support Unita. But as spring 1994 began, nearly three years after the Bush administration boasted of its "significant foreign-policy success," the continuation of horrors in Angola caused Brittain to write: "Every year since the mid-1980s, I have interviewed dozens of displaced peasants who described attacks on their villages by Unita, kidnapping of young men and boys, looting, beatings, and killings, while in hospital beds the rows of mutilated women bore witness to the mining of their fields. Defectors from Unita told more chilling stories of mass rallies at the headquarters in Jamba where women were burned alive as witches. These were not stories the outside world wanted to hear about Unita, whose leader was regularly received at the White House."[25]

In October 1990, during the lead-up to the Gulf War, a Democratic congressman from northern California, Tom Lantos, teamed up with an Illinois Republican to stage an informal hearing with enormous impact. "It was a propaganda exercise for the national media, and it succeeded wildly in mobilizing U.S. support for the war," media analyst John Stauber recalls. The audacity was notable: "Tom Lantos knew that the lying 15-year-old girl who claimed to have seen Iraqi soldiers kill 15 newborns by tossing them from their hospital incubators [in Kuwait] was in fact the daughter of the Kuwaiti ambassador to the U.S., a member of the royal family. Lantos kept her identity secret, and this PR scam became the defining event that convinced the U.S. Congress to support the war."[26]

President George H. W. Bush embraced the incubator tale as a valuable part of the agenda-building repertoire. At one midterm campaign stop in late October, he said that "they had kids in incubators, and they were thrown out of the incubators so that Kuwait could be systematically dismantled."[27] Overall, syndicated columnist Mary McGrory pointed out later, the president "mentioned the 22 babies 'thrown on the floor like firewood' six times. . . . He spoke of the unspeakable in Massachusetts, in Hawaii, in Des Moines, in Dallas and in Dhahran."[28] As the *St. Louis Post-Dispatch* reported, "Seven senators mentioned the horror story when they voted to authorize war against Iraq."[29]

The snow job was so deftly executed that even Amnesty International initially backed up the story. At any rate, "John Healey, executive director of Amnesty International USA, took vehement exception to the president's use of the Amnesty report," McGrory wrote. "Amnesty, he said, had provided Washington with innumerable reports about Iraqi atrocities—about torture, executions and rapes—for 12 years. Nobody paid the slightest attention." McGrory observed: "There is no question that the Kuwaitis were treated abominably by the invading Iraqi forces. The atrocities are too well-documented to be doubted. But when agents for human-rights groups finally got to Kuwait after the war, Middle East Watch, a human rights group, said the incubator story was 'totally false,' and Amnesty backed off its certification, saying it found no proof."[30]

Often, the same officials responsible for deplorable past deeds are called in to provide analysis of present ones. To a large extent, the news media facilitate future wars by failing to confront some history.

Without a hint of intended irony, the *NewsHour* on PBS concluded its program on September 9, 2003, with a warm interview of Henry Kissinger and then a segment about a renowned propagandist for the Nazi war machine. Kissinger talked about his latest book. Then a professor of German history talked about Leni Riefenstahl, the pathbreaking documentary filmmaker who had just died at age 101.

The conversation was cozy with Kissinger, the man who served as the preeminent architect of U.S. foreign policy during the last half-dozen years of the Vietnam War. Tossed his way by host Jim Lehrer, the questions ranged from softball to beach ball. And when the session ended, Lehrer went beyond politeness: "Dr. Kissinger, good to see you. Thank you for being with us. Good luck on your book."

But once in a while, a mainstream news outlet summons the gumption necessary to explore grim truth about the powerful in our midst. That's what happened in February 2001 when *NewsHour* correspondent Elizabeth Farnsworth interviewed Kissinger about his direct contact with General Augusto Pinochet, the Chilean dictator who came to power in a military coup on September 11, 1973. Kissinger was President Nixon's national security adviser at the time. Nearly three years after that coup—which overthrew the elected socialist president, Salvador Allende—Kissinger huddled with General Pinochet in Chile. By then, Kissinger was in his third year as secretary of state; by then, thousands of political prisoners had died, and many more had been tortured, at the hands of the Pinochet regime. At the 1976 meeting, a declassified memo says, Kissinger told Pinochet: "We are sympathetic with what you are trying to do here."

Farnsworth confronted Kissinger about the memo's contents during the 2001 interview. She asked him point-blank about the discussion with Pinochet: "Why did you not say to him, 'You're violating human rights. You're killing people. Stop it.'?"

Kissinger replied: "First of all, human rights were not an international issue at the time, the way they have become since. That was not what diplomats and secretaries of state and presidents were saying generally to anybody in those days." He added that at the June 1976 meeting with Pinochet, "I spent half my time telling him that he should improve his human rights performance in any number of ways." But the American envoy's concern was tactical. As Farnsworth noted in her reporting: "Kissinger did bring up human rights violations, saying they were making it difficult for him to get aid for Chile from Congress."[31]

During the last quarter of a century, Kissinger became quite wealthy as an international consultant and member of numerous boards at huge corporations, including media firms. Along the way, he accumulated many friends in high media places. When Washington Post Company owner Katharine Graham wrote her autobiography, she praised Kissinger as a dear friend and all-around wonderful person.[32]

As it happened, the *NewsHour* interview with Kissinger on September 9, 2003, came just two days before the thirtieth anniversary of the coup in Chile. Although declassified documents show that Kissinger was deeply involved in making that coup possible, Lehrer's hospitality was such that the anchor did not mention it. Minutes later, during another *NewsHour* interview, historian Claudia Koonz was aptly pointing out that Riefenstahl "saw herself as a documentary maker, not as a propagandist. But what she understood so much before anyone else is that the best propaganda is invisible. It looks like a documentary. Then you realize all you're seeing is glory, beauty and triumph, and you don't see the darker side."

6

This Is Not at All about Oil or Corporate Profits

On August 15, 1990—two weeks after the Iraqi invasion of Kuwait—President George H. W. Bush expressed great concern about oil as the Pentagon moved to deploy troops and weaponry to the Persian Gulf. Of course, the confrontation was about "our own national security interests" along with ensuring "peace and stability," but there was something more at stake. "We are also talking about maintaining access to energy resources that are key—not just to the functioning of this country, but to the entire world," the president said. "Our jobs, our way of life, our own freedom and the freedom of friendly countries around the world would all suffer if control of the world's great oil reserves fell into the hands of Saddam Hussein," he declared.[1] But by autumn the official story had shifted. Confronted by protesters while speaking at a fund-raiser in Des Moines, the president had this rejoinder: "You know, some people never get the word. The fight isn't about oil. The fight is about naked aggression that will not stand."[2] Addressing a Republican crowd in Vermont a week later, Bush flatly said that "it isn't oil that we're concerned about. It is aggression. And this aggression is not going to stand."[3]

Papering over corporate interests with humanitarian ones is standard media operating procedure for presidents and their administrations along with many pundits. On the last day of November 2003, with U.S. troops occupying Iraq, *New York Times* columnist Thomas Friedman gushed that "this war is the most important liberal, revolutionary U.S. democracy-building project since the Marshall Plan." He lauded the war as "one of the noblest things this country has ever attempted abroad." Friedman did not mention the estimated 112 billion barrels of oil under the sand in Iraq.

Selling weaponry and a vast array of supplies to the Pentagon is central to the gargantuan military-contractor business. And ongoing transfers of arms to other countries also enrich many corporations. Those profitable achievements provide the wherewithal to help sustain wars on several continents. Globally, the United States leads the world in international sales of weapons. The Congressional Research Service reported that U.S. arms sales topped $14.5 billion during 2003—with the United States alone cashing in on 56.7 percent of all weapons sales worldwide. While the global total for weapons deals dropped from the previous year, the United States increased its amount by about $1 billion. And arms merchants certainly did not forget the neediest. For the year, the U.S. arms sales included $6.2 billion in contracts with developing countries, where societies could least afford big expenditures for weapons.[4]

When the government of a developing nation is in sync with Washington's priorities, what it has to offer includes a lot more than buying weapons or agreeing to deals for extraction of natural resources on terms beneficial to U.S. interests. After war ushers in a regime to Uncle Sam's liking, a country is much more apt to provide a lucrative market for American products—whether Big Macs, Disney movies, household appliances, or earth-moving equipment—along with loans and other financial transactions. Along the way, as in Iraq after the 2003 invasion, the big reconstruction contracts awarded by Washington (and funded by U.S. taxpayers) are heavily weighted toward politically connected American firms.

The public arguments in favor of war do not usually include zeal to serve corporate interests. But once in a blue moon, politicians opt to openly illuminate such motives, as when—during congressional debate in January 1991, a few days before the Gulf War began—Senator Warren Rudman grounded the prevailing lofty arguments with a factor more crude. "Can anyone reasonably assert," he asked, "that it would serve our interests to mortgage the production and pricing levels of nearly one-half of the world's proven oil reserve to the whims of an ambitious tyrant? I think not."[5]

A dozen years later, weeks before the invasion of Iraq, liberal *Washington Post* columnist Richard Cohen launched a barrage of invective against a member of Congress who had dared to identify oil as "the strongest incentive" for the impending war. Cohen claimed to be shocked shocked shocked. The first word of his column was "liar." From there, he peppered his piece with references to Representative Dennis Kucinich as an "indomitable demagogue" and a "fool" who was "repeating a lie."[6] But Cohen would have done well to reread a front page of his own newspaper. Five months earlier, on September 15, 2002, a page-one *Post* story carried the headline "In Iraqi War Scenario, Oil Is Key Issue; U.S. Drillers Eye Huge Petroleum Pool." In the article, Ahmad Chalabi, the exile leader of the U.S.-backed Iraqi National Congress, said that he favored the creation of a United States–led consortium to develop oil fields in a post-Saddam Iraq: "American companies will have a big shot at Iraqi oil."

The same *Post* article quoted former CIA director James Woolsey—a Chalabi supporter who, according to a *Legal Times* story, had been on the payroll of Chalabi's group. Woolsey said: "France and Russia have oil companies and interests in Iraq. They should be told that if they are of assistance in moving Iraq toward decent government, we'll do the best we can to ensure that the new government and American companies work closely with them. If they throw in their lot with Saddam, it will be difficult to the point of impossible to persuade the new Iraqi government to work with them." As business pages had often indicated, it was actually quite reasonable to identify oil as very important in U.S. policy toward Iraq. But in political news coverage, and among all but a few mainstream pundits, such talk was in general disrepute.

On Wall Street, financial analysts were inclined to be much more candid than politicians or political reporters. "Think of Iraq as a military base with a very large oil reserve underneath," said Fadel Gheit, an expert on the oil industry for Oppenheimer & Company. He added: "You can't ask for better than that." After more than a quarter century of tracking the oil business, Gheit commented: "Think of Iraq as virgin territory. . . . It is the superstar of the future. That's why Iraq becomes the most sought-after real estate on the face of the earth."[7] A *Toronto Star* columnist and author, Linda McQuaig, cited internal documents that the Bush administration had used for policy formulation (papers not intended for public viewing but released due to a successful lawsuit). In spring 2001, high-ranking Bush officials and oil firm execs pored over a map showing details of "Exploration Blocks" and other intricacies of Iraq's oil fields. Meeting in secret, the energy task force—chaired by Vice President Dick Cheney—had also examined a chart that featured information about sixty-three oil companies from thirty nations under the heading "Foreign Suitors for Iraqi Oilfields." The documents, McQuaig wrote, "suggest that those who took part in the Cheney task force—including senior oil company executives—were very interested in Iraq's oil and specifically in the danger of it falling into the hands of eager foreign oil companies, rather than into the rightful hands of eager U.S. oil companies. As the documents show, prior to the U.S. invasion, foreign oil companies were nicely positioned for future involvement in Iraq, while the major U.S. oil companies, after years of U.S.-Iraqi hostilities, were largely out of the picture." Of course, for oil corporations based in the United States, that picture would change drastically after the invasion.[8]

While evaded or downplayed in standard political journalism, the inseparability of major corporate interests and foreign affairs is taken for granted by policy players.[9] Perhaps there is some symbolism in the career path of Margaret Tutwiler, a longtime State Department spokeswoman who in December 2003 took the post of "undersecretary of state for public affairs" (previously filled by advertising whiz Charlotte Beers). Tutwiler stayed in that role, dubbed "America's chief of public relations" by the New York Times, for only half a year before joining the private sector—at the New York Stock Exchange, where her title became "executive vice president for communications and government relations."[10]

American journalists don't hesitate to probe the nefarious goals of a Washington-designated enemy leader, as when a Newsweek cover story featured "Milosevic—The Face of Evil—His Mind and Motives."[11] In sharp contrast, reporting on overall corporate motivations of U.S. policy tends to be evasive (aside from some of the business press). Profiteering by specific firms may become controversial, but the more generic conflicts of interest are evidently too routine to raise journalistic eyebrows.

In an essay near the close of the 1990s, National Public Radio correspondent Sylvia Poggioli noted that the countries of the Balkans as well as eastern and central Europe had been under close Western scrutiny during the decade. Yet, she pointed out, "too often their most zealous monitors have been free-market missionaries whose democracy-building yardstick is limited to privatization of industry and the creation of a consumer society."[12] Frequently touted in glowing terms ("globalization," "modernization," "free trade," "economic reform"), high on Washington's global agenda is the aim of making the world safe for lucrative corporate investment. But when an administration presents its current war as an exercise in altruism, supporters may bristle at any charge that motivations include geo-political positioning, future use of far-flung military bases, gaining markets, economic leverage, or advantageous access to natural resources such as oil. While pointing to possibly selfish motives of other nations (as in the case of Russian and French opposition to invading Iraq in 2003), the mainstream U.S. press shies away from putting too fine a point on evidence that a war greatly benefits special interests in the United States.

Such circumspect coverage occurs in the context of media outlets dominated by large corporations. Steady consolidation of ownership and the hefty clout of advertising (along with corporate "underwriting" of public TV and radio programs) combine to limit the range of information and debate in news media. Ongoing pressures—economic, ideological, and governmental—constrain the work of mainline journalists, whose efforts routinely suffer from self-censorship, a very big problem in societies with press freedoms. "Circus dogs jump when the trainer cracks his whip, but the really well-trained dog is the one that turns his somersault when there is no whip," George Orwell observed.[13] Media critic Herbert Schiller described dynamics that apply to the bulk of news coverage: "In truth, the strength of the control process rests in its apparent absence. The desired systemic result is achieved ordinarily by a loose though effective institutional process." Schiller went on to cite "the education of journalists and other media professionals, built-in penalties and rewards for doing what is expected, norms presented as objective rules, and the occasional but telling direct intrusion from above. The main lever is the internalization of values."[14] Self-censorship has long been one of journalism's most insidious and least discussed hazards. And when journalists defer to the prevalent spin on matters of war and peace, they participate in a process that eases the country into one war after another.

The financial benefits of war extend well beyond what usually comes to mind when we think of military contracts. Destructive effects of warfare open up myriad opportunities to make a killing. So it was not a particularly conspicuous story in mid-March 2004 when the *San Francisco Chronicle*'s business section reported some good financial news for the household of a U.S. senator: "Perini Corp., a Massachusetts construction company partially owned by the investment firm of California Senator Dianne Feinstein's husband, landed a $500 million contract Friday to repair southern Iraq's electricity grid. . . . Feinstein's husband, Richard Blum, controls about 24 percent of Perini shares through his investment firm, Blum Capital Partners."[15] The bonanza for the Feinstein-Blum duo was part of the latest bounty from a cornucopia of big deals coming out of the war for American firms. The U.S. officials divvying up the contracts brushed aside well-founded complaints that Iraqis were ready, willing, and able to do such reconstruction projects at a fraction of the cost to U.S. taxpayers.

Feinstein's spouse was into something big in financial terms. Democrats made election-year hay about the fact that Halliburton, a company that Dick Cheney ran shortly before becoming vice president, was cashing in on U.S. government reconstruction contracts in Iraq. But the net for profit-taking in the invasion aftermath was cast wide. "Perini is one of several American firms mobilized to restore Iraq's electricity under a series of contracts issued by the Pentagon this week," the *Chronicle* noted. "On Friday, Washington Group International won a $500 million contract to restore power in northern Iraq. The Pentagon is selecting firms to perform $5 billion of reconstruction work, including repairs to damaged hospitals, courthouses and water systems."[16] Of course, those hospitals, courthouses, and water systems had been damaged largely because of the war. After being paid big bucks to help implement the destruction, various portions of the American corporate sector were also paid handsomely to assist with repairs and to help keep the military operations rolling.[17]

When annual reports came off the press in 2004, quite a few reflected megaprofits in hand and on the horizon. As usual, corporate beneficiaries of warfare ranged widely in size.

- Orbit International Corp., a small business making high-tech products for use by the navy, air force, army, and marines, had increased its net sales by nearly $2.4 million during the previous two years, to about $17.1 million—and the war future was bright. "Looking ahead," CEO Dennis Sunshine reported, "Orbit's Electronics and

Power Unit Segments expect to continue to benefit from the expanding military/defense and homeland security marketplace."[18] In its yearly report to federal regulators, the firm acknowledged: "We are heavily dependent upon military spending as a source of revenues and income. Accordingly, any substantial future reductions in overall military spending by the U.S. government could have a material adverse effect on our sales and earnings."[19]

- A much larger corporation, Engineered Support Systems, Inc., had quadrupled its net revenues between 1999 and 2003, when they reached $572.7 million. In early 2004, the company proclaimed itself to be "rapidly approaching revenues of $1 billion and beyond." The growth was impressive. "Fueled by a steady steam [sic] of strategic acquisitions," the firm reported, it "has emerged as a leading designer, manufacturer and supplier of integrated military electronics, support equipment and technical and logistics services for all branches of America's armed forces and certain foreign militaries, homeland security forces and selected government and intelligence agencies." For the title of its 2003 annual report, the company chose "On Active Duty."[20] A statement signed by the corporation's top officers declared: "As we have always said, rapid deployment of our armed forces drives our business. That has never been more true than today with our military personnel actively engaged in Iraq and Afghanistan and stationed in dozens of countries around the globe."[21] And, company president Jerry Potthoff assured investors, "our long-term success doesn't necessarily depend on America being at war or being engaged in large-scale operations such as those currently under way in Iraq and Afghanistan. Our nation's military is deployed in over 130 countries, so our products and personnel are deployed, as well. As long as America remains the world's policeman, our products and services will help them complete their missions."[22]

- With revenues of just over $26.2 billion in 2003, the gigantic Northrop Grumman put out an annual report on the year with a decidedly upbeat tone, asserting that "our nation's recent conflicts in Afghanistan and Iraq have borne out Northrop Grumman's strategic vision of the changing nature of warfare. With the bases of many neighboring foreign countries closed to us, it was largely sea-basing provided by the Navy and air strikes from distant land bases that allowed us to project force globally without, in President Bush's words, 'asking for a permission slip.'"[23] The corporation reported: "In terms of the portfolio, Northrop Grumman is situated in the 'sweet spot' of U.S. defense and national security spending. We believe the depth and breadth of our programs and leading-edge technologies, and their strategic alignment with the transformation of our military in the 21st century, give us the best-positioned portfolio in our industry."[24]

War: how sweet it can be. The CEO of Engineered Support Systems, Jerry Daniels, used the same saccharine jargon in his firm's annual report to describe its enviable position. "We're really in a sweet spot within the defense market," he exulted. "Today, our armed forces are increasingly being pushed out of large, permanent overseas bases, forced to conduct military operations both from the continental United States and from alternate temporary bases around the world. In addition, the military is outsourcing more and more of its non-warfighting services to civilian contractors like Engineered Support. Both of these trends are working to our advantage."[25]

These are not isolated slices of the corporate sector or just unusual winnings from a particular war. *New York Times* reporter Chris Hedges, in his Q&A-format book *What Every Person Should Know About War*, wrote that in just one year (2002) the Defense Department "spent $170.8 billion with military contractors such as Boeing and Lockheed Martin." One way or another, the red-white-and-blue war machine cuts a lot of paychecks. With 627,000 civilians directly on the U.S. military's payroll, "the defense industry employs another 3 million." Military business lobbying groups spend upward of $1 million per week, in addition to election campaign contributions. Hedges posed this question: "Does the military industry help make defense spending decisions?" His answer: "Yes."[26]

After September 11, 2001, Russia's president found that the White House was flashing a green light for the Kremlin to pursue the grisly war in Chechnya. Under the "war on terrorism" heading, Vladimir Putin and George W. Bush proceeded to engage in a mutual winkathon about conflicts they were pleased to portray as antiterror imperatives. "Not surprisingly, since 9/11 President Putin has struggled to pry the Chechen secessionist movement from history," regional policy analyst Raffi Khatchadourian pointed out two years later. "Ignoring its nationalist origins, he has argued that Chechen violence is a 'link' in the 'same chain of acts by international terrorists' who targeted the United States. And Washington has so far given him a pass on this (just as Russia, returning the favor, has chosen not to interfere with recent U.S. troop deployments in Central Asia). True, some militants in Chechnya—such as the late, infamous Khattab— have established ties with global Islamist terror networks. But the crisis in Chechnya ultimately remains local."[27]

Among the U.S. troop deployments that would have been more difficult before 9/11 was the stationing of GIs in Georgia, a country with a compelling strategic location—and not just for providing air bases to use in future U.S. military operations. The Bush administration proclaimed Georgia to be in urgent need of reinforcements against terrorism. But, as Khatchadourian observed, "given the nature of the training, it's more likely they were deployed to help secure Georgia as a link in Washington's coveted 'east–west energy corridor' for shuttling oil and gas from the Caspian Sea to world markets." Overall in the Caucasus and central Asia, "Washington's primary interests are energy and security—the familiar story of oil and war— but will that bring much-needed stability and democracy?"[28] On the ground, in daily life, events grimly answer such questions. For American policymakers and national-security journalists, the problems are apt to remain somewhat abstract, while people in the region endure the human costs of war and political suppression.

In October 2003, facing large-scale street protests, Azerbaijan's ill dictator Heidar Aliyev turned the reins of power over to his son Ilham. A bogus election, complete with arrests and physical attacks on opponents, provided thin window dressing along the way. "The repression machine is firing all its cylinders," said a leader of the opposition.[29] Swiftly after the close of the "election," Deputy Secretary of State Richard Armitage called the new dictator, Ilham Aliyev, to congratulate him on a "strong performance at the polls."[30]

As it happened, Armitage was a founding member of the board for the U.S.–Azerbaijan Chamber of Commerce. And, with extensive oil reserves in Azerbaijan, there was plenty more commerce to be anticipated. The political warmth from Armitage toward Azerbaijan's ruling elites was extended in tandem with military help.

7

They Are the Aggressors, Not Us

Judgments at Nuremberg and precepts of international law forbid launching aggressive war. "We must make clear to the Germans that the wrong for which their fallen leaders are on trial is not that they lost the war, but that they started it," said Supreme Court justice Robert L. Jackson, representing the U.S. government at the International Conference on Military Trials, when World War II finally ended. He added that "no grievances or policies will justify resort to aggressive war. It is utterly renounced and condemned as an instrument of policy."[1]

A fierce advocate of international law, Senator Wayne Morse had no patience for double standards. In 1964 he told a national TV audience: "I don't know why we think, just because we're mighty, that we have the right to try to substitute might for right. And that's the American policy in Southeast Asia—just as unsound when we do it as when Russia does it."[2] Morse was crying out in Washington's wilderness as escalation of the Vietnam War accelerated.

Sometimes the White House praises "international law" while violating it, as in the case of the Johnson administration and Vietnam. "There are those who complain of the loss of sovereignty involved in membership in the United Nations, or in the Organization of American States, or in NATO, or in signing any international treaty," Vice President Hubert Humphrey said while the Vietnam War raged. "But without the rule of law, the rule of the jungle prevails."[3]

A recurring media motif is to dwell on painful aspects of wielding power, such as the reported anguish of shouldering a heavy burden that requires making life-or-death decisions as commander in chief. Presidents have encouraged such media coverage, which sometimes cues the public to extend more empathy toward the man who gives the orders to drop bombs than toward the people underneath those bombs. "The exercise of power in this century has meant for all of us in the United States not arrogance but agony," President Lyndon Johnson said in 1966. "We have used our power not willingly and recklessly ever, but always reluctantly and with restraint."[4] (Less widely publicized was Henry Kissinger's comment quoted in the *New York Times* on January 19, 1971: "Power is the great aphrodisiac.") The inversion of victimizer and victim is common in wartime media coverage.

Even while repeatedly unleashing Pentagon firepower, presidents have been fond of portraying themselves as victims of aggression by a foe all too willing to exploit American moderation. After years of bombing Vietnam with massive ferocity, President Johnson sounded a warning in early 1968 as he told fellow Americans: "And the other side must not take advantage of our restraint as they have in the past. This nation simply cannot accept anything less without jeopardizing the lives of our men and of our allies."[5]

While inflicting extreme military violence, presidents are inclined to depict extreme passivity as the only other option, raising the specter of gargantuan Uncle Sam tied down by Lilliputians of the world. "If when the chips are down, the world's most powerful nation . . . acts like a pitiful, helpless giant," President Richard Nixon contended on April 30, 1970, as he announced the U.S. invasion of Cambodia, "the forces of totalitarianism and anarchy will threaten free nations and free institutions throughout the world." The frequent message: The alternative to war is disastrous surrender. "My fellow Americans," Nixon said on November 3, 1969, "I am sure you can recognize from what I have said that we really only have two choices open to us if we want to end this war." After that speech, which made an appeal to a "great silent majority," the president's popularity rating spiked up 12 points.[6]

Statements about adhering to international principles are sometimes effusive when the U.S. government can laud its legalisms and wage war, too. "Our commitment to international law and to international organizations has been demonstrated anew," Republican senator Richard G. Lugar boasted on January 17, 1991, with the Gulf

War just under way. Such self-praise for the U.S. government is bipartisan. Months later, in the afterglow of war, Democratic senator Bill Bradley voiced satisfaction: "International law provides the basis for action when one country invades another."[7] But the burlesque quality of such dedication to "international law" was inadvertently satirized shortly thereafter by powerful senator Jesse Helms when he stated: "The Israeli possession of Judaea and Samaria has stronger claim to validity under international law and historical precedent than that of any Arab state. As a Baptist, I feel very strongly about that."[8]

In November 2002, while the Pentagon geared up for the invasion of Iraq, more than three hundred law professors in the United States signed a statement pointing out that "the international rule of law is not a soft luxury to be discarded whenever leaders find it convenient or popular to resort to savage violence."[9] Six months later, with U.S. forces occupying Iraq, the secretary-general of Amnesty International charged: "The United States continues to pick and choose which bits of its obligations under international law it will use, and when it will use them."[10]

Paradoxically, the kinds of arguments made to oppose a war on the grounds of its unwinnability are likely to help fuel that war—and the next ones. With the underpinnings of war prerogatives unchallenged, a logical response is that wars must be fought more effectively to assure a clear victory. That's what I. F. Stone was driving at when he wrote, a few years into the Vietnam War, in mid-February 1968: "It is time to stand back and look at where we are going. And to take a good look at ourselves. A first observation is that we can easily overestimate our national conscience. A major part of the protest against the war springs simply from the fact that we are losing it. If it were not for the heavy cost, politicians like the Kennedys [Robert and Edward] and organizations like the ADA [the liberal Americans for Democratic Action] would still be as complacent about the war as they were a few years ago."[11]

Stone made another point that several decades later could have served as an apt critique of outraged claims from pundits and politicians who described the aggressive U.S. war on Iraq as unprecedented. "For all the poppycock about the Vietnamese war clashing with our past traditions," Stone wrote, "we have long been an imperialistic people. The Truman Doctrine and the Johnson Doctrine are only extensions of the Monroe Doctrine, new embodiments of that Manifest Destiny to which our expansionists appealed in a less cautious day. Bolivar once said that we plagued Latin America in the name of liberty; today we do it to a growing sector of the world. Everywhere we talk liberty and social reform but we end up by allying ourselves with native oligarchies and military cliques—just as we have done in Vietnam. In the showdown, we reach for the gun."[12]

But the conventional media wisdom says that Uncle Sam's gun is not the first to leave its holster. In 1999, summing up, *Newsweek* flatly reported that "America has not started a war in this century."[13] And the baseline of U.S. military intervention is actually reinforced as acceptable when critics of a new war claim that the current militaristic transgression is extraordinary and out of sync with the normality of the nation's foreign policy. Such revision of history affirms garden-variety wars of intervention. When Howard Dean was a candidate for the 2004 Democratic presidential nomination while trumpeting opposition to the invasion of Iraq, his campaign issued a statement that faulted an opponent for backing "a Bush-Cheney policy where, for the first time in American history, we commit to war before exhausting our efforts to commit to peace."[14] In response, the author of a widely read book on U.S. history, Howard Zinn, commented: "Instances of the U.S. government spurning peace efforts and going to war include the Korean War, the Vietnam War, the first Gulf War, the bombing of Afghanistan."[15]

Reaching for the gun is routinely seen as a benevolent—or at least necessary—activity for the present day. In a front-page *New York Times* analysis piece a year after the invasion of Iraq, under the headline "A Solemn Call for Toughness in a Time of Peril," the only quote from a source outside of the Bush administration came near the end, from historian Richard Norton Smith: "A majority of Americans want to believe that what we have done in Iraq is admirable, necessary, and in the long run good for us and the peace of the world. But they need reminding, they need credible advocacy and they need reassurance that those in charge have a game plan."[16] The following week, a *Times* editorial expressed confidence in "the fortitude of average citizens, who are able to accept the cost of war whenever they are confident that the cause is right."[17]

But no matter what most Americans wanted to believe or were

able to accept, the Iraq war had entered its second year without indications that public opinion would curtail the U.S. role in the bloodshed anytime soon. Skewed by the exact wording of the questions cooked up, opinion-poll results could be sliced and diced many different ways. In late April 2004, even while some polling indicated that most people in the United States would favor the idea of sending more U.S. troops to augment the 135,000 already in Iraq, an editor of the *New Republic* was citing poll data that showed "a record 65 percent believe the level of American casualties in Iraq is 'unacceptable.'"[18] Meanwhile, the hazed clarity offered by a *Time* magazine cover story was encapsulated in a bromide near the close: "The *Time*/CNN poll last week showed only 24 percent of Americans now view the military campaign in Iraq to be 'unsuccessful'; on the other hand, more than half say the U.S. should maintain or increase the number of troops in Iraq. The relative public equanimity gives the Bush administration precious time to try to get things right."[19] In the months that followed, the poll numbers would shift to become more negative toward the Iraq war. Yet there was a kind of near-inevitability in the air—hardly unprecedented—assuming that as a practical matter the war would need to go on quite a bit longer. The distant mirror of Vietnam could provide a grim reflection.

During a CBS News broadcast in the spring of 1967, while the president was preparing to partially approve General William Westmoreland's request for deployment of additional troops to Vietnam, correspondent Mike Wallace reported that "one high-ranking official who reflects the feeling in top [U.S. military] circles in Saigon . . . . said he thought the enemy was willing to take a million casualties, which at the current ratio would mean 200,000 U.S. casualties, with at least 25,000 killed, and that figure may be conservative." Continuing his on-air report, Wallace recounted the conversation:

"Will the American people accept those losses?" I wondered.
"Do they have any choice?" was his rejoinder.
"Then the real war out here is just beginning?" I asked.
The official nodded his head in assent.[20]

From the standpoint of media and politics, launching the war was not very difficult and stopping it was extremely difficult. Like a runaway vehicle, a war's momentum can overcome any number of obstacles. As it happened, Mike Wallace's chilling report from Saigon went on the air just three days before a gathering of Americans, estimated at up to three hundred thousand or more, marched against the war through streets of New York City. That was the spring when Martin Luther King Jr., joining with the peace protests, declared: "I never intend to adjust myself to the madness of militarism."[21] But even though active opposition grew to involve millions of Americans during the late 1960s, the U.S. war in Southeast Asia persisted for several more years. Three decades after that war ended, its instructive meaning was up for grabs across the U.S. political spectrum as the Iraq war accelerated.

8

If This War Is Wrong, Congress Will Stop It

It's a classic pattern: Some in Congress raise concerns. On the record, hearings include cautionary testimony. Impassioned oratory and debates ensue on Capitol Hill, with at least a few senators and representatives fretting aloud about a possible "quagmire" and whether sufficient planning has gone into an "exit strategy." In both chambers there are calls for the White House to consult with the congressional leadership, which the president promises to do. A resolution in favor of war is introduced, debated, and passed, amid assurances that the Congress has not approved a blank check and can count on consultation in the future. Supporters of going to war cite the public record while more vaguely referring to the ominous significance of classified intelligence briefings. In such times of national crisis, many say that support for the president is essential, that the American people expect no less.

The Gulf of Tonkin Resolution gave President Johnson authority "to take all necessary measures to repel any armed attack against the forces of the United States and to prevent further aggression." It was to be followed by several other resolutions from Capitol Hill in the next decades that also stopped short of a declaration of war—yet relinquished congressional responsibilities by deferring to presidential power to make war as the man in the Oval Office saw fit.

It all seemed very clear. "American Planes Hit North Vietnam After 2d Attack on Our Destroyers; Move Taken to Halt New Aggression," said a *Washington Post* headline on August 5, 1964. That same day, the front page of the *New York Times* reported: "President Johnson has ordered retaliatory action against gunboats and 'certain supporting facilities in North Vietnam' after renewed attacks against American destroyers in the Gulf of Tonkin."

But there was no "second attack" by North Vietnam—no "renewed attacks against American destroyers." By reporting official claims as absolute truths, American journalism opened the floodgates for the Vietnam War.

The official story was that North Vietnamese torpedo boats launched an "unprovoked attack" against a U.S. destroyer on "routine patrol" in the Gulf of Tonkin on August 2—and that North Vietnamese PT boats followed up with a "deliberate attack" on a pair of U.S. ships two days later. But the truth was very different. Rather than being on a routine patrol August 2, the U.S. destroyer *Maddox* was actually engaged in aggressive intelligence-gathering maneuvers—in sync with coordinated attacks. "The day before, two attacks on North Vietnam . . . had taken place," wrote scholar Daniel C. Hallin. Those assaults were "part of a campaign of increasing military pressure on the North that the United States had been pursuing since early 1964."[1]

On the night of August 4, the Pentagon stated that a second attack by North Vietnamese PT boats had occurred earlier that day in the Tonkin Gulf—a report cited by President Johnson as he went on national TV that evening to announce a momentous escalation in the war: air strikes against North Vietnam. But Johnson ordered U.S. bombers to "retaliate" for a North Vietnamese torpedo attack that never happened.

Prior to the U.S. air strikes, top officials in Washington had reason to doubt that any August 4 attack by North Vietnam had occurred. Cables from the U.S. task force commander in the Gulf of Tonkin, Captain John J. Herrick, referred to "freak weather effects," "almost total darkness," and an "overeager sonarman" who "was hearing ship's own propeller beat." Herrick advised against jumping to conclusions: "Review of action makes many reported contacts and torpedoes fired appear doubtful. . . . Suggest complete evaluation before any further action."[2] One of the navy pilots flying overhead that night was squadron commander James Stockdale. "I had the best seat in the house to watch that event," he recalled many years later, "and our destroyers were just shooting at phantom targets—there were no [North Vietnamese] PT boats there."[3]

But Johnson's speech of August 4, 1964, won accolades from editorial writers. The *New York Times* proclaimed that the president "went to the American people last night with the somber facts," while the *Los Angeles Times* urged Americans to "face the fact that the Communists, by their attack on American vessels in international waters, have themselves escalated the hostilities."

The *Washington Post* featured a prominent news analysis, headlined "Firm Stand Is Warning to Hanoi." That August 5 article recited the White House line in a journalistic voice: "The United States turned loose its military might on North Vietnam last night to prevent the Communist leaders in Hanoi and Peking from making the mistaken decision that they could attack American ships with impunity. But the initial United States decision was for limited action, a sort of tit-for-tat retaliation, and not a decision to escalate the war in Southeast Asia."[4]

However, as Hallin has pointed out, "it certainly was not the case that the first air strike against North Vietnam was merely a 'tit-for-tat' retaliation. The administration had been moving throughout 1964 toward a fundamental change in American policy. The covert operations begun in February were part of a systematic program of 'increasingly escalating pressure' on North Vietnam." Hallin observed that journalists had "a great deal of information available which contradicted the official account [of Tonkin Gulf events]; it simply wasn't used."[5] Ironically, the obscured story of attacks on North Vietnam by South Vietnamese gunboats was itself a cover story. Those attacks had been, in Daniel Ellsberg's words, "entirely U.S. operations."[6]

On August 6—two days after the second purported incident in the Gulf of Tonkin—Secretary of Defense Robert McNamara testified at a joint closed session of the Foreign Relations and Armed Services committees of the Senate. McNamara claimed that the two U.S. vessels, the *Maddox* and the *Turner Joy*, "returned the fire" that had been directed at them in the form of "torpedoes" and "automatic weapons fire." Flanked by General Earle Wheeler, he spun out the tale. When Senator Frank Lausche asked "how many of the torpedoes were set in motion and what small arms were used," this exchange followed:

McNamara: "It is difficult to estimate. This was a very dark night. The attack was carried out during the night, the hours of darkness.

It was a premeditated attack, a preplanned attack. It was described as an ambush in the reports from the commanders, but because it was night it is very difficult to estimate the total amount of fire."

Senator Lausche: "The shots were again initiated by the North Vietnamese?"

McNamara: "Yes."

General Wheeler: "That's correct."[7]

At the joint committee's session that day, a gadfly in the ointment was Senator Wayne Morse of Oregon. "Early that morning, a Pentagon officer telephoned a startling tip to Morse," journalist Stanley Karnow wrote two decades later. "The officer, whose identity Morse would never divulge, revealed that the *Maddox* had indeed been involved in the covert South Vietnamese raids against North Vietnam."[8] But when Senator Morse raised the issue, Defense Secretary McNamara responded by lying: "Our navy played absolutely no part in, was not associated with, was not aware of, any South Vietnamese actions, if there were any. . . . I say this flatly. This is a fact."[9]

For the Johnson administration, the rigorously deceptive behind-closed-doors testimony was part of a dissembling approach that cinched a congressional resolution for war. The blitz was multi-pronged, with no aspect more important than manipulative use of television, radio, and major print outlets. Setting the pace for administration officials with a relentless media drumbeat, Johnson did not hesitate to follow up the first news accounts of Tonkin Gulf attacks with quick and facile rhetoric of the injured mighty party. He told a national TV audience: "This new act of aggression, aimed directly at our own forces, again brings home to all of us in the United States the importance of the struggle for peace and security in Southeast Asia."[10]

Media reliance on official sources facilitated the Vietnam War, as it would many other wars in the next four decades. Such reliance was the professional norm—and a shoddy rendition of journalism. As media researcher Hallin points out: "The assumptions and routines of what is often known as 'objective journalism' made it exceedingly easy for officials to manipulate day-to-day news content. There was little 'editorializing' in the columns of major American newspapers at the time of the Tonkin Gulf incident: most of the reporting, in the best tradition of objective journalism, 'just gave the facts.' But they were not just *any* facts. They were *official* facts, facts about what the president said and what 'officials here believe.' The effect of 'objectivity' was not to free the news of political influence, but to open wide the channel through which official influence flowed."[11]

Confident of near-unanimous passage, the White House pushed ahead for a congressional vote on August 7. In the absence of independent journalism or congressional skepticism, the Gulf of Tonkin Resolution—the closest thing there ever was to a declaration of war against North Vietnam—sailed through Congress. Two courageous senators, Morse of Oregon and Ernest Gruening of Alaska, provided the only "no" votes.

During his fall campaign for a full presidential term, Johnson was intent on easing any concerns that he might be leading the country into war with Vietnam. "We are not about to send American boys 9,000 or 10,000 miles away from home to do what Asian boys ought to be doing for themselves," he said on October 21, 1964.[12] The next spring he ordered a drastic escalation of the war. Between 1964 and 1965, the U.S. troop levels in South Vietnam went from 23,000 to 185,000.[13]

The people in charge of military bureaucracies, I. F. Stone noted a few years after the Gulf of Tonkin Resolution, "play incidents up or down like an organist depending on whether they want to make or avoid war. Faked or exaggerated, the Tonkin incidents were used for a war buildup the White House and Pentagon wanted."[14] More than two decades later, during the Gulf War, former war correspondent Sydney Schanberg warned journalists not to forget "our unquestioning chorus of agreeability when Lyndon Johnson bamboozled us with his fabrication of the Gulf of Tonkin incident." Schanberg blamed not only the press but also "the apparent amnesia of the wider American public." And he remarked: "We Americans are the ultimate innocents. We are forever desperate to believe that this time the government is telling us the truth."[15]

In July 1998 I asked a number of *Washington Post* staffers whether the newspaper ever retracted its Gulf of Tonkin reporting. Finally, the trail led to someone with a definitive answer. "I can assure you that there was never any retraction," said Murrey Marder, a reporter who wrote much of the *Washington Post*'s political coverage of Tonkin Gulf events in August 1964. He added: "If you were making a retraction, you'd have to make a retraction of virtually everyone's entire coverage of the Vietnam War."

Marder remembered the story that the South Vietnamese navy had been shelling North Vietnamese coastal islands just prior to the reported attacks by North Vietnam on U.S. ships in the Tonkin Gulf. But the propaganda machinery was in high gear: "Before I could do anything as a reporter, the *Washington Post* had endorsed the Gulf of Tonkin Resolution." The news coverage of events in the Tonkin Gulf "was all driven by the White House," recalled Marder, who was a *Post* reporter from 1946 to 1985. "It was an operation—a deliberate manipulation of public opinion. . . . None of us knew, of course, that there had been drafted, months before, a resolution to justify American direct entry into the war, which became the Gulf of Tonkin Resolution." He told me: "If the American press had been doing its job and the Congress had been doing its job, we would never have been involved in the Vietnam War."

Daniel Ellsberg recounts that after a few years of working on Vietnam policies as a U.S. government insider, he "realized something crucial: that the president's ability to escalate, his entire strategy throughout the war, had depended on secrecy and lying and thus on his ability to deter unauthorized disclosures—truth telling—by officials."[16]

Appearing on the CBS program *Face the Nation* in 1964, Wayne Morse objected when journalist Peter Lisagor told him: "Senator, the Constitution gives to the president of the United States the sole responsibility for the conduct of foreign policy."

Senator Morse responded sharply. "Couldn't be more wrong," he broke in. "You couldn't make a more unsound legal statement than the one you have just made. This is the promulgation of an old fallacy that foreign policy belongs to the president of the United States. That's nonsense." When Lisagor prodded him ("To whom does it belong then, Senator?"), Morse did not miss a beat: "It belongs to the American people. . . . And I am pleading that the American people be given the facts about foreign policy."

The questioner persisted: "You know, Senator, that the American people cannot formulate and execute foreign policy."

Morse became positively indignant. "Why do you say that? . . . I have complete faith in the ability of the American people to follow the facts if you'll give them. And my charge against my government is, we're not giving the American people the facts."[17]

"It is a commonplace that 'you can't keep secrets in Washington' or 'in a democracy,' that 'no matter how sensitive the secret, you're likely to read it the next day in the *New York Times*.' These truisms are flatly false," Daniel Ellsberg wrote in 2002. "They are in fact cover stories, ways of flattering and misleading journalists and their readers, part of the process of keeping secrets well. . . . [T]he overwhelming majority of secrets do not leak to the American public. This is true even when the information withheld is well known to an enemy and when it is clearly essential to the functioning of the congressional war power and to any democratic control of foreign policy. The reality unknown to the public and to most members of Congress and the press is that secrets that would be of the greatest import to many of them can be kept from them reliably for decades by the Executive Branch, even though they are known to thousands of insiders."[18]

When war backers want Congress to defer to presidential enthusiasm for sending troops into action, the repertoire of justification often includes references to the ultimate information and judgment residing in the White House. A week before the Gulf War began, the avowedly moderate Senator Warren Rudman was serving as a loyal Republican. "The president's personal relationships with the leaders of the allied states are unparalleled," he said. "Having masterfully forged a fragile multinational coalition, he is the one who can best gauge its cohesion and durability."[19] On the same day, Senator Jesse Helms used the timeworn argument of "national interest," saying that "the president has dispatched over 400,000 American military personnel to the Persian Gulf to protect the national interest. We must support the president in the course he has laid out."[20]

Playing follow the leader, many a member of Congress simply abdicates responsibility to the White House. Consider this statement by Democratic senator Joseph Biden on January 24, 1991, a week into the Gulf War: "Therefore, I believe, since I do not have any moral objection to what we are doing—I just thought it was less wise to do it this way than the way I preferred to do it—that it is my obligation to do all that I can to support the president and support the fighting women and men in the field. He is the commander in chief. We gave him the authority. We gave him the constitutional equivalent of a declaration of war. As the commander in chief, he is required to exercise that responsibility as he sees fit. I am not a military expert, and it would be presumptuous of me to suggest how that war, now that it is under way, should be conducted, and I will not. I will follow his lead and judgment on that."

In late May 1999, the president of the United States openly violated the War Powers Act—and the national media yawned.

The war powers law, enacted in 1973, requires congressional approval if the U.S. military is to engage in hostilities for more than sixty days. As that deadline passed on May 25, 1999—while large-scale bombing of Yugoslavia continued—some members of the House spoke up. "Today, the president is in violation of the law," California Republican Tom Campbell said. "That is clear." And Ohio Democrat Dennis Kucinich added, "The war continues unauthorized, without the consent of the governed."

But sophisticated journalists in the nation's capital just shrugged. To them—and to the Clinton administration—the law was irrelevant and immaterial, a dead letter undeserving of serious attention. In a dark time of push-button warfare, with more and more eyes getting adjusted to shadowy maneuvers, it was possible to discern a pattern of contempt for basic democratic principles.

Forget all that high-sounding stuff in the civics textbooks. Unable to get Congress to vote for the ongoing air war, the president insisted on continuing to bomb Yugoslav cities and towns, destroying bridges and hospitals, electrical generators and water systems. Boasting of the Pentagon's might, he pursued a Pax Technocratica with remote-control assurance.

Attorney Walter J. Rockler, a former prosecutor at the Nuremberg War Crimes Trials more than half a century earlier, was outraged. On May 23, in an essay for the *Chicago Tribune* that cut against the prevalent media grain, he denounced "our murderously destructive bombing campaign in Yugoslavia." He challenged what was being done in the name of Americans: "The notion that humanitarian violations can be redressed with random destruction and killing by advanced technological means is inherently suspect. This is mere pretext for our arrogant assertion of dominance and power in defiance of international law. We make the nonnegotiable demands and rules, and implement them by military force."

With enormous help from mass media, the White House is routinely able to marginalize Congress and the public on matters of war and peace. In effect, reporters and pundits depict top U.S. officials as beleaguered experts whose jobs are difficult enough without intrusive pressures from commoners. The American people have served mostly as spectators while peace and war hang in the balance.

Three days after 9/11, with a lone dissenting vote from Representative Barbara Lee, Congress passed a resolution that stated: "The president is authorized to use all necessary and appropriate force against those nations, organizations, or persons he determined planned, authorized, or aided the terrorist attacks that occurred on September 11, 2001, or harbored such organizations or persons."[21] The attack on Afghanistan began a few weeks later.

Noting that "the scope was global, the time frame infinite," Lee explained later: "Congress was not voting to declare war; it was voting to give almost unlimited authority to the president to pursue the perpetrators of September 11 and any of their supporters anywhere. I could not support such a broad, open-ended grant of warmaking power."[22] But every other member of Congress went along with the blank check for war—an incomparably easier vote to cast. Of course, hundreds of them reserved the right to complain later that they had been grievously misled.

During the lead-up to the Iraq invasion, diplomatic feints were very important for media consumption—and for political cover on Capitol Hill. Quite a few Democrats, reluctant to vote for the war resolution but even more reluctant not to, hung their hats on the spurious pretense that the Bush administration would use the mid-October 2002 congressional resolution as a bargaining chip at the diplomatic table. Instead, George W. Bush's team simply pocketed the chip and went on their way to war. With scant credibility, after the war was turning out badly under the political lights, some Democrats claimed that they'd meant for Bush to use Congress's resolution for diplomatic leverage instead of as a green light to go ahead with the invasion.

"The president's ability to decide when and where to use America's military power is now absolute," Michael Kinsley observed as the invasion of Iraq ended in (temporary) triumph. "Congress cannot stop him. That's not what the Constitution says, and it's not what the War Powers Act says, but that's how it works in practice."[23]

9

If This War Is Wrong, the Media Will Tell Us

After eight years in the White House, Dwight D. Eisenhower delivered his farewell address on January 17, 1961. The former general warned of "an immense military establishment and a large arms industry." He added that "we must guard against the acquisition of unwarranted influence, whether sought or unsought, by the military-industrial complex."

Several decades after President Eisenhower spoke, that complex is extremely profitable. The United States military's regular budget—well over $1 billion per day—includes a wide array of line items providing large income streams for weapons contractors and a plethora of other companies heavily reliant on sales of goods and services to the Defense Department. Politicians are often swayed by the economic clout of the military business, the political power of its allies, and the vehement reach of its advocates in news media, a sector increasingly dominated by a few huge corporations. One way or another, a military-industrial complex now extends to much of corporate media. In the process, firms with military ties routinely advertise in news outlets. Often, media magnates and people on the boards of large media-related corporations enjoy close links—financial and social—with the military industry and Washington's foreign-policy establishment.

Sometimes a media-owning corporation is itself a significant weapons merchant. In 1991, when my colleague Martin A. Lee and I looked into the stake that one major media-invested company had in the latest war, what we found was sobering: NBC's owner, General Electric, designed, manufactured, or supplied parts or maintenance for nearly every major weapons system used by the United States during the Gulf War—including the Patriot and Tomahawk cruise missiles, the Stealth bomber, the B-52 bomber, the AWACS plane, and the NAVSTAR spy satellite system. "In other words, when correspondents and paid consultants on NBC television praised the performance of U.S. weapons, they were extolling equipment made by GE, the corporation that pays their salaries."[1] During just one year, 1989, General Electric had received close to $2 billion in military contracts related to systems that ended up being utilized for the Gulf War. Fifteen years later, the company still had a big stake in military spending. In 2004, when the Pentagon released its list of top military contractors for the latest fiscal year, General Electric ranked eighth, with $2.8 billion in contracts.[2]

The descent into war is greatly smoothed by deferrals of tough news coverage. Napoleon recognized the dynamic two centuries ago when he asserted that it wasn't necessary to censor the news, it was sufficient to delay the news until it no longer mattered. During the first half of 1992—a year and more after the Gulf War—the ABC show *Nightline* and other major U.S. news outlets got around to reporting on the Bush administration's role in building up Saddam Hussein's financial and military power. In contrast, a relatively small media outlet, the *Village Voice*, had published the essence of that story—"Gulfgate: How the U.S. Secretly Armed Iraq"—back in December 1990, a month before the Gulf War began.[3]

Given the extent of shared sensibilities and financial synergies within what amounts to a huge military-industrial-media complex, it shouldn't be surprising that—whether in the prelude to the Gulf War of 1991 or the Iraq invasion of 2003—the USA's biggest media institutions did little to illuminate how Washington and business interests had combined to strengthen and arm Saddam Hussein during many of his worst crimes. "In the 1980s and afterward, the United States underwrote 24 American corporations so they could sell to Saddam Hussein weapons of mass destruction, which he used against Iran, at that time the prime Middle Eastern enemy of the United States," Ben Bagdikian wrote in *The New Media Monopoly*, the 2004 edition of his landmark book on the news business. "Hussein used U.S.-supplied poison gas" against Iranians and Kurds "while the United States looked the other way. This was the same Saddam Hussein who then, as in 2000, was a tyrant subjecting dissenters in his regime to unspeakable tortures and committing genocide against his Kurdish minorities."[4] In corporate medialand, history could be supremely relevant when it focused on Hussein's torture and genocide, but the historic assistance he got from the U.S. government and American firms was apt to be off the subject and beside the point.[5]

No matter what limits the White House seeks to impose on media reporting and access to troops in wartime, the judgments made by American reporters and editors ultimately do far more to filter the news coverage and views that reach the public. Vietnam "was the first war in which reporters were routinely accredited to accompany military forces yet not subject to censorship," Daniel Hallin has noted.[6] The authorities in Washington figured they could expect correspondents not to wander too far in terms of content; "the integration of the media into the political establishment was assumed to be secure enough that the last major vestige of direct government control—military censorship in wartime—could be lifted."[7]

Some reporters exercised a significant degree of independence. And, Hallin concluded, "this did matter: in 1963, when American policy in Vietnam began to fall apart, the media began to send back an image that conflicted sharply with the picture of progress officials were trying to paint. It would happen again many times before the war was over. But those reporters also went to Southeast Asia schooled in a set of journalistic practices which, among other things, ensured that the news would reflect, if not always the views of those at the very top of the American political hierarchy, at least the perspectives of American officialdom generally."[8] The absence of government censorship "did not mean the absence of restrictions on the flow of information that might have damaged public support for American policy in Vietnam."[9] Hallin identified two key factors at work in sustaining "the system of 'control' that kept the media 'in line' with the war effort"[10]—what he described as "the routines of journalism, and the ideological assumptions journalists shared with officials, as part of the political mainstream in the early to middle 1960s."[11]

Despite all the changes in news media since then, a filtration process remains crucial. Strong economic pressures are especially significant—and combine with powerful forces for conformity at times of nationalistic fervor and military action. "Even if journalists, editors, and producers are not superpatriots, they know that appearing unpatriotic does not play well with many readers, viewers, and sponsors," media analyst Michael X. Delli Carpini has commented. "Fear of alienating the public and sponsors, especially in wartime, serves as a real, often unstated tether, keeping the press tied to accepted wisdom."[12] Journalists in American newsrooms don't have to worry about being taken out and shot; the constraining fears are apt to revolve around peer approval, financial security, and professional advancement.

The attitudes of reporters covering U.S. foreign-policy officials are generally similar to the attitudes of those officials. "Most journalists who get plum foreign assignments already accept the assumptions of empire," according to longtime foreign correspondent Reese Erlich. (I traveled to Iraq with him in September 2002, and we later coauthored a book.) He added, "I didn't meet a single foreign reporter in Iraq who disagreed with the notion that the U.S. and Britain have the right to overthrow the Iraqi government by force. They disagreed only about timing, whether the action should be unilateral, and whether a long-term occupation is practical."[13] After decades of freelancing for major U.S. news organizations, Erlich offered this blunt conclusion: "Money, prestige, career options, ideological predilections—combined with the down sides of filing stories unpopular with the government—all cast their influence on foreign correspondents. You don't win a Pulitzer for challenging the basic assumptions of empire."[14]

Far from restraining the reliance on war as an instrument of foreign policy, the widespread media support for corporate "globalization" boosts the view that the U.S. government must strive to bring about favorable conditions in international affairs. The connections between military might and global commercial market share are not shouted from Washington's rooftops, but the links are solid. With matter-of-fact approval, Thomas Friedman wrote in his 1999 book *The Lexus and the Olive Tree*: "The hidden hand of the market will never work without a hidden fist. McDonald's cannot flourish without McDonnell Douglas, the designer of the U.S. Air Force F-15. And the hidden fist that keeps the world safe for Silicon Valley's technologies to flourish is called the U.S. Army, Air Force, Navy and Marine Corps."[15]

In the aftermath of the December 1989 Panama attack, *Washington Post* reporter Patrick E. Tyler wrote that it was "an invasion that almost everybody acknowledges was poorly covered by the news media because reporters were barred from accompanying the troops."[16] Forty-eight hours after the assault began, *Newsday* had reported: "During the first day of the invasion, the impression was that the media pool, which arrived a few hours after the heaviest fighting had abated, was being held 'captive,' said John Stacks, chief of correspondents for *Time* magazine, echoing complaints made by others. 'They might as well have been in Washington, except that the weather's different,' he said."[17] Days later the *Boston Globe* published a dispatch from Panama City that reported: "Unlike the 1983 U.S. military intervention in Grenada, this one is open to coverage by American journalists. But they have discovered that this newfound freedom, for the most part, has been illusory. The U.S. government, after acquiescing to demands that it open Panama to coverage, has made it all but impossible for journalists to do their jobs during much of the last week." The article, by staff reporter Walter V. Robinson, said that "more than 100 members of the news media opted to take a military flight home [on December 23], many of them without ever filing a story." From the invasion's second day until its fourth, "armed guards had prevented reporters from leaving the U.S. military installations where they had been confined . . . in many cases without food and in nearly all cases without a place to sleep other than on concrete or linoleum floors." In many instances, the result was "a lack of information that has been reflected in the coverage of the U.S. intervention."[18] This was a polite journalistic way of saying that the U.S. government had done a great job of manipulating the flow of information.

Overall, while some reporters expressed displeasure with the limits, few journalists or news organizations did any more than gripe about them. The restrictive media "pool" system for the invasion of Panama amounted to a dry run for the much larger Gulf War.

In January 1991, the Pentagon imposed strict curbs on journalistic access to the Gulf War. American military activities in the region were mostly off-limits to reporters. Defense Department censors cleared photos, video footage, and battlefield dispatches. Reporters were only allowed to travel in pools accompanied by U.S. military escorts. A *New York Times* correspondent, Malcolm Browne, complained that "the pool system is turning journalists into essentially unpaid employees of the Department of Defense."[19] The president of CBS News, Eric W. Ober, was caustic: "The new guidelines guarantee pack journalism—the worst form of reporting—and allow the military to orchestrate and control the news before it reaches the American people."[20] But such objections amounted to little more than grumbles as major American news outlets handled the Gulf War to the evident satisfaction of the White House and the Pentagon.

Patrick J. Sloyan, who covered the war as a *Newsday* correspondent, has recalled that once the air bombardment got under way, "the media was fed carefully selected footage by [General Norman] Schwarzkopf in Saudi Arabia and [General Colin] Powell in Washington, D.C. Most of it was downright misleading." And Sloyan described "limitations imposed on reporters on the battlefield" during the war: "Under rules developed by [Defense Secretary Dick] Cheney and Powell, journalists were not allowed to move without military escorts. All interviews had to be monitored by military public affairs escorts. Every line of copy, every still photograph, every strip of film had to be approved—censored—before being filed. And these rules were ruthlessly enforced."[21] But, then as now, the most pernicious restrictions remained self-imposed. Whatever the journalistic grievances, workday concepts of professionalism have included parroting Pentagonspeak.

By the time of the Gulf War, retired colonels, generals, and admirals had become mainstays in network TV studios during wartime. Language such as "collateral damage" flowed effortlessly between journalists and military men, who shared perspectives on the occasionally mentioned and rarely seen civilians killed by U.S. firepower. At the outset of the Gulf War, NBC's Tom Brokaw echoed the White House and a frequent chorus from U.S. journalists by telling viewers: "We must point out again and again that it is Saddam Hussein who put these innocents in harm's way."[22] When those innocents got a mention, the U.S. government was often depicted as anxious to avoid hurting them. A couple of days into the war, Ted Koppel told ABC viewers that "great effort is taken, sometimes at great personal cost to American pilots, that civilian targets are not hit."[23] Two weeks later, Brokaw was offering assurances that "the U.S. has fought this war at arm's length with long-range missiles, high-tech weapons . . . to keep casualties down."[24]

With such nifty phrasing, no matter how many civilians might die as a result of American bombardment, the U.S. government—and by implication, its taxpayers—could always deny the slightest responsibility. And a frequent U.S. media message was that Saddam Hussein would use civilian casualties for propaganda purposes, as though that diminished the importance of those deaths. With the Gulf War in its fourth week, Bruce Morton of CBS provided this news analysis: "If Saddam Hussein can turn the world against the effort, convince the world that women and children are the targets of the air campaign, then he will have won a battle, his only one so far."[25] In American televisionland, when Iraqi civilians weren't being discounted or dismissed as Saddam's propaganda fodder, they were liable to be rendered nonpersons by omission. On a day that two thousand bombing runs occurred over Baghdad, anchor Ted Koppel reported: "Aside from the Scud missile that landed in Tel Aviv earlier, it's been a quiet night in the Middle East."[26]

News coverage of the Gulf War in U.S. media was sufficiently laudatory to the warmakers in Washington that a former assistant secretary of state, Hodding Carter, remarked: "If I were the government, I'd be paying the press for the kind of coverage it is getting right now."[27] A former media strategy ace for President Reagan put a finer point on the matter. "If you were going to hire a public relations firm to do the media relations for an international event," said Michael Deaver, "it couldn't be done any better than this is being done."[28]

When the media watch group FAIR conducted a survey of network news sources during the Gulf War's first two weeks, the most frequent repeat analyst was ABC's Anthony Cordesman. Not surprisingly, the former high-ranking official at the Defense Department and National Security Council gave the warmakers high marks for being trustworthy. "I think the Pentagon is giving it to you absolutely straight," Cordesman said.[29] The standard media coverage boosted the war. "Usually missing from the news was analysis from a perspective critical of U.S. policy," FAIR reported. "The media's rule of thumb seemed to be that to support the war was to be objective, while to be antiwar was to carry a bias." Eased along by that media rule of thumb was the sanitized language of Pentagonspeak as mediaspeak: "Again and again, the mantra of 'surgical strikes against military targets' was repeated by journalists, even though Pentagon briefers acknowledged that they were aiming at civilian roads, bridges and public utilities vital to the survival of the civilian population."[30]

As the Gulf War came to an end, people watching CBS saw Dan Rather close an interview with the 1st Marine Division commander by shaking his hand and exclaiming: "Again, General, congratulations on a job wonderfully done!"[31]

Chris Hedges covered the Gulf War for the *New York Times*. More than a decade later, he wrote in a book: "The notion that the press was used in the war is incorrect. The press wanted to be used. It saw itself as part of the war effort."[32] Truth-seeking independence was far from the media agenda. "The press was as eager to be of service to the state during the war as most everyone else. Such docility on the part of the press made it easier to do what governments do in wartime, indeed what governments do much of the time, and that is lie."[33] Variations in news coverage did not change the overwhelming sameness of outlook: "I boycotted the pool system, but my reports did not puncture the myth or question the grand crusade to free Kuwait. I allowed soldiers to grumble. I shed a little light on the lies spread to make the war look like a coalition, but I did not challenge in any real way the patriotism and jingoism that enthused the crowds back home. We all used the same phrases. We all looked at Iraq through the same lens."[34]

In late April 1999, with the bombing of Yugoslavia in its fifth week, many prominent American journalists gathered at a posh Manhattan hotel for the annual awards dinner of the prestigious Overseas Press Club. They heard a very complimentary speech by Richard Holbrooke, one of the key U.S. diplomats behind recent policies in the Balkans. "The kind of coverage we're seeing from the *New York Times*, the *Washington Post*, NBC, CBS, ABC, CNN and the newsmagazines lately on Kosovo," he told the assembled media professionals, "has been extraordinary and exemplary."[35] Holbrooke had good reasons to praise the nation's leading journalists. That spring, when the Kosovo crisis exploded into a United States–led air war, news organizations functioned more like a fourth branch of government than a Fourth Estate. The pattern was familiar.

Instead of challenging Orwellian techniques, media outlets did much to foist them on the public. Journalists relied on official sources—with nonstop interviews, behind-the-scenes backgrounders, televised briefings, and grainy bomb-site videos. Newspeak routinely sanitized NATO's bombardment of populated areas. Correspondents went through linguistic contortions that preserved favorite fictions of Washington policymakers.

"NATO began its second month of bombing against Yugoslavia today with new strikes against military targets that disrupted civilian electrical and water supplies"—the first words of the lead article on

the *New York Times* front page the last Sunday in April 1999—accepted and propagated a remarkable concept, widely promoted by U.S. officials: The bombing disrupted "civilian" electricity and water, yet the targets were "military."[36] Never mind that such destruction of infrastructure would predictably lead to outbreaks of disease and civilian deaths. On the newspaper's op-ed page, columnist Thomas Friedman made explicit his enthusiasm for destroying civilian necessities: "It should be lights out in Belgrade: Every power grid, water pipe, bridge, road and war-related factory has to be targeted."[37]

American TV networks didn't hesitate to show footage of U.S. bombers and missiles in flight—but rarely showed what really happened to people at the receiving end. Echoing Pentagon hype about the wondrous performances of Uncle Sam's weaponry, U.S. journalists did not often provide unflinching accounts of the results in human terms. Reporter Robert Fisk of London's *Independent* managed to do so: "Deep inside the tangle of cement and plastic and iron, in what had once been the make-up room next to the broadcasting studio of Serb Television, was all that was left of a young woman, burnt alive when NATO's missile exploded in the radio control room. Within six hours, the [British] Secretary of State for International Development, Clare Short, declared the place a 'legitimate target.' It wasn't an argument worth debating with the wounded—one of them a young technician who could only be extracted from the hundreds of tons of concrete in which he was encased by amputating both his legs. . . . By dusk last night, 10 crushed bodies—two of them women—had been tugged from beneath the concrete, another man had died in hospital and 15 other technicians and secretaries still lay buried."[38]

In the spring of 1999, as usual, selected images and skewed facts on television made it easier for Americans to accept—or even applaud—the exploding bombs funded by their tax dollars and dropped in their names. "The citizens of the NATO alliance cannot see the Serbs that their aircraft have killed," the *Financial Times* noted.[39] On American television, the warfare appeared to be wondrous and fairly bloodless.

As for recent history, the TV networks rendered it murky, the *Financial Times* observed: "Distortion of important background by Western broadcasters, whether intentional or not, has also helped NATO's cause." The newspaper added: "The stated aims of NATO's bombing campaign have also been muddied, by both heads of government and the Western media. A common phrase heard on the lips of correspondents of CNN . . . is 'forcing Yugoslav President Slobodan Milosevic to return to the negotiating table.' Yet Madeleine Albright, U.S. secretary of state, and Robin Cook, British foreign minister, made it clear after the breakdown of peace talks . . . that the autonomy deal offered by the West—and signed by the Kosovo Albanians—was no longer negotiable. There was in reality no table to return to."[40]

Ever since the start of NATO's bombing blitz, the regime in Belgrade had maintained control of Serbia's press—and American journalists scornfully reported on the propaganda role of Yugoslavian news media. Yet the U.S. mainstream media's reflexive deference to official sources and outlooks produced an overwhelming flood of sanitized coverage. As a popular euphemism for the continuous bombing, "air campaign" was a phrase that hardly conveyed what happened when bombs exploded in populated areas.

On April 5, when TV networks convened experts to discuss the war on Yugoslavia, viewers could see hawkish senator John McCain at 9:00 P.M. on CNN's *Larry King Live*, at 10:00 P.M. on Fox News Channel, at 11:00 P.M. on PBS's *Charlie Rose* show, and at 11:30 P.M. on ABC's *Nightline* with Ted Koppel. Researchers at FAIR quipped that the senator's whereabouts between 10:30 and 11:00 P.M. could not be determined.

When Thomas Friedman reflected on the first dozen days of what he called NATO's "surgical bombing," he engaged in easy punditry. "Let's see what 12 weeks of less than surgical bombing does," he wrote.[41] Sleek B-2 Stealth bombers and F-117A jets kept appearing in file footage on TV networks. Journalists talked with keen anticipation about Apache AH-64 attack helicopters on the way; military analysts told of the great things such aircraft could do.[42] Reverence for the latest weaponry was acute.[43]

Mostly, the American television coverage of the Iraq invasion was akin to scripted "reality TV," starting with careful screening of participants. CNN was so worried about staying within proper bounds that it cleared on-air talent with the Defense Department, as CNN executive Eason Jordan later acknowledged: "I went to the Pentagon myself several times before the war started and met with important people there and said, for instance—'At CNN, here are the generals we're thinking of retaining to advise us on the air and off about the war'—and we got a big thumbs-up on all of them. That was important."[44]

During the war that followed, the "embedding" of about seven hundred reporters in spring 2003 was hailed as a breakthrough. Those war correspondents stayed close to the troops invading Iraq, and news reports conveyed some vivid front-line visuals along with compelling personal immediacy. But with the context usually confined to the warriors' frame of reference, a kind of reciprocal bonding quickly set in.

"I'm with the U.S. 7th Calvary along the northern Kuwaiti border," CNN's embedded Walter Rodgers told viewers during a typical report. "We are in what the army calls its attack position. We have not yet crossed into Iraq at this point. At that point, we will tell you, when we do, of course, that we will cross the line of departure. What we are in is essentially a formation, much the way you would have seen with the U.S. Calvary in the nineteenth-century American frontier. The Bradley tanks, the Bradley fighting vehicles are behind me. Beyond that perimeter, we've got dozens more Bradleys and MI A1 main battle tanks."[45]

With American troops moving into action, CNN's Aaron Brown emphasized that he and his colleagues "wish them nothing but safety."[46] He did not express any such wish for the Iraqi people in harm's way.

The launch of a war is always accompanied by tremendous media excitement, especially on television. A strong adrenaline rush pervades the coverage. Even formerly reserved journalists tend to embrace the spectacle, providing a proud military narrative familiar to Americans, who have seen countless movies and TV shows conveying such story lines. War preparations may have proceeded amid public controversy, but White House strategists are keenly aware that a powerful wave of "support our troops" sentiment will kick in for news coverage as soon as the war starts.

Serving as bookends for U.S.-led wars in the 1990s, a pair of studies by FAIR marked the more narrow discourse once the U.S. military went on the attack. Whether the year was '91 or '99, whether the country under the U.S. warplanes was Iraq or Yugoslavia, major U.S. media outlets facilitated Washington's efforts to whip up support for the new war. During the first two weeks of the Gulf War, voices of

domestic opposition were all but excluded from the nightly news programs on TV networks. (The few strong denunciations of the war that
made it onto the air were usually from Iraqis.) In total, FAIR found,
only 1.5 percent of the sources were identified as American antiwar
demonstrators; out of 878 sources cited on the newscasts, just one was
a leader of a U.S. peace organization.[47] Eight years later, the pattern
was similar: in the spring of 1999, FAIR studied coverage during the
first two weeks of the bombing of Yugoslavia and found "a strong
imbalance toward supporters of NATO air strikes." Examining the
transcripts of two influential TV programs, ABC's *Nightline* and the
PBS *NewsHour with Jim Lehrer*, FAIR documented that only 8 percent of the 291 sources were critics of NATO's bombing. Forty-five
percent of sources were current or former U.S. government (including
military) officials, NATO representatives, or NATO troops. On *Nightline*, the study found, no U.S. sources other than Serbian Americans
were given airtime to voice opposition.[48]

Summarizing FAIR's research over a fifteen-year period, sociologist Michael Dolny underscored the news media's chronic "overre-
liance on official sources," and he also emphasized that "opponents of
war are underrepresented compared to the percentage of citizens
opposed to military conflict."[49] Those patterns were on display in
spring 2003 with the Iraq invasion, when FAIR conducted a study of
the 1,617 on-camera sources who appeared on the evening newscasts
of six U.S. television networks during the first three weeks of the war.
"Nearly two-thirds of all sources, 64 percent, were prowar, while 71
percent of U.S. guests favored the war. Antiwar voices were 10 percent
of all sources, but just 6 percent of non-Iraqi sources and only 3 percent of U.S. sources. Thus viewers were more than six times as likely
to see a prowar source as one who was antiwar; counting only U.S.
guests, the ratio increases to 25 to 1."[50]

Less than 1 percent of the U.S. sources were antiwar on *CBS
Evening News* during the Iraq war's first three weeks. Meanwhile,
as FAIR's researchers commented wryly, public television's PBS *News-
Hour with Jim Lehrer* "also had a relatively low percentage of U.S.
antiwar voices—perhaps because the show less frequently features on-
the-street interviews, to which critics of the war were usually rele-
gated."[51] During the invasion, the major network studios were
virtually off-limits to vehement American opponents of the war.

As usual, the enthusiasm for war was extreme on Fox News Channel. After a preinvasion makeover, the fashion was similar at MSNBC. (In a timely manner, that cable network had canceled the nightly *Donahue* program three weeks before the invasion began. A leaked in-house report said that Phil Donahue's show would present a "difficult public face for NBC in a time of war. . . . He seems to delight in presenting guests who are antiwar, anti-Bush and skeptical of the administration's motives." The danger, quickly averted, was that the show could become "a home for the liberal antiwar agenda at the same time that our competitors are waving the flag at every opportunity."[52]) At the other end of the narrow cable-news spectrum, CNN cranked up its own prowar fervor. Those perspectives deserved to be heard. But on the large TV networks, such voices were so dominant that they amounted to a virtual monopoly in the "marketplace of ideas."

On March 24, 1999, about an hour before the first missiles struck Yugoslavia, viewers heard a Fox News Channel anchor make an understandable slip: "Let's bring in our Pentagon spokesman—excuse me, our Pentagon correspondent." Soon all the networks were filled with footage of U.S. planes taking off from bases in Italy and England. And across television screens, a parade of former military officers began. A retired Marine Corps general named Richard Neal—transformed into a "CNN military analyst"—bedazzled an anchor with lingo such as "neutralize," "take out," and "collateral damage."[53] Many analysts hailed the "combat debut" of the B-2 Stealth bomber. It was par for the media course when *NewsHour with Jim Lehrer* correspondent Margaret Warner introduced a panel: "We get four perspectives now on NATO's mission and options from four retired military leaders."[54]

When the first missiles explode into public view, even many broadcast channels join in the nonstop coverage. There are live feeds from far away, camera shots of targeted areas, and special effects with extra sizzle because they're real acts of war, in real time. At that point, journalists seem to be conveying that the moments for doubts and divisive debate have passed, at least for now, as the Pentagon conducts war on behalf of us all. Frequent long briefings from Washington combine with similar news conferences from overseas; with so many high-ranking medaled men in uniform behind podiums and in front of TV studio cameras, distinctions between military officers and reporters blur. Journalists become part of the rooting section for the home team of America.

Retired generals were well represented in network studios when the bombing of Afghanistan started the second week of October 2001. On CNN, former NATO supreme commander Wesley Clark teamed up with Major General Don Shepperd to explain military strategies; they were sharing their insights as employees of AOL Time Warner.[55] Far away, missiles were flying and bombs were exploding— but on television, a sense of equilibrium prevailed, the tones calm, the correspondents self-composed. News bulletins crawled across the bottom of the screen, along with invitations to learn more, such as "Take a 3-D look at U.S. military aircraft at CNN.com." At Pentagon briefings, the language of Defense Secretary Donald Rumsfeld projected a war without end: "In this battle against terrorism, there is no silver bullet." In keeping with assurances of surgical air strikes, Rumsfeld echoed the metaphor: "Terrorism is a cancer on the human condition."[56]

As the Iraq invasion began, NBC's star anchor Tom Brokaw seemed unembarrassed as he engaged in boosterism. Speaking on-air with a military analyst, Brokaw said: "Admiral McGinn, one of the things that we don't want to do is to destroy the infrastructure of Iraq, because in a few days we're going to own that country."[57] In early April, on the same network, in the midst of the invasion carnage, Katie Couric said on NBC's *Today* show: "Well, Commander Thompson, thanks for talking with us at this very early hour out there. And I just want you to know, I think Navy SEALs rock."[58]

In the wake of September 11, 2001, the White House repeatedly sent news executives and working journalists an unsubtle message: exercise too much independence and you'll risk accusations of giving aid and comfort to the terrorist enemy. While breaking new ground in news management, the Bush administration indicated from the outset that it envisioned a war without end. Television networks in particular seemed to be running scared.[59]

With the overwhelming bulk of news organizations already inclined to serve as amplification systems for Washington in times of crisis, the White House found itself in a strong position to retool and oil the machinery of domestic propaganda after September 11. When confronted with claims about "coded messages" that Osama bin Laden and his henchmen might be sending via taped statements—as though other means, such as the Internet, did not exist—TV network executives fell right into line.

Tapes of Al Qaeda leaders provided a useful wedge for the administration to hammer away at the wisdom of (government-assisted) self-censorship. Network executives from ABC, CBS, NBC, Fox, and CNN were deferential in an October 10 conference call with Condoleezza Rice. The conversation was "very collegial," White House press secretary Ari Fleischer told journalists.[60] The result was an agreement, the *New York Times* reported, to "abridge any future videotaped statements from Osama bin Laden or his followers to remove language the government considers inflammatory." It was, the *Times* added, "the first time in memory that the networks had agreed to a joint arrangement to limit their prospective news coverage."[61] News Corp. magnate Rupert Murdoch, speaking for Fox, promised: "We'll do whatever is our patriotic duty."[62] CNN, owned by the world's largest media conglomerate, AOL Time Warner, was eager to present itself as a team player: "In deciding what to air, CNN will consider guidance from appropriate authorities."[63]

"Guidance" from "appropriate authorities" is exactly what the president's strategists had in mind—brandishing a club without quite needing to swing it. As longtime White House reporter Helen Thomas noted in a column, "To most people, a 'request' to the television networks from the White House in wartime carries with it the weight of a government command. The major networks obviously saw it that way."[64] The country's TV news behemoths snapped to attention and saluted the commander in chief. "I think they gave away a precedent, in effect," said James Naughton, president of the Poynter Institute for Media Studies. "And now it's going to be hard for them not to do whatever else the government asks."[65]

Ostensibly concerned about coded messages, administration spinmeisters were after much more sweeping leverage over all types of mainstream media.[66] The compliant network execs explained that the coded-messages matter "was only a secondary consideration," the *New York Times* recounted. "They said Ms. Rice mainly argued that the tapes enabled Mr. bin Laden to vent propaganda intended to incite hatred and potentially kill more Americans."[67] There was, of course, no need to curtail the broadcasting of propaganda that might incite hatred and potentially kill more Afghans.

TV and radio executives were acutely aware that the Federal

Communications Commission—more corporate-friendly than ever—
would frown on independent behavior in the industry. The FCC
chair, Michael Powell, was more conservative than his father, the secretary of state. With media conglomerates seeking even more deregu-
lation to assist with mergers and boost market share, there were
powerful incentives to go along with any "request" or preference
from the Bush administration about limiting war coverage.

Just before the bombing of Afghanistan got under way on October
7, 2001, the *Washington Post* reported that U.S. intelligence officials
had informed members of Congress that the Al Qaeda network was
very likely to strike again soon in the United States. It was hardly startling news—Attorney General John Ashcroft had already said as
much on television—but alarm bells went off at the White House, and
CIA director George Tenet swung into action to wave the *Post* away
from further unauthorized reporting.[68] Tenet "had been forced to persuade the newspaper not to publish even more sensitive material,"
according to the *New York Times*.[69] The next day, the *Times* quoted
the *Post*'s executive editor, Leonard Downie Jr., who said that—"a
handful of times" during the month since September 11—administration officials called the *Post* and "raised concerns that a specific story
or more often that certain facts in a certain story, would compromise
national security." Those calls were fruitful, Downie said: "In some
instances we have kept out of stories certain facts that we agreed
could be detrimental to national security and not instrumental to our
readers, such as methods of intelligence collection."[70]

But it was the content of collected intelligence and other secrets
that the officials often seemed most anxious to keep under wraps. A
frequent explanation was that details of U.S. troop movements had to
be tightly controlled. But the administration was eager to withhold
information that, if made public, could undermine Washington's
prowar position.

Gauging the overall effects of the U.S. government's media-related
initiatives, the Committee to Protect Journalists made this assessment
in its annual report about 2001: "The actions taken by the Bush
administration seemed to embolden repressive governments around
the world to crack down on their own domestic media. In Russia, a
presidential adviser said President Vladimir Putin planned to study
U.S. limitations on reporting about terrorists in order to develop rules
for Russian media."[71]

When civilian casualties gradually increased during the first days of bombing Afghanistan, the U.S. government took action—not by curtailing the carnage but by foreclosing public access to detailed photos that otherwise would have been available from space. "The Pentagon has spent millions of dollars to prevent Western media from seeing highly accurate civilian satellite pictures of the effects of bombing in Afghanistan," the London-based *Guardian* reported. At issue were photos from the Ikonos satellite, taking pictures at such high resolution that "it would be possible to see bodies lying on the ground after last week's bombing attacks." When the Defense Department moved to prevent media access to such pictures, it did not invoke provisions of American law allowing "shutter control" over U.S.-launched civilian satellites in wartime. Instead, the *Guardian* reported, "the Pentagon bought exclusive rights to all Ikonos satellite pictures of Afghanistan off Space Imaging, the company which runs the satellite. The agreement was made retrospectively to the start of the bombing raids." Because photos of the human toll in Afghanistan from the air war "would not have shown the position of U.S. forces or compromised U.S. military security," the *Guardian* explained, "the ban could have been challenged by news media as being a breach of the First Amendment."[72]

In autumn 2001, buying up all of the satellite's pictures proved to be a much more effective way to thwart media access than seeking a legal ban would have been. The Pentagon was determined to guard against embarrassing visual disclosures such as the satellite photos that the *St. Petersburg Times* had obtained a decade earlier. Those photos, casting doubt on presidential claims that Iraqi troops were positioned to invade Saudi Arabia, hadn't gotten enough media attention to cause major problems for the administration. But why take the chance?

The press corps mostly served as a conduit for the government's news flow, complete with grainy video supplied by the U.S. military to illustrate bombing of Afghanistan. But journalists pushed for more interaction with top officials. A week and a half into the air war, Pentagon correspondents got an affirmative response to requests for formal spoon-feeding at day-in, day-out news conferences. Secretary of Defense Rumsfeld was understandably upbeat. "Let's hear it for the essential daily briefing, however hollow and empty it might be," he said. "We'll do it."[73]

Many observers were suspicious that the Pentagon engaged in an aggressive form of news management with a devastating November 13 missile attack on the Al-Jazeera bureau in Kabul. In a postmortem assessment months later, the Committee to Protect Journalists was skeptical of the official explanations. "The U.S. military described the building as a 'known' Al Qaeda facility without providing any evidence," the CPJ report said. "Despite the fact that the facility had housed the Al-Jazeera office for nearly two years and had several satellite dishes mounted on its roof, the U.S. military claimed it had no indications the building was used as Al-Jazeera's Kabul bureau."[74] With its antipathy toward Al-Jazeera's reporting well established, the U.S. government seemed to be "dispatching" the news in a deadly sense, an impression later reinforced during the invasion and occupation of Iraq when, on several occasions, journalists with Al-Jazeera and other troublesome Arab correspondents were killed by U.S. fire.

For a long time, policymakers in Washington had been hostile to Al-Jazeera. The satellite TV network's coverage of the Iraq war, widely seen in the Arab world, was quite a contrast to the coverage on American television. As *Time* magazine observed: "On U.S. TV it means press conferences with soldiers who have hand and foot injuries and interviews with POWs' families, but little blood. On Arab and Muslim TV it means dead bodies and mourning."[75]

Among all the assessments of U.S. news coverage of the Vietnam War, none has stood the test of time better than the 1986 book *The "Uncensored War": The Media and Vietnam* by communications professor Daniel Hallin, a meticulous researcher.[76] Interviewed in early November 2003, with the Iraq occupation in the midst of turning into a large-scale war against a growing insurgency, Hallin compared media treatment of the two wars and saw similar patterns. "As you begin to get a breakdown of consensus, especially among political elites in Washington, then the media begin asking more questions," he said. In the case of Iraq, "the Democrats were mostly silent for a long time on this war, and when things began to bog down, they started asking questions. There were divisions within the Bush administration, and then the media starts playing a more independent role."[77]

To a notable degree, reporters seem to await signals from politicians and high-level appointees to widen the range of discourse. "They need confirmation that this issue is part of the mainstream political discussion in the U.S.," Hallin commented. "Journalists are very keyed into what their sources are talking about. Political reporters define news worthiness in part by what's going to affect American politics in the sense of who gets elected the next time around. But it isn't absolutely only elites. I think it also makes a difference that polls show the public divided, and that there are problems of morale among soldiers in Iraq. But the first thing that the journalists look to is: 'What are the elites debating in Washington?' That's what really sets the news agenda. . . . It's the self-conception of media in our society that they are this watchdog. But frequently they depart from it, and they depart from it most of all in the case of war."[78]

In late April 2003, a few weeks after Saddam statues began to fall in Baghdad, MSNBC correspondent Ashleigh Banfield caused a stir when she spoke on a college campus in Kansas. "There are horrors that were completely left out of this war," she said. "So was this journalism or was this coverage? There is a grand difference between journalism and coverage, and getting access does not mean you're getting the story, it just means you're getting one more arm or leg of the story. And that's what we got, and it was a glorious, wonderful picture that had a lot of people watching and a lot of advertisers excited about cable news. But it wasn't journalism, because I'm not so sure that we in America are hesitant to do this again, to fight another war, because it looked like a glorious and courageous and so successful terrific endeavor, and we got rid of a horrible leader: We got rid of a dictator, we got rid of a monster, but we didn't see what it took to do that."[79] Four days later, responding to a flap over Banfield's remarks, a spokeswoman for NBC management admonished the fleetingly errant reporter in the course of issuing an apology: "She and we both agreed that she didn't intend to demean the work of her colleagues, and she will choose her words more carefully in the future."[80]

The Banfield-in-Kansas episode sounded familiar: In a wartime frenzy, TV correspondents blend in with the prevailing media scenery. Later, a few briefly uttered words of regret, although next time around they revert to more or less the same pattern of cheerleading the current war. (Mark Twain remarked that it was easy to quit smoking —he'd done it thousands of times.)

When Dan Rather told BBC television that American journalists were intimidated after 9/11, he said: "There was a time in South

Africa that people would put flaming tires around people's necks if they dissented. And in some ways the fear is that you will be 'necklaced' here, you will have a flaming tire of lack of patriotism put around your neck. Now it is that fear that keeps journalists from asking the toughest of the tough questions." Rather was speaking on May 16, 2002. He called what was going on "a form of self-censorship" and added that "I do not except myself from this criticism." Rather described some of the internal process: "It starts with a feeling of patriotism within oneself. It carries through with a certain knowledge that the country as a whole—and for all the right reasons—felt and continues to feel this surge of patriotism within themselves. And one finds oneself saying: 'I know the right question, but you know what? This is not exactly the right time to ask it.'"[81]

During that BBC interview, Rather was outspoken: "Limiting access, limiting information to cover the backsides of those who are in charge of the war, is extremely dangerous and cannot and should not be accepted. And I am sorry to say that, up to and including the moment of this interview, that overwhelmingly it has been accepted by the American people. And the current administration revels in that, they relish that, and they take refuge in that."[82] But the following spring, Dan Rather fully joined in the overall media boosterism during his coverage of the Iraq invasion. And days after Baghdad fell, Rather went on the CNN program *Larry King Live* and emphasized his professional allegiance. "Look, I'm an American," Rather said. "I never tried to kid anybody that I'm some internationalist or something. And when my country is at war, I want my country to win, whatever the definition of 'win' may be. Now, I can't and don't argue that that is coverage without a prejudice. About that I am prejudiced."[83]

10

Media Coverage Brings War into Our Living Rooms

Many people like to think that television conveys the horrors of war. That assumption may be comforting, but it's absurd. Watching TV resembles experiencing war in much the same way that watching a marathon is like running one. Television sets don't explode, and walls don't fall; viewers don't bleed, aren't crushed, and won't be killed on the spot. A key reality of the war experience—tremendous fear—is absent from the viewing experience. Shots are not fired at us; they're edited for us, a process that filters out the footage and statements that producers consider to be too grisly or otherwise disturbing. It's a popular illusion—the idea that today's media coverage of war tells it like it is—but we don't really get more than the images approved by careful editors.

Planners in Washington can't very well call the next war "Operation Enormous Death and Suffering." The PR job ahead involves making the war seem to be as much as possible like the uplifting name given to it.[1]

Though they rose to much more public prominence with the advent of cable television, "Operation" names were popular with the Pentagon during the Vietnam War. Later, a war lasting just weeks might have a single name for its entirety. But the long war in Vietnam included an uncounted number of names for military ventures. "Two words sum up the beginnings of our military campaign to subdue the Mekong Delta. One is futility and the other brutality," the independent journalist I. F. Stone wrote. "The first invasion, launched with a tremendous air and naval bombardment, and an equally sensational splurge of publicity, was Operation Dockhouse V. It has just fizzled out. . . . Any time the Pentagon runs out of the glamourous names it gives these operations, we'd suggest a code name suited to this combination of monstrous power with dim intelligence. Why not Operation Dinosaur?"[2] But the war was officially going well at the time—January 1967—and few journalists had much use for such critical perspectives.

The invasion of Grenada in 1983 got the brand name Operation Urgent Fury. The 1986 bombing of Libya was Operation El Dorado Canyon. The invasion of Panama in 1989 went forward under the name Operation Just Cause. Scarcely a year later came Desert Shield, the "defensive" setup for Desert Storm, a.k.a. the Gulf War. At the end of the decade, the bombing of Yugoslavia was Operation Allied Force. For the attack on Afghanistan in October 2001, the Bush administration provided the tag Operation Infinite Justice, but—after learning that Muslims found it offensive for claiming to supplant Allah's role—the war's promoters in Washington rebranded it Operation Enduring Freedom.

Operation Iraqi Freedom was not far behind.

War planners rely on huge gaps between the horrendous realities of warfare and the news reporting about it. Even when carnage was at its height in Vietnam, correspondent Michael Herr later wrote, the U.S. media "never found a way to report meaningfully about death, which of course was really what it was all about. The most repulsive, transparent gropes for sanctity in the midst of the killing received serious treatment in the papers and on the air. The jargon of Progress got blown into your head like bullets, and by the time you waded through all the Washington stories and all the Saigon stories, all the Other War stories and the corruption stories and the stories about brisk new gains in ARVN effectiveness, the suffering was somehow unimpressive. And after enough years of that, so many that it seemed to have been going on forever, you got to a point where you could sit there in the evening and listen to the man say that American casualties for the week had reached a six-week low, only eighty GI's had died in combat, and you'd feel like you'd just gotten a bargain."[3]

A persistent myth is that television was responsible for bringing discontent with the Vietnam War into American homes and fomenting antiwar sentiment. An effect of the mythology has been to pressure journalists not to overstep their perceived bounds in coverage of subsequent wars. But during the 1960s and in later decades, TV news has played a much larger role in promoting and accepting wars than in challenging them. Even the apex of supposedly critical television reporting on Vietnam was hardly a catalyst for aversion to the war. Citing "three systematic studies of network television coverage of Vietnam," researcher Daniel Hallin summarized the findings: "All reject the idea that the living-room war meant graphic portrayals of violence on a daily basis, or that television was consistently negative toward U.S. policy or led public opinion in turning against the war."[4]

In autumn 1973, several months after the final withdrawal of U.S. combat troops from Vietnam, *TV Guide* published a major series of investigative articles by journalist Edward Jay Epstein. He reviewed kinescopes and transcripts from ABC, CBS, and NBC—the only American television networks to speak of during that period—over an eleven-year time span beginning in 1962. "It is generally assumed that the constant exposure of this war on television was instrumental in shaping public opinion," Epstein noted. "It has become almost a truism, and the standard rhetoric of television executives, to say that television, by showing the terrible truth of war, caused the disillusionment of Americans with the war."[5]

But Epstein pointed out that after half a dozen years of TV coverage in the early and mid-1960s, most Americans still supported the war: "The Gallup 'trend' poll, for example, indicates that until mid-1967 the number of Americans who agreed with the decision to send American ground troops to Vietnam actually increased, despite television's coverage." In fact, "almost every major poll taken through 1967 showed widespread support for American involvement in the war."[6] When *Newsweek* commissioned a Harris poll to zero in on how television affected public opinion about the war, 64 percent replied that the TV coverage had actually increased their support for the war, compared to just 26 percent who indicated that it had boosted their opposition. In *Newsweek*'s words, "TV had encouraged a decisive majority of viewers to support the war."[7]

Epstein debunked the assumption that the Vietnam War "was covered, and exposed, with the same vigilance and skepticism in the critical years of commitment (1962–1967) as it has been in the last stages of protest and withdrawal (1969–1973)."[8] Well-known exceptions were quite different from the routine TV news fare: "Almost every discussion of television's early coverage of the war touches on what has been rightly called, by CBS News executive William Small, 'the single most famous bit of reporting in South Vietnam'—the burning of the huts at Cam Ne. On August 5, 1965, the *CBS Evening News* carried a dramatic film story, narrated by Morley Safer, which showed U.S. Marines using their cigarette lighters to set fire to Vietnamese thatched huts in the village of Cam Ne. The report immediately became a cause célèbre. . . . The fact that this particular journalistic endeavor is now celebrated by virtually everyone who writes on the subject does not, however, mean that it exemplified the coverage of the war during this period. On the contrary, in examining network newscasts and scripts from 1962 to 1968, I could find few other comparable instances of indiscriminate American destruction or brutality"—even though "hundreds of South Vietnamese villages were destroyed and evacuated in 'relocation programs' during this period."[9] Epstein mentioned that other extensive research had ended up with very similar results: "The same conclusion was reached also by Professor Lawrence Litchy of the University of Wisconsin, who systematically analyzed network kinescopes of this period. Professor Litchy concludes that instances, such as Cam Ne, shown on television of American brutality toward the South Vietnamese 'could be counted on one hand.'"[10]

Attentive news watchers might see disquieting information in the press about the escalating war in Vietnam. From early on, some disturbing coverage did occur. But the overall reporting, political analysis, and commentaries were overwhelmingly tilted in favor of the war, so the context of troubling stories fed assumptions that whatever suffering occurred was the price that had to be paid. Yet careful readers were bound to run across snippets like these once in a while:

- American pilots "are given a square marked on a map and told to hit every hamlet within the area. The pilots know they sometimes are bombing women and children."

  —*Washington Post*, March 13, 1965

- "A United States military spokesman outlined today for the first time some of the combat rules set down for American Marines fighting in South Vietnam. . . . 'Marines do not burn houses or villages unless those houses or villages are fortified,' he said. When a reporter remarked that a great majority of the villages in Vietnam were fortified to some degree, the spokesman looked up from the text and said, 'I know it.'"

—*New York Times*, August 5, 1965

- "In Bien Hoa province south of Saigon on August 15 United States aircraft accidentally bombed a Buddhist pagoda and a Catholic church . . . it was the third time their pagoda had been bombed in 1965. A temple of the Cao Dai religious sect in the same area has been bombed twice this year.

  "In another delta province there is a woman who has both arms burned off by napalm and her eyelids so badly burned that she cannot close them. When it is time for her to sleep her family puts a blanket over her head. The woman had two of her children killed in the air strike that maimed her.

  "Few Americans appreciate what their nation is doing to South Vietnam with airpower . . . this is strategic bombing in a friendly allied country . . . innocent civilians are dying every day in South Vietnam."

  —*New York Times*, September 5, 1965[11]

A United Press International dispatch that summer, with a Chan Son dateline, included this passage: "'I got me a VC, man. I got at least two of them bastards.' The exultant cry followed a 10-second burst of automatic-weapons fire yesterday, and the dull crump of a grenade exploding underground. The Marines ordered a Vietnamese corporal to go down into the grenade-blasted hole to pull out their victims. The victims were three children between 11 and 14—two boys and a girl. Their bodies were riddled with bullets. . . . 'Oh, my God,' a young Marine exclaimed. 'They're all kids.'"[12] If such reportage is difficult to read now, presumably it wasn't easier for people reading it at breakfast tables in 1965. For that matter, every U.S. war since then has sparked at least a small amount of American news coverage of horrific results. But the vast bulk of war reporting is flattened by pallid words; circumscribed images; and, quite routinely, implicit and explicit justifications for the war.

Media insistence on downplaying the horrors of a war helps to promote it. Yet we should acknowledge that depicting war's anguish may do little or nothing to prevent more of the same. Such depictions can actually fuel enthusiasm for war. "Photographs of an atrocity may give rise to opposing responses," Susan Sontag has observed. "A call for peace. A cry for revenge. Or simply the bemused awareness, continually restocked by photographic information, that terrible things happen."[13]

Visual images may be among the most powerful messages we receive about war, but those graphic messages still leave it to us to assign them meaning. And we, in turn, assess meaning not so much because of what's in front of our eyes as what's behind them—our assumptions and attitudes—influenced and shaped, probably more than we would prefer to admit, by cues from political leaders, pundits, and reporters who function as role models with their reactions, including what they say and don't say.

Recalling the initial coverage of the Vietnam War, NBC correspondent Floyd Kalber commented: "To the degree that we in the media paid any attention at all to that small, dirty war in those years, we almost wholly reported the position of the government."[14] In 1965, Walter Cronkite lauded "the courageous decision that Communism's advance must be stopped in Asia and that guerrilla warfare as a means to a political end must be finally discouraged."[15]

During the middle period of the war, with hundreds of thousands of U.S. soldiers in South Vietnam, the coverage was so centered on Americans that Vietnamese people received media treatment as little more than walk-on extras in their own country. "From 1965 to 1968, few interviews can be found with South Vietnamese military or civilian leaders, and the Vietcong and North Vietnamese were almost nonexistent on American television newscasts," Epstein recounted.[16] During that period, network correspondent Howard K. Smith later recalled, "Television covered only one-third of the war—the American third."[17]

"As soon as American troops were committed to combat in large numbers," Hallin said, "television coverage focused overwhelmingly on one central story: American boys in action."[18] His research also found that "only about 22 percent of all film reports from Southeast Asia in the period before the [early 1968] Tet offensive showed actual combat, and often this was minimal—a few incoming mortar rounds or a crackle of sniper fire (perhaps followed by distant film of air strikes called in to 'take out' the unseen enemy). A similar percentage, about 24 percent, showed film of the dead or wounded, and again this might be no more than a brief shot of a wounded soldier being lifted onto a helicopter."[19]

Relying heavily on U.S. government sources who claimed American progress was evident in Vietnam, the TV coverage through 1967 tended to be reassuring. "The early picture of the war on television was truncated in an even more serious sense: all three networks had very definite policies about showing graphic film of wounded American soldiers or suffering Vietnamese civilians," Epstein reported. "Producers of the NBC and ABC Evening News programs said that they ordered editors to delete excessively grisly or detailed shots because they were not appropriate for a news program shown at dinnertime. A former producer of the *CBS Evening News* said that they also had a network policy of not showing 'identifiable' American soldiers before their families were notified, and that the anchorman was supposed to warn the audience if especially 'gruesome shots' were to be shown. According to former CBS News president Fred W. Friendly, these network policies 'helped shield the audience from the true horror of the war.' And although large numbers of Americans were wounded throughout this period, the net effect of these policies, though perhaps not intentional, was to severely restrict the coverage of wounded Americans"—except, Epstein added, "in the anchormen's weekly totals."[20]

For the first years of the Vietnam War, the upbeat claims from U.S. officials dominated news coverage. In retrospect, wrote one academic analyst of media, Michael X. Delli Carpini, "It is clear that the United States military, intentionally or not, systematically underreported the strength of the opposition and overreported the number of 'kills.' It is also clear that the press corps, with few exceptions, accepted these official numbers and reported them dutifully to the American public until the Tet offensive."[21] Hallin cites a study of six newspapers that varied in size and politics: "Historian Clarence Wyatt found that papers varied a good deal in their coverage, reflecting different political orientations, but overall the familiar pattern could be seen: a heavy dependence on official information before Tet, and greater independence, to a limited degree, later in the war."[22] Like most Americans, evidently, news managers want to see their country win wars but may become restive when victory seems elusive.

As the war went on in the late 1960s, people could argue about whether the USA's setbacks were primarily military or psychological, but the reality was that many Americans and many more Vietnamese people were being killed and wounded. Television news became more downbeat—and, in the wake of the Tet offensive early in 1968, Walter Cronkite famously decried the war as a "bloody stalemate."[23] In a one-hour CBS television special that aired on February 27, he opined that the solution would come through negotiations rather than victory. Perhaps most startling to viewers was Cronkite's unhopeful tone: "It seems now more certain than ever that the bloody experience of Vietnam is to end in a stalemate. This summer's almost certain standoff will either end in real give-and-take negotiations or terrible escalation; and for every means we have to escalate, the enemy can match us. . . . And with each escalation, the world comes closer to the brink of cosmic disaster. To say that we are closer to victory today is to believe, in the face of the evidence, the optimists who have been wrong in the past. To suggest we are on the edge of defeat is to yield to unreasonable pessimism. To say that we are mired in stalemate seems the only realistic, yet unsatisfactory, conclusion."[24]

That kind of discourse, to be sure, was a significant shift from the denial and cheerleading of previous years. But Cronkite's script was filled with regret that "we" could not escalate without "the enemy" being able to "match us"—and while many have cited that broadcast as the pivotal moment when the country's most trusted journalist came out against the war, his evident anguish was much more centered on America's military failures than on its moral ones. Even though the overall tenor of Vietnam coverage became more critical, "the media never questioned American motives or the policymaking system itself," Delli Carpini pointed out after the war. "They merely questioned the soundness of the tactics and whether the benefits of this protracted, bloody war outweighed the rising costs."[25]

Scarcely a year after Cronkite's prime-time (and quickly fabled) lament, the networks were losing interest in the carnage even while it continued unabated. The incoming Nixon administration was eager to divert attention to peace talks set for Paris, and in general the networks were willing to oblige.

The negotiations served as a diversion from the continuing war. While deaths of Americans and Southeast Asians were not appreciably reduced, the network focus moved away from the ongoing bloodshed. At NBC, for instance, "although combat footage was sent to New York from the Saigon bureau every day for two months following the [early November 1968 U.S.] decision [initiating peace negotiations in Paris], it was aired only three times on the evening news. The preceding year, when there had been almost the same number of American combat deaths during the same period, combat stories were shown almost every night of the week."[26] With the media wisdom now determining that the main Vietnam story was about the negotiations, NBC News producer Robert Northshield said that "combat stories seemed like a contradiction and would confuse the audience."[27] As Epstein found: "Similar decisions were made at the other networks. . . . Even though the negotiations in Paris failed to produce any tangible results at that time, the actual war continued to be phased out by the networks."[28]

A typical approach was embodied in edicts handed down at ABC, where the executive producer of the evening news, Av Westin, put out a March 1969 memo that explained: "I have asked our Vietnam staff to alter the focus of their coverage from combat pieces to interpretive ones, pegged to the eventual pull-out of the American forces. This point should be stressed for all hands." In a telex to the network's Saigon bureau, Westin gave the news of his decree to the news correspondents: "I think the time has come to shift some of our focus from the battlefield, or more specifically American military involvement with the enemy, to themes and stories under the general heading 'We Are on Our Way Out of Vietnam.' "[29]

As the White House gradually pulled troops from Vietnam, the media shifted farther away from the actual destruction of people, villages, farmland, and ecosystems—even while the U.S. air war and coordinated ground assaults in Vietnam, Cambodia, and Laos persisted at a very high rate of killing. "By 1970, consistent with U.S. policy, the main story on all three networks had become the withdrawal of American troops," Delli Carpini writes. "When negotiations failed to produce results, the media blamed the North Vietnamese."[30] Daniel Hallin concurs: "In each story the onus for lack of progress toward peace is removed entirely from the Nixon administration and put onto the North Vietnamese."[31]

It turned out to be a terribly long good-bye; large numbers of U.S. troops remained in Vietnam for years longer. At the negotiating table, the American media establishment knew which side it was on, as reflected in anchor David Brinkley's explanation that reached millions of Americans via NBC News on October 8, 1970: "President Nixon's new peace plan for Vietnam was formally offered at the Paris peace talks today, and the Communists reacted with sneers, wisecracks, and sarcasm. But actually that's about what was expected of them; no one thought that was their final reaction, and the American ambassador said he was not discouraged. . . . [I]t's taken for granted they will talk seriously some time later. In this country the president's plan has won wide support and approval in both parties."[32]

In October 2001, CNN chairman Walter Isaacson wanted to prevent any implication of undue sympathy for the victims of Pentagon bombs. "It seems perverse to focus too much on the casualties or hardship in Afghanistan," he said in a memo ordering his staff to accompany any grim images of Afghan civilians with the message that U.S. bombing was in retaliation for the Taliban harboring terrorists. As if viewers might otherwise forget September 11, the CNN chief explained: "You want to make sure that when they see civilian suffering there, it's in the context of a terrorist attack that caused enormous suffering in the United States."[33]

But few American viewers or readers saw much about "civilian suffering there" due to the bombing. The *Panama City News Herald* in Florida seemed to clumsily distill the predilections of many news outlets across the country when an internal memo warned the daily's editors: "DO NOT USE photos on Page 1A showing civilian casualties from the U.S. war on Afghanistan. Our sister paper in Fort Walton Beach has done so and received hundreds and hundreds of threatening e-mails and the like. . . . DO NOT USE wire stories which lead with civilian casualties from the U.S. war on Afghanistan. They should be mentioned further down in the story. If the story needs rewriting to play down the civilian casualties, DO IT. The only exception is if the U.S. hits an orphanage, school or similar facility and kills scores or hundreds of children."[34]

Such admonitions from media managers might seem heavy-handed. But they're quite harmonious with the sensibilities of foreign-policy officials in Washington. It was unremarkable when Colin Powell, then chairman of the Joint Chiefs of Staff, gave an interview at the Pentagon on March 22, 1991, and indicated that he could not be bothered about how many Iraqis had died as a result of the U.S.-led attacks during the six-week Gulf War. He said: "It's really not a number I'm terribly interested in."[35] On the same day, the Associated Press cited estimates from official U.S. military sources that the war had killed a hundred thousand Iraqi people. But high-profile American leaders preferred to avoid mentioning even antiseptic numbers that might convey the scope of the war's human toll.

Distance from consequences is pronounced when bombs arrive from thousands of feet in the air. Typically, on the third night of bombing in December 1998, CNN's Christiane Amanpour repeatedly told viewers that Baghdad was having a "dramatic" night.[36] When the smoke cleared, many journalists spoke of "collateral damage" without quite mentioning dead Iraqi civilians. (In effect: *If necessary, don't spare them. But spare us the grisly details.*) During four long nights, while cruise missiles exploded in Baghdad and other populated areas of Iraq, millions of children were among those who lay awake.

"The hijacking of language is fundamental to war," Chris Hedges wrote after many years as a war correspondent. "It becomes difficult to express contrary opinions. There are simply not the words or phrases to do it. We all speak with the same clichés and euphemisms."[37] Along the way, the vocabulary of journalism is part of the warmaking lexicon for dramatic scripts: "Life in wartime becomes theater. All are actors. Leaders, against the backdrop of war, look heroic, noble. Pilots who bail out of planes shot down by the enemy and who make their way back home play cameo roles. The state, as we saw in the Persian Gulf War or Afghanistan, transforms war into a nightly television show. The generals, who are no more interested in candor than they were in Vietnam, have at least perfected the appearance of candor. And the press has usually been more than willing to play the dupe as long as the ratings are good."[38]

Meanwhile, Hedges points out, the media show is a fantasy in which "the images of war handed to us, even when they are graphic, leave out the one essential element of war—fear. There is, until the actual moment of confrontation, no cost to imagining glory. The visual and audio effects of films, the battlefield descriptions in books, make the experience appear real. In fact the experience is sterile. We are safe. We do not smell rotting flesh, hear the cries of agony, or see before us blood and entrails seeping out of bodies. We view, from a distance, the rush, the excitement, but feel none of the awful gut-wrenching anxiety and humiliation that come with mortal danger. It takes the experience of fear and the chaos of battle, the deafening and disturbing noise, to wake us up, to make us realize that we are not who we imagined we were, that war as displayed by the entertainment industry might, in most cases, as well be ballet. But even with this I have seen soldiers in war try to recreate the fiction of war, especially when a television camera is around to record the attempted heroics. The result is usually pathetic."[39]

Avowedly, the main targets for the bombing of Afghanistan in late 2001 were people in the bin Laden network. "We will rout them out and . . . starve them out," Donald Rumsfeld said, just before closing a news conference with a ringing declaration: "We are determined not to be terrorized."[40]

"That last quote says it all," MSNBC anchor Brian Williams interjected a moment later, before going to "NBC military analyst" Bernard Trainor. Like other ex-generals on network retainers, Trainor consistently used the word "we" to describe U.S. military actions. ("We now have the capability . . .") High-tech maps and video graphics were profuse during the explications of war-game scenarios. Former diplomats were network players, too. On NBC, Richard Holbrooke—a media favorite who had engineered the diplomatic run-up to the bombing of Yugoslavia a couple of years earlier—chatted with Tom Brokaw while using a pointer and a brightly lit map to elucidate geopolitical dynamics.

Crawling across the bottoms of cable TV screens, snippets of quotes blurred together, with bin Laden proclaiming that believers would triumph, Bush declaring "may God continue to bless America," and the Taliban accusing the United States of "terrorist" attacks. As time went on, the adversaries increasingly seemed to be talking each other's language.

The on-screen logos, spangled in red, white, and blue, exuded pride in a nation resurgent. CBS had opted for "America Fights Back." NBC and MSNBC were using "America Strikes Back." At times, MSNBC switched to an alternate buzz phrase: "Homeland Defense." Within days, networks were showing footage of bombers taking off from aircraft carriers, en route to Afghanistan. MSNBC's viewers saw footage of warheads with "NYPD" scrawled on them; in the background, an American flag fluttered on deck. And so, a bait-and-switch process of patriotic imagery was near completion. For weeks, in the aftermath of the horrendous events of September 11, the public had embraced Old Glory as a symbol of grief, human solidarity, and love of country. Now the ubiquitous American flag was being affixed to military means of destruction.

"This will be a long war," President George W. Bush promised.[41] The TV networks were ready to do their part. As *Los Angeles Times* critic Howard Rosenberg wrote several weeks into the bombing of Afghanistan, the interior decor of the televised universe amounted to wall-to-wall props for war unbound: "Propaganda of all kinds, from newscasters saluting themselves to national leaders lobbying the public, is the furniture of TV." From White House officials to network anchors, the lines between government and media blurred to the vanishing point. In a mid-November 2001 column, Rosenberg recounted the latest airing of ABC's *Good Morning America*, during which "hosts Diane Sawyer and Charles Gibson ran themselves up the flagpole when telecasting from the returning aircraft carrier *Enterprise*, which launched the first air strikes against Afghanistan. 'This is the first time an entire U.S. broadcast has come from a U.S. carrier at sea,' someone said. A nice idea were it not for Admiral Gibson being decked out in Navy threads."[42]

For the warmakers, it was surely heartening to see TV news professionals acting like part of the U.S. military. The ostensibly most liberal network, CNN, was unabashedly with the war program. As Rosenberg noted, "CNN keeps running thunderous promos that sell its war coverage as 'Saving Private Ryan II.' And what juxtapositions. One day, anchor Kyra Phillips was selling CNN's extended live coverage of police chasing a flaming lumber truck in Dallas as significant news . . . and the next crouching on one of those floor maps while reviewing U.S. battle military strategy in Afghanistan."[43]

During the Iraq war in 2003, there were instances of exceptional journalism in the mainstream U.S. press. A few reporters, notably Anthony Shadid of the *Washington Post* and Ian Fisher of the *New York Times*, wrote vivid accounts of what the Pentagon's firepower did to Iraqi people on the ground. Newsmagazines provided a number of grisly pictures. Only a closed heart could be unmoved by those stories and photos. But our country seemed to remain largely numb.

"Information about what is happening elsewhere, called 'news,' features conflict and violence—'If it bleeds, it leads' runs the venerable guideline of tabloids and 24-hour headline news shows—to which the response is compassion, or indignation, or titillation, or approval, as each misery heaves into view," Susan Sontag commented.[44] Her book *Regarding the Pain of Others* challenges common assumptions about the powerful effects of camerawork, whether in print or on television or on museum walls. A strength of her analysis is that it helps to clarify the social role of the photograph: "its meaning—and the viewer's response—depends on how the picture is identified or misidentified; that is, on words."[45] The book points out: "In the current political mood, the friendliest to the military in decades, the pictures of wretched hollow-eyed GIs that once seemed subversive of militarism and imperialism may seem inspirational. Their revised subject: ordinary American young men doing their unpleasant, ennobling duty."[46]

We're likely to overestimate the clarity of media visuals. Sontag noted that "the image as shock and the image as cliché are two aspects of the same presence."[47] When she acknowledged that "harrowing photographs do not inevitably lose their power to shock," Sontag immediately added: "But they are not much help if the task is to understand."[48]

The publication date of *Regarding the Pain of Others* came in March 2003, just days before the U.S. government launched its war on Iraq. The Pentagon's PR innovation of "embedding" reporters and photographers during the war did not reduce the validity of Sontag's assessment when describing "the preferred current American way of warmaking." She wrote: "Television, whose access to the scene is limited by government controls and by self-censorship, serves up the war as images. The war itself is waged as much as possible at a distance, through bombing, whose targets can be chosen, on the basis of instantly relayed information and visualizing technology, from continents away."[49] And photographic images "cannot be more than an invitation to pay attention, to reflect, to learn, to examine the rationalizations for mass suffering offered by established powers. Who caused what the picture shows? Who is responsible? Is it excusable? Was it inevitable? Is there some state of affairs which we have accepted up to now that ought to be challenged?"[50]

In newsrooms and studios, quite a few macho exemplars—serving behind computer screens and in front of TV cameras—reliably cheered the war effort during the invasion of Iraq. Along the way, they managed to keep a stiff upper lip about the suffering of others. Such courage is inexhaustible and sometimes awesome. "The American public knows the importance of this war," Fox News pundit and *Weekly Standard* executive editor Fred Barnes told viewers a few days after the invasion began. "They are not as casualty sensitive as the weenies in the American press are."[51]

The Defense Department engaged in notable fakery about the circumstances of her wartime trauma, but the young army private Jessica Lynch was left with terribly real injuries. Her authorized biography—*I Am a Soldier, Too*—described the damage, much of it lasting. "Her right arm was shattered between her shoulder and her elbow, and the compound fracture shoved slivers of bone through muscles, nerves and skin, leaving her right hand all but useless. Her spine was fractured in two places, causing nerve damage that left her unable to control her kidneys and bowels. Her right foot was crushed. Her left leg had broken into pieces above and below the knee, also a compound fracture, and splintered bone had made a mess of the nerves and left her without feeling in that limb."[52]

Thousands of other Americans who followed orders into Iraq also sustained life-changing wounds. They were soldiers, too. For those individuals, any media attention faded.

Many pundits seemed most appreciative of the dead, not only silent but also forever out of sight. War boosters don't have to worry about words or actions from dead soldiers. A fatality tells no tale; those who paid "the ultimate price" can't say they feel cheated. But the wounded are a different story. Their suffering is not only in the past. And they might not be silent.

There were many stories to be told about men and women returning home. "In reading the casualty reports, I have been struck by how many of the wounded lose arms and legs," Sydney Schanberg wrote in the *Village Voice*. "Ironically, while the new torso armor keeps soldiers alive, they are often left with maimed bodies and onerous futures. We'll be seeing those survivors soon, wearing prosthetic limbs. Let us hope we don't look away."[53]

But for the most part, journalists do look away—toward any number of stories with less gloomy endings. At the same time, the White House has tried to downplay the wounded, preferring to treat them as middle-distance props of patriotism, bathed in soft, vague light. A protracted focus on the suffering of grievously injured soldiers and their loved ones might evoke tough questions about a war continuing to cause such human anguish.

Officials have strived to dim the media spotlights when the ultimately sacrificed are laid to rest. After six months of occupation in Iraq, the Pentagon implemented new regulations at Arlington National Cemetery: "Reporters are no longer permitted to stand at the rear of the mourners during the service," and microphones "are not permitted . . . anywhere near the grave site."[54] The new rules at the cemetery were in harmony with a twelve-year-old ban on media coverage of flag-draped coffins arriving at Dover Air Force Base in Delaware; since 1991 the solemn honor-guard ceremonies for the caskets were being conducted out of public view, in compliance with regulations that prohibited media photos of military coffins returning to the United States.[55] When the invasion of Iraq began, the Pentagon explicitly barred media coverage of "deceased military personnel returning to or departing from" airports.[56] Those rules caused a private employee to lose her job a year later, in April 2004, when a military contractor took action against Tami Silicio, "a Kuwait-based cargo worker whose photograph of flag-draped coffins of fallen U.S. soldiers was published in Sunday's edition of the *Seattle Times*," that newspaper reported. Working for Maytag Aircraft, she got fired after publication of the photo, which showed more than twenty coffins about to leave Kuwait for the United States. A Pentagon spokesperson explained: "We've made sure that all of the installations who are involved with the transfer of remains were aware that we do not allow any media coverage of any of the stops until [the casket] reaches its final destination."[57]

One of the leading warriors in the Washington press corps, Charles Krauthammer, kept encouraging the commander in chief to let the good wartimes roll. Praising Bush for staying away from the coffins of American soldiers, Krauthammer warned in a December 2003 *Time* magazine column that "the enemy's entire war objective" is "to inflict pain." And so, he claimed, "that is why it would be a strategic error to amplify and broadcast that pain by making great public shows of sorrow presided over by the president himself."[58] Such rationales for diverting media attention from casualties of war were, no doubt, greatly appreciated by White House senior adviser Karl Rove, serving as the president's key political strategist.

The dead could be swiftly lowered into the ground while the president stayed safely out of camera range. Wounded men and women needed to be acknowledged, visited, thanked. "This weekend, at a Fort Hood hospital, I presented a Purple Heart to some of our wounded, had the honor of thanking them on behalf of all Americans," President Bush said very soon after beginning a major news conference in mid-April 2004.[59] The mention of medals was a way of conveying that the wounded had not been taken for granted, that high-level due diligence had been expended in hopes that the circles of pain could be squared away. While Bush was keeping his distance from funerals, *Newsweek* noted a year after the invasion that "Bush does appear from time to time with the families of dead or wounded soldiers."[60] The *Washington Post* reported later in the spring that "the administration has limited damaging images of the cost of war in Iraq. While the president has met privately with the families of many of the war victims, Bush has not attended any funeral for fallen service members."[61]

With many Americans contemptuous of the official rationales for starting the war in the first place, media stories about injured GIs stoked the smoldering anger. "A growing number of young men and women were returning from Iraq and trying to resume lives that were interrupted by war and then minced by tragedy," the *New York Times* reported in a profile of a twenty-four-year-old army sergeant, Jeremy Feldbusch, who was near Baghdad when an exploding shell propelled steel shrapnel through his right eye and into his brain.[62] He was in a coma for five weeks. Later, the young man learned that he was getting a Bronze Star and a Purple Heart. And he was blind.

Such occasional news stories were fleeting reminders of the pain and anguish that others—soldiers and civilians—would forever bear. To dwell on their suffering might undermine the latest war and the next one. "Those who pay the price, those who are maimed forever by war, are shunted aside, crumpled up and thrown away," Chris Hedges wrote in 2004. "They are war's refuse. We do not want to see them. We do not want to hear them. They are doomed, like wandering spirits, to float around the edges of our consciousness, ignored, even reviled. The message they bear from war is too painful for us to absorb. . . . If we really knew war, what war does to minds and bodies, it would be harder to wage. This is why the essence of war, which is death and suffering, is so carefully hidden from public view. . . . We taste a bit of war's exhilaration but are safe, spared the pools of blood, the wailing of a dying child."[63]

During the first days of the Iraq invasion, many American journalists emphasized the idea of their own extraordinary latitude. To a significant degree, the war was marketed as a war that was not being marketed. Forrest Sawyer, anchoring the nightly news on CNBC, put it this way: "Now, this is certainly not your father's Gulf War. Last time, you remember, the government essentially shut reporters down as much as they could. In fact, they had them holed up up in Dahrahn, Saudi Arabia, and if you went out 100 kilometers outside without a minder, you were arrested. Well, this time reporters, as we have seen, have been broadcasting live from any number of places. They have been, as they put it, embedded with the military. And they have been able to broadcast, on at least some occasions, with very few restrictions."[64]

"I can tell you that these soldiers have been amazing to us," said NBC correspondent David Bloom, on the move with the 3rd Infantry in southern Iraq as the invasion got under way.[65] Bloom devoted some words to affirming his professionalism. ("Obviously we're trying to maintain our objectivity and report factually what we see and hear here. . . . As a journalist, you have to maintain some distance. If there are problems that they encounter, we'll report those as well and let you know what's going on here, both the good things and the bad things."[66]) But the intensifying bond with the American troops overwhelmed the pro forma disclaimers. The soldiers he was covering "have done anything and everything that we could ask of them," Bloom said, "and we in turn are trying to return the favor by doing anything and everything that they can ask of us. But as far as the relationship is concerned, we are about as one with this force as you could possibly be."[67]

Minutes after dawn spread daylight across the Iraqi desert, embedded CNN correspondent Walter Rodgers was on the air with a live report. Another employee of the network, former U.S. general Wesley Clark—on the job in a TV studio back home—asked his colleague a question. When Rodgers responded, he addressed Clark as "General" and "Sir."

That deferential tone pretty much summed up the overall relationship between American journalists and the U.S. military on major TV

networks. Correspondents in the field bonded with troops to the point that their language was often indistinguishable. Meanwhile, no matter what tensions existed, reporters seemed basically comfortable with Pentagon sources. And what passed for debate was rarely anything more than the second-guessing of military decisions. It was kind of okay to question how—but not why—the war was being fought. Within the bounds of mass media, during the first days of the invasion, the loudest questioning voices demanded to know whether the U.S. government had miscalculated by failing to deploy enough troops from the outset.

Exceptional reports on American television, conspicuous for their rarity, asked deeper questions. On the ABC program *Nightline*, correspondent John Donvan shed light on what "embeds" routinely missed. Rather than traveling under the Pentagon's wing, Donvan and other intrepid "unilaterals" ventured out on their own. In his case, the results included an illuminating dispatch from the Iraqi town of Safwan. "Just because the Iraqis don't like Saddam, doesn't mean they like us for trying to take him out," Donvan explained. "To the contrary. Although people started out talking to us in a friendly way, after a while it became a little tense. These people were mad at America, very mad. And they wanted us to know why. It was because, they said, people in town had been shot at by the United States." Declining to travel in tandem with U.S. troops, Donvan was able and willing to report on views not apt to be expressed by Iraqis looking down the barrels of the invaders' guns: "Why are you taking over Iraq? That's how the people in this crowd saw it—takeover, not liberation."[68]

In contrast to the multitudes of embedded American reporters, Donvan was oriented toward realities underneath fleeting images. Instead of zooming along on the media fast track, he could linger: "In short, if embeds are always moving with the troops, unilaterals get to see what happens after they've passed through." The visible anger of Iraqi people had roots in events that usually get described in antiseptic and euphemistic terms by U.S. media outlets. "What else did we see by going in as unilaterals? The close-up view of collateral damage. The U.S. says it's trying to limit injuries to civilians. It is, however, hard not to take it personally when that collateral damage is you." Donvan reported on a wounded Iraqi man, evidently a bus driver, who had lost his wife over the weekend: "She was collateral damage. So were his two brothers. So were his two children."[69]

Media tacticians at the Pentagon had reason to view the embedding as a success. Later, some journalists sounded a bit rueful. *Los Angeles Times* reporter David Zucchino recalled his experiences while embedded with the 101st Airborne. He had good "access," he said, but that access "could be suffocating and blinding." Zucchino commented: "Often I was too close, or confined, to comprehend the war's broad sweep. I could not interview survivors of Iraqi civilians killed by U.S. soldiers or speak to Iraqi fighters trying to kill Americans. I was not present when Americans died at the hands of fellow soldiers in what the military calls 'frat,' for fratricide. I had no idea what ordinary Iraqis were experiencing. I was ignorant of Iraqi government decisions and U.S. command strategy."[70]

Overall, the Bush administration benefited from good PR, and the public suffered from bad journalism. There were exceptional instances of reportage—including from some embedded journalists—but as a practical matter the innovation oiled the military's spin machinery. "The close quarters shared by journalists and troops inevitably blunted reporters' critical edge," the Committee to Protect Journalists concluded after the smoke and mirrors cleared. "There were also limits on what types of stories reporters could cover, since the ground rules barred journalists from leaving their unit."[71] Meanwhile, journalists who were not imbedded with the invading military "faced a multitude of hazards and restrictions, limiting the reporting from non-U.S. military perspectives," the committee said. In some cases, those journalists "faced outright harassment from U.S. forces."[72]

On April 8, 2003, in Baghdad, a U.S. missile hit the Al-Jazeera office, taking the life of Tareq Ayub, a thirty-four-year-old Jordanian journalist. On the same day, a U.S. tank fired a shell at the Palestine Hotel, where most foreign journalists were then based in Baghdad. The assault killed Taras Protsyuk of the Reuters news agency and José Couso of the Spanish network Telecinco. The explanations from the Pentagon were not credible. "U.S. Central Command first said troops came under fire from the [hotel] lobby, while the field commander said whatever fire had been headed toward his troops was wiped out with a single tank round into the upper floors of the hotel," the AFX news agency reported. "But after a journalist questioned why the tank shot the upper floors when fire had come from the lobby, Central Command issued a revised statement saying there had been 'significant enemy fire.'"[73] However, the journalists who were eyewitnesses flatly contradicted that claim, saying no weapons fire had emanated from the hotel. "There was no shooting at all," said French TV cameraman Herve de Ploeg. "Then I saw the turret turning in our direction and the carriage lifting. It faced the target." He insisted, "It was not a case of instinctive firing."[74]

The U.S. government's response was to scold journalists for trying to do their jobs. "We continue to warn news organizations about the dangers," said Defense Department spokeswoman Victoria Clarke, who had been credited with invention of the embedding concept. She added: "We've had conversations over the last couple of days, news organizations eager to get their people unilaterally into Baghdad. We are saying it is not a safe place, you should not be there."[75] The key word in her statement was "unilaterally"—as opposed to "embedded" with U.S. troops. Decoding the Pentagon's message to journalists wasn't too difficult: if you don't play by our rules, you're much more likely to find yourself wounded or dead.

A year after the invasion, Marine Corps spokesman Lieutenant Colonel Rick Long told a University of California symposium: "The reason we embedded so many journalists is that we wanted to dominate the information environment. We wanted to beat any kind of disinformation or propaganda by beating them at their own game."[76] Although such statements assessed the embedding of reporters in Iraq as a past experience, the practice was continuing.

In early April 2004—three weeks after the Marine lieutenant colonel's thinly veiled gloat about "beating them at their own game" in the category of "disinformation or propaganda"—the national NPR program *All Things Considered* aired an on-the-scene description from Eric Niiler, a reporter with member station KPBS who was accompanying the 1st Marine Division as it fought to gain control of Fallujah. The report was more stenographic than journalistic. His first words were: "What I understand from the commanders here . . ." And his account of events seemed to be largely based on statements by those he later referred to as "Marine commanders here." To the casual listener, it might have sounded like Niiler was actually a Marine himself, as when he began his response to a question from the NPR anchor by saying, "Well, what's happened is that in the areas where we patrolled today, it's really very quiet."[77]

. . .

In 2004, the U.S. public was not very knowledgeable about global views of the war. At the Program on International Policy Attitudes, director Steven Kull said: "Despite polling showing that the majority of world public opinion is opposed to the U.S. war with Iraq, only 41 percent [of Americans] were aware that this is the case. Among those who knew that world public opinion opposed the U.S. going to war with Iraq, only 25 percent thought that going to war was the right decision."[78] Ignorance or unconcern about the opinions of people elsewhere in the world seemed to make it easier for Americans to support U.S. military action. And in some instances, we can assume, supporting the war was a disincentive to learn or care what others on the planet thought about it all.

A follow-up study found that most Americans who got their news from commercial TV harbored at least one of three "misperceptions" about the Iraq war—that weapons of mass destruction had been discovered in Iraq, that evidence closely linking Iraq to Al Qaeda had been found, or that world public opinion approved of the U.S. invasion. Fox News viewers were the most confused about key facts, with 80 percent embracing at least one of those misperceptions. The study found a correlation between being misinformed and being supportive of the war.[79]

11

Opposing the War Means Siding with the Enemy

During the mid-1960s, as President Lyndon Johnson escalated the Vietnam War, he grew accustomed to defaming Americans who voiced opposition. They were prone to be shaky and irresolute, he explained—and might even betray the nation's servicemen. "There will be some Nervous Nellies," he predicted on May 17, 1966, "and some who will become frustrated and bothered and break ranks under the strain. And some will turn on their leaders and on their country and on our fighting men."

Blaming dissent at home for problems on the battlefield became a standard tactic for easing PR problems while the Vietnam War went from bad to worse. At the time, I. F. Stone called it "the oldest alibi of frustrated generals—they could have won the war if it hadn't been for those unpatriotic civilians back home."[1] In April 1967, a month when several hundred thousand Americans participated in antiwar protests, General William Westmoreland spoke to an Associated Press luncheon and asserted that—despite "repeated military defeats"—the Vietnamese Communist enemy was able to continue the anti-U.S. struggle "encouraged by what he believes to be popular opposition to our efforts in Vietnam."[2]

Delivering a speech in mid-March 1968, President Johnson contended that as long as the foe in Vietnam "feels that he can win something by propaganda in the country—that he can undermine the leadership—that he can bring down the government—that he can get something in the Capital that he can't get from our men out there—he is going to keep on trying." Johnson went on: "But I point out to you that the time has come when we ought to unite, when we ought to stand up and be counted."[3] LBJ's successor, Richard Nixon, was quick to brandish similar innuendos. "Let us be united for peace," Nixon said early in his presidency. "Let us be united against defeat. Because let us understand: North Vietnam cannot defeat or humiliate the United States. Only Americans can do that."[4]

To this kind of argument, Stone had a ready rebuttal. Although the United States enjoyed advantages over North Vietnam that included vastly greater wealth, a sevenfold larger population, and incalculably superior technological power, the inherent long-term commitments of the two sides were tilted in opposite directions. Read thirty-five years later, Stone's words seemed to describe not only the Vietnam War but also the war in Iraq as bloodshed intensified there in 2004: "For us the war is a nuisance. For them the war is a matter of life-and-death. They are prepared to die for their country. We are prepared to die for our country too—if it were attacked—but not for the mere pleasure of destroying theirs. This is why they have the advantage of morale. . . ." In the face of such basic realities, Stone contended, "self-deception has been the characteristic of our leadership in this war from its beginning."[5]

In times of war, pressures for conformity intensify, as Daniel Ellsberg became acutely aware well before leaking the Pentagon Papers. In October 1969, he joined with five other national security analysts at the Rand Corporation to sign and release a letter that said: "We believe that the United States should decide now to end its participation in the Vietnam War, completing the total withdrawal of our forces within one year at the most."[6] When the letter appeared on the *Washington Post*'s editorial page, a companion op-ed article by a former State Department official criticized it while a *Post* editorial attacked the Rand employees' letter directly, describing them three times as "hardcore critics" and once as "extreme." Such media treatment was to be expected, but what took Ellsberg aback was the pattern of responses from his colleagues at Rand, a nonprofit haven for engineers and policy analysts charged with independent research for the U.S. government.

Ellsberg recalls receiving memos from about seventy people at Rand: "It couldn't be called a controversy, because nearly all of them were on the same side, against our action, making the same points. With two or three exceptions, every one of them was negative, often very hostile, angry, reproachful, disdainful, accusatory. Moreover—this is what most surprised me, what I was least prepared for—hardly one took issue with the substance of our letter or even addressed it, unless in a sentence or two, dismissing our argument as shallow or unsupported. More commonly, each memo writer indicated that he (these were virtually all men, as were nearly all the professionals at Rand then) opposed the continuation of the war as much as we did, before going on to say, as one put it, that our action showed 'a sense of almost complete irresponsibility toward your colleagues at Rand, the corporation itself, and quite possibly, the welfare of the country.'"[7] The colleagues attacked "in tones ranging from cold to furious."[8]

Martin Luther King Jr. also found that former allies could become incensed when he went out of his way to challenge the war. In his "Beyond Vietnam" speech delivered at New York's Riverside Church on April 4, 1967, King called the United States "the greatest purveyor of violence in the world today." From Vietnam to South Africa to Latin America, he said, the U.S. was "on the wrong side of a world revolution." King asked why the United States was suppressing revolutions "of the shirtless and barefoot people" in the Third World, instead of supporting them. That kind of talk draw barbs and denunciations from media quarters that had applauded his efforts to end racial segregation. *Time* magazine called the speech "demagogic slander that sounded like a script for Radio Hanoi."[9] The *Washington Post* warned that "King has diminished his usefulness to his cause, his country, his people."[10]

Ever since the loss of the war in Vietnam, a myth has blamed antiwar activism in the United States.[11] When correspondent Chris Wallace, then with ABC, interviewed former Vietnam War commander Westmoreland in October 1990 during the lead-up to the Gulf War, one of Wallace's questions went like this: "General Westmoreland, it's become almost a truism by now that you didn't lose the Vietnam War so much in the jungles there as you did in the streets in the United States. How worried should the president and the Pentagon be now about this new peace movement?"[12]

When the Gulf War began, snappy phrases like "blame America first" were a popular way to vilify dissenters. "What we cannot be proud of, Mr. Speaker, is the unshaven, shaggy-haired, drug culture, poor excuses for Americans, wearing their tiny, round wire-rim glasses, a protester's symbol of the blame-America-first crowd, out in front of the White House burning the American flag," Representative Gerald B. H. Solomon said on January 17, 1991.

A dozen years later, amid a very large outpouring of protest before the invasion of Iraq, the media coverage of the demonstrators was often cartoonish. "A substantial portion of Americans (and others around the world) were in the streets protesting this venture before the shooting started," journalist William Greider wrote a year after the invasion. "The media generally dismissed them and often carica-tured the protesters as aging hippies on a sixties nostalgia trip. It's a pity reporters didn't listen more respectfully. Virtually every element of what has gone wrong in Iraq was cited by those demonstrators as among the reasons they opposed the march to war."[13]

The Vietnam War became such an enduring archetype of wartime disaster that even mild comparisons between Vietnam and Iraq caused President George W. Bush to bristle and reach for the rhetorical blun-derbuss. Suggestions about learning from the past were met not only with denial but also with the charge that analogies would undermine our troops while giving aid and comfort to foreign foes. At a prime-time news conference on April 13, 2004, a reporter asked Bush about the increasingly heard comparison:

Q: "Mr. President, April is turning into the deadliest month in Iraq since the fall of Baghdad, and some people are comparing Iraq to Vietnam and talking about a quagmire. Polls show that support for your policy is declining and that fewer than half of Americans now support it. What does that say to you? And how do you answer the Vietnam comparison?"

Bush: "I think the analogy is false. I also happen to think that analogy sends the wrong message to our troops and sends the wrong message to the enemy."

Strong critics of U.S. foreign policy are likely to encounter charges of "anti-Americanism." Such epithets often raise the specter of irra-tional hostility toward the United States. A more subtle implication might be that zeal to wage aggressive war is an inherently American trait. (At times it also seems that male support for war is assumed to be properly masculine.[14]) Yet accepting militarism runs directly counter to the views of vast numbers of American citizens. Even at the height of domestic support for the war on Iraq in early spring 2003, pollsters discovered that fully a quarter of the population was opposed.

Referring to the "anti-American" buzz phrase, former USIA specialist Nancy Snow calls it "a favorite name-calling device to stain the reputation of someone who disagrees with official policies and positions. It conjures up old red-baiting techniques that stifle free speech and dissent on public issues. It creates a chilling effect on people to stop testing the waters of our democratic right to question the motives of our government."[15] During a typical outburst, in early 2003 before the Iraq invasion, Rush Limbaugh told his radio audience: "I want to say something about these anti-war demonstrators. No, let's not mince words, let's call them what they are—anti-American demonstrators."[16] Weeks later, former congressman Joe Scarborough, a Republican rising through the ranks of national TV hosts, said on MSNBC: "These leftist stooges for anti-American causes are always given a free pass. Isn't it time to make them stand up and be counted for their views, which could hurt American troop morale?"[17]

Today, in an era when the sun never sets on deployed American troops, the hoary epithet is a rhetorical weapon against dissenters, foreign and domestic. The elastic "anti-American" label stretches along a wide gamut. The routine aim is to disparage and stigmatize what displeases policymakers in Washington. Thus, applied to targets overseas, "anti-American" has spanned from al-Qaeda terrorists, to angry Iraqis tiring of occupation, to recalcitrant German and French leaders, to Labour Party backbenchers in Britain's House of Commons.[18] Naturally, Americans deemed to be insufficiently supportive of U.S. government policies also qualify.[19]

In many cases, fear of being called "anti-American" seems to cripple the ability or willingness of U.S. journalists to confront officials who are determined to wage war. Likewise, politicians are quite aware that if they step too far out of line, they're liable to be accused of lacking patriotism and giving comfort to the enemy.

Early in the autumn of 2002, when a media frenzy erupted about Representative Jim McDermott's live appearance from Baghdad on ABC's *This Week* program, what riled the punditocracy as much as anything was his last statement during the interview: "I think the president would mislead the American people."[20] First to wave a media dagger at the miscreant was George Will, a regular on the television show. Within minutes, on the air, he denounced "the most disgraceful performance abroad by an American official in my lifetime."[21] But the syndicated columnist was just getting started.

Back at his computer, Will churned out a piece that appeared in the *Washington Post* two days later, ripping into McDermott and a colleague on the trip, Representative David Bonior. "Saddam Hussein finds American collaborators among senior congressional Democrats," Will wrote. There was special venom for McDermott in the column. Will could not abide the spectacle of a congressperson casting doubt on George W. Bush's utter veracity: "McDermott's accusation that the president—presumably with Cheney, Powell, Rumsfeld, Rice and others as accomplices—would use deceit to satisfy his craving to send young Americans into an unnecessary war is a slander."[22]

The country's media echo chamber rocked with countless reprises of Will's bugle call. One of the main reasons for the furor was widespread media denial that "the president would mislead the American people." An editorial in the *Rocky Mountain News* fumed that "some of McDermott's words, delivered via TV, were nothing short of outrageous."[23] In Georgia, the *Augusta Chronicle* went farther: "For a U.S. congressman to virtually accuse the president of lying while standing on foreign soil—especially the soil of a nation that seeks to destroy his nation and even tried to assassinate a former U.S. president—is an appallingly unpatriotic act."[24]

Nationally, on the Fox News Channel, the one-man bombast factory Bill O'Reilly accused McDermott of "giving aid and comfort to Saddam while he was in Baghdad." O'Reilly said that thousands of his viewers "want to know why McDermott would give propaganda material to a killer and accuse President Bush of being a liar in the capital city of the enemy."[25] A syndicated column by Cal Thomas followed with similar indignation: "We have seen Representatives Jim McDermott of Washington and David Bonior of Michigan—the Bozos of Baghdad—accuse President Bush of lying for political gain about Iraq's threat to civilization."[26]

But such attacks did not come only from right-wing media stalwarts. Plenty of middle-road journalists were happy to go the way of the blowing wind. During one of her routine appearances on Fox television, National Public Radio political correspondent Mara Liasson commented on McDermott and Bonior: "These guys are a disgrace. Look, everybody knows it's 101, politics 101, that you don't go to an adversary country, an enemy country, and badmouth the United

States, its policies and the president of the United States. I mean, these guys ought to, I don't know, resign."[27]

Yet the president of the United States not only "would" mislead the American people, he actually did—with the result of a horrendous war. However, when the evidence became incontrovertible, the pundits who had gone after McDermott with a vengeance did not publicly concede that he'd made a valid and crucial point. To use George Will's inadvertently apt words, it was prescient to foresee that "the president—presumably with Cheney, Powell, Rumsfeld, Rice and others as accomplices—would use deceit to satisfy his craving to send young Americans into an unnecessary war." If a mainstream political journalist like Mara Liasson was so quick to suggest that McDermott resign for inopportunely seeking to prevent a war, why didn't she later advocate that the president resign for dishonestly promoting a war?

By late 2002, the U.S. government was clearly preparing for war with Iraq. And controversies about words and actions of some famous Americans seemed to be metaphors for broader pressure to accept the war agenda.

In December, days after the release of a strong antiwar statement by numerous well-known entertainers, a trip to Baghdad by actor and director Sean Penn drew a large media spotlight—and added fuel to a public debate on whether celebrities should venture from the art of make-believe to the flash-point realities of politics. Often overlooked was the simple and illuminating fact that celebrities rarely get into public-relations trouble for aligning themselves with popular views. Surface arguments about proper celebrity behavior are usually markers for hostility toward sharp divergence from conventional media wisdom. The problem was not with celebrities expressing themselves—the catalyst for uproar was the antiwar outlook being expressed. (Many of Penn's critics who insisted that actors should stay out of politics had enthusiastically voted for Ronald Reagan.) During the late 1960s, with the establishment still solidly lined up behind the Vietnam War, actor John Wayne rarely faced charges of overstepping when he voiced enthusiasm for the war. But when singer Eartha Kitt, attending a White House event about young people in 1968, publicly said that the war was wrong, the resulting furor was so intense that it harmed her career.

If Penn had gone to a U.S. military base in the Persian Gulf region to show his support for the anticipated war on Iraq, it was hard to imagine that America's cable news channels would be filled with the kind of fierce arguments that raged about his peace-oriented trip to Baghdad. There was far more than a whiff of prowar correctness in the media air. Wanting celebrities to stay in line figured into a larger pattern—the assumption that going along with war preparations could be equated with a sign of patriotism and civic virtue.

As a multitude of pundits could attest, it was not difficult to find rationales for writing off just about any opponents of plans for imminent war. Paul Loeb, author of *Soul of a Citizen*, remarked that admonishing celebrities to know their place is a form of the cynicism that short-circuits genuine debate across the society: "Ordinary citizens can't speak up because they don't know enough; young people are dismissed as naive; older people we're told are trying to re-live the '60s; academics are just eggheads; religious people are unrealistic; immigrants are suspects; celebrities are airheads and so on."[28]

Sean Penn emphasized his belief that matters of war and peace were much too important to be left to the authorities to manage—and that all of us should seek out a wide array of facts and perspectives. "I would hope that all Americans will embrace information available to them outside conventional channels," Penn said.[29] And he spoke of his own desire—"both as an American and as a human being"—to fulfill "the obligation to accept some level of personal accountability for the policies of my government, both those I support and any that I may not."[30] Perhaps the most important moments of Penn's trip to Iraq (which I accompanied him on) came during a UNICEF-guided tour of schools in the Saddam City area of Baghdad, as we visited with hundreds of children. "My trip here is to personally record the human face of the Iraqi people so that their blood—along with that of American soldiers—would not be invisible on my own hands," Penn said at a news conference the next day. He had made the journey "to find my own voice on matters of conscience."[31] For people in all walks of life, any such authentic search must withstand the pressures for conformity and popularity. As Eartha Kitt commented long after speaking her mind about the Vietnam War at the White House: "If you walk through life needing everybody to love you, you will never do anything."[32]

Not long before the invasion of Iraq, when Dixie Chicks lead singer Natalie Maines, a Texan, said she was ashamed to be from the same state as Bush, the ensuing controversy did not do much harm to sales of their music, but the Dixie Chicks had a sharp drop in radio airplay. "What's clear is that in these days of highly concentrated media ownership," the Chicago area's *Daily Herald* reported, "there is an immense amount of pressure to not make waves."[33] Voicing support for the Dixie Chicks as "terrific American artists expressing American values by using their American right to free speech," rocker Bruce Springsteen condemned "the pressure coming from the government and big business to enforce conformity of thought concerning the war and politics."[34]

Public support for the Vietnam War and the postinvasion Iraq war would have eroded faster if the U.S. news media had been less constrained in the framing of debates and the flow of information.[35] Self-reinforcing media dynamics often fuel the momentum of a war rather than counter it. Presidents—and for that matter, pundits—do not like to admit that they were wrong. And loved ones are understandably loath to believe that their child or partner died needlessly, without meaningful purpose. (On May 5, 2004, a typical story appeared on the front page of the *Marin Independent Journal* in California under a headline with quotation marks around it: "He Didn't Die in Vain." The article was about the death of Christian F. Kilpatrick, a twenty-five-year-old former army Ranger killed in Iraq while working as a contractor. The piece quoted his girlfriend, Tara Scott: "Everybody should know he didn't die in vain. He died as a hero.") Staying within the usual channels, the media current exerts a powerful pull on journalists, politicians, and the society as a whole. Perseverance for victory—or at least avoidance of humiliating defeat—seems to be the least we can do.

During the Vietnam era, "news coverage in the later years of the war was considerably less positive than in the early years, but not nearly so consistently negative as the conventional wisdom now seems to hold," professor Daniel Hallin wrote in the mid-1980s. "If news coverage largely accounted—at least as an 'intervening variable'—for the growing public desire to get out of the war, it probably also accounts for the fact that the Nixon administration was able to maintain majority support for its Vietnam policies through four years of war and for the fact that the public came to see the war as a 'mistake' or 'tragedy,' rather than the crime the more radical opposition believed it to be."[36]

To a significant extent, media coverage enables people to project their own views into the mix, and sometimes mistakenly assume that others are getting the same message. Often the mixed messages of an anchor script or a correspondent's stand-up report seem carefully honed to have something for everyone and to alienate few viewers outright. This can lead to complacency among those who figure that what's obvious to them has been obvious to the news media and is therefore well on the way to becoming commonly understood. "One of the traditional findings of research on the effects of mass communication," Hallin pointed out, is that "because of selective perception, the media will often tend merely to reinforce people's existing attitudes." And so "Vietnam news was ambiguous and contradictory enough, especially after the beginning of 1968, that both hawks and doves could easily have found material to support their own views of the war." And those views were apt to be projected onto the TV news reporters. Citing a 1968 study, Hallin wrote that "75 percent of respondents who considered themselves 'hawks' on the war thought Walter Cronkite was also a 'hawk.' Somewhat more thought Huntley and Brinkley were 'hawks.' But a majority of 'doves' thought each of the three anchors was a 'dove.'"[37]

During this period of upheaval, protests against the war in Southeast Asia grew swiftly in size and impact across the country. But the substance of antiwar positions typically got short shrift in news coverage. "Journalists often made a point in later years to promote moderation," Hallin wrote. "But ironically this meant that the theme of violence often dominated reports of protests in which there was none: 'Today's protest was *different*,' began one report on the Moratorium, 'peaceful, within the law, and not confined to a radical minority.' And violence still drew coverage. [Walter] Cronkite began one report on college anti-war protests by saying, 'The Cambodia development set off a new round of anti-war demonstrations on U.S. campuses, and not all of them were peaceful.' The film report, not surprisingly, was about one of the ones that was *not* peaceful, and dealt mainly with the professionalism shown by the authorities who restored order."[38]

A problem for antiwar activists—and a boon for war supporters—was a pattern of media coverage that skirted the reasons why people were seeking to stop the war. The TV news usually excluded actual statements from them. Hallin found that "64 percent of film reports on the anti-war movement contained no substantial discussion of the war. Only 16 percent of film reports on anti-war marches and rallies had film of speeches with natural sound. When they were shown, representatives of the anti-war movement often appeared only for a few seconds."[39] And the slant was steeply uphill. "On those rare occasions . . . when the underlying reasons for American intervention were discussed explicitly, what journalists did was to defend the honorableness of American motives."[40]

As the withdrawal of U.S. troops from Vietnam continued, while American bombing persisted at sky-high levels in Southeast Asia, media coverage of antiwar actions diminished at home. In late summer 1972, major media outlets played down protests at the Republican National Convention in Miami Beach. The contrast was great with the news coverage of antiwar protests in Chicago streets outside the Democrats' 1968 convention. "More demonstrators turned out in Miami this year than in Chicago four years ago," wrote media analyst Danny Schechter. "Almost twice as many ended up getting arrested. The demonstrations themselves represented a much more diverse group of people, and many of the protests were among the more creative in conception. Only this time when the 'whole world was watching,' they saw the imported youth galleries chanting 'four more years' rather than the photographs of Vietnamese horror being carried in the streets. In their postmortems, the television commentators assured their audiences that the protest movement had had its last hurrah. . . . Few of the activists were interviewed; little of what they had written or said was reported or taken seriously."[41]

Several years before the Iraq invasion, Barbara Ehrenreich wrote that "war has dug itself into economic systems, where it offers a livelihood to millions, rather than to just a handful of craftsmen and professional soldiers. It has lodged in our souls as a kind of religion, a quick tonic for political malaise and a bracing antidote to the moral torpor of consumerist, market-driven cultures."[42] Calling present-day antiwar movements "admittedly feeble undertakings compared to that which they oppose," Ehrenreich described them as "reactive and ad hoc, emerging, usually tardily, in response to particular wars, then ebbing to nothing in times of peace. They are fuzzy-minded, moralistic, and often committed to cartoonish theories of the sources of war—that it is a product of capitalism, for example, or testosterone or some similar flaw."[43]

Much of that description still applied midway through the first decade of the twenty-first century—though the estimated 10 million people who demonstrated worldwide to express prewar opposition to the invasion of Iraq indicated some real progress in becoming less reactive or tardy. Even before that, Ehrenreich concluded in her book *Blood Rites: Origins and History of the Passions of War*, such activism was vitally instructive. "But for all their failings," she wrote, "anti-war movements should already have taught us one crucial lesson: that the passions we bring to war can be brought just as well to the struggle *against* war. There is a place for courage and solidarity and self-sacrifice other than in the service of this peculiarly bloody institution, this inhuman 'meme'—a place for them in the struggle to shake ourselves free of it. . . . And we will need all the courage we can muster. What we are called to is, in fact, a kind of war. We will need 'armies,' or at least networks of committed activists willing to act in concert when necessary, to oppose force with numbers, and passion with forbearance and reason. We will need leaders—not a handful of generals but huge numbers of individuals able to take the initiative to educate, inspire, and rally others. We will need strategies and cunning, ways of assessing the 'enemy's' strength and sketching out the way ahead. And even with all that, the struggle will be enormously costly. Those who fight war on this war-ridden planet must prepare themselves to lose battle after battle and still fight on, to lose security, comfort, position, even life."[44]

12

This Is a Necessary Battle in the War on Terrorism

On July 24, 1964—two weeks before pushing the Gulf of Tonkin Resolution through Congress—President Lyndon Johnson responded emphatically to a proposal from French president Charles de Gaulle to reconvene the Geneva conference in search of peaceful solutions for Vietnam and the rest of Southeast Asia. De Gaulle's new overture had come on the heels of similar proposals—also without preconditions—from the Soviet Union and from U.N. Secretary-General U Thant. The initial responses from the Communist Chinese and North Vietnamese governments were positive. But Johnson would have none of it. The conference that De Gaulle had in mind, Johnson declared, would be a gathering "to ratify terror."[1]

Overall, during the Vietnam War, "The theme of terrorism directed against civilians was central to television's image of the enemy," Daniel Hallin's research found.[2] While he "never encountered a television story . . . that dealt primarily, or at any substantial length, with the political tactics, history, or program of the North Vietnamese or the NLF," Hallin discovered that "television coverage of the North Vietnamese and NLF focused on terror to the almost total exclusion of politics."[3]

Traveling from New York City in late September 2001, on a prescheduled book tour, author Joan Didion spoke to audiences in several cities on the West Coast. Those two weeks, she ended up writing, "turned out to be nothing I had expected, nothing I had ever before experienced, an extraordinarily open kind of traveling dialogue, an encounter with an America apparently immune to conventional wisdom."[4]

In the wake of 9/11, "these people to whom I was listening—in San Francisco and Los Angeles and Portland and Seattle—were making connections I had not yet in my numbed condition thought to make: connections between [the American] political process and what had happened on September 11, connections between our political life and the shape our reaction would take and was in fact already taking. These people recognized that even then, within days after the planes hit, there was a good deal of opportunistic ground being seized under cover of the clearly urgent need for increased security. These people recognized even then, with flames still visible in lower Manhattan, that the words 'bipartisanship' and 'national unity' had come to mean acquiescence to the administration's preexisting agenda—for example the imperative for further tax cuts, the necessity for Arctic drilling, the systematic elimination of regulatory and union protections, even the funding for the missile shield—as if we had somehow missed noticing the recent demonstration of how limited, given a few box cutters and the willingness to die, superior technology can be."[5]

Much of the media coverage focused on outsized glorification of people who had lost their lives or shown courage on September 11. "In fact," Didion contended, "it was in the reflexive repetition of the word 'hero' that we began to hear what would become in the year that followed an entrenched preference for ignoring the meaning of the event in favor of an impenetrably flattening celebration of its victims, and a troublingly belligerent idealization of historical ignorance."[6] To observe the political manipulation of 9/11 after the towers collapsed was to witness a multidimensional power grab exercised largely via mass media. By the end of 2002, Didion concisely and incisively described what occurred: "We had seen, most importantly, the insistent use of September 11 to justify the reconception of America's correct role in the world as one of initiating and waging virtually perpetual war."[7] Instead of, even in theory, being a war to end all wars, the new war for America would be a war to end peace.

Like many of his colleagues in the upper reaches of the Bush administration, Defense Secretary Rumsfeld went out of his way to stress that this war—with no single nation to defeat and no finite enemy to vanquish—would be open-ended. On September 27, 2001, a *New York Times* op-ed piece under Rumsfeld's byline emphasized the theme: "Some believe the first casualty of any war is the truth. But in this war, the first victory must be to tell the truth. And the truth is, this will be a war like none other our nation has faced." Written two weeks after 9/11, the short Rumsfeld essay was an indicative clarion call. And, from the outset, the trumpet was sounding inside a tent pitched large enough to accommodate any number of configurations: "This war will not be waged by a grand alliance united for the single purpose of defeating an axis of hostile powers. Instead, it will involve floating coalitions of countries, which may change and evolve." Purporting to be no-nonsense, the message from the Pentagon's civilian head was expansive to the point of limitlessness: "Forget about 'exit strategies'; we're looking at a sustained engagement that carries no deadlines." If the concepts of deadlines and exit strategies were suddenly obsolete, so too was the idea that disfavored historical contexts should or could matter a heck of a lot.

"The phrase 'War on Terrorism' is itself a propaganda message," Nancy Snow has commented. "By design, it elevates the language of conflict, suggesting that all other options (negotiation, international courts of justice, international policing) have been exhausted, when the reality is that they were never seriously considered."[8] At once, the proclaimed war on terrorism was to be unending, and impervious to information or analysis that might encourage critical scrutiny. As soon as the basic premises of the ongoing war were accepted, the irrelevance of any inconvenient part of the historical record was a given. And so, when Rumsfeld's essay in the *New York Times* told a still-shocked nation that it was embarking on "a war against terrorism's attack on our way of life"—an attack coming from foes "committed to denying free people the opportunity to live as they choose"—some questions were off-limits. Such as: Perhaps the attack was more against our foreign policy than against our domestic "way of life" or our opportunity to live as we choose? (Scandinavian countries, for instance, were not notably different in the extent or character of their freedoms compared to the United States, yet those nations did not seem to be in much danger of an al-Qaeda attack.) Explorations along that line were out of bounds. "By accepting the facile cliché that the battle under way against terrorism is a battle against evil, by easily branding those who fight us as the barbarians, we, like them, refuse to acknowledge our own culpability," journalist Chris Hedges observed. "We ignore real injustices that have led many of those arrayed against us to their rage and despair."[9]

In the aftermath of 9/11, warning shots became routine against mentioning aspects of history that others deemed best forgotten or never learned. "There was the frequent deployment of the phrase 'the Blame America Firsters,' or 'the Blame America First crowd,' the wearying enthusiasm for excoriating anyone who suggested that it could be useful to bring at least a minimal degree of historical reference to bear on the event," Didion wrote. "There was the adroit introduction of convenient straw men. There was Christopher Hitchens, engaging in a dialogue with Noam Chomsky, giving himself the opportunity to generalize whatever got said into 'the liberal-left tendency to "rationalize" the aggression of September 11.' There was Donald Kagan at Yale, dismissing his colleague Paul Kennedy as 'a classic case of blaming the victim,' because the latter had asked his students to try to imagine what resentments they might harbor if America were small and the world dominated by a unified Arab-Muslim state. There was Andrew Sullivan, warning on his Web site that while the American heartland was ready for war, the 'decadent left in its enclaves on the coasts' could well mount 'what amounts to a fifth column.' There was the open season on Susan Sontag—on a single page of a single issue of the *Weekly Standard* that October she was accused of 'unusual stupidity,' of 'moral vacuity,' and of 'sheer tastelessness'—all for three paragraphs in which she said, in closing, that 'a few shreds of historical awareness might help us understand what has just happened, and what may continue to happen'; in other words that events have histories, political life has consequences, and the people who led this country and the people who wrote and spoke about the way this country was led were guilty of trying to infantilize its citizens if they continued to pretend otherwise."[10]

Meanwhile, numerous reporters seemed content to provide stenographic services for official U.S. sources under the guise of journalism. During a September 17 appearance on David Letterman's show, the CBS news anchor Dan Rather laid it on the line. "George Bush is the president," Rather said, "he makes the decisions." Speaking as "one American," the newsman added: "Wherever he wants me to line up, just tell me where. And he'll make the call." Cokie Roberts, well known as a reporter-pundit for NPR and ABC, appearing on the Letterman show a few weeks later, gushed: "I am, I will just confess to you, a total sucker for the guys who stand up with all the ribbons on and stuff, and they say it's true and I'm ready to believe it. We had

General Shelton on the show the last day he was chairman of the Joint Chiefs of Staff and I couldn't lift that jacket with all the ribbons and medals. And so when they say stuff, I tend to believe it."[11]

Long after September 11, 2001, most U.S. reporting seemed to be locked into a zone that excluded unauthorized ironies. It simply accepted that the U.S. government could keep making war on "terror" by using high-tech weapons that inevitably terrorized large numbers of people. According to routine news accounts, just about any measures deemed appropriate by Washington fit snugly under the rubric of an ongoing war that might never end in any of our lifetimes.[12] Against the current, a daily paper in Florida published a forthright statement on March 2, 2002. "The nation's loyalty is turning into groupthink," the *Daytona Beach News-Journal* editorialized. "How else explain a president who, playing on the war's most visceral slogan, gets away with justifying an obscene corporate tax cut as 'economic security,' a build-up of defense industry stock as 'homeland security,' and an exploitative assault on the nation's most pristine lands as 'energy security'? How else explain his contempt for Congress, his Nixonian fixation on secrecy, his administration's junta-like demeanor in Washington since September?" The editorial warned that "without robust dissent, democracy might as well pack up and head for the hills." And it accurately described the status quo nearly six months after 9/11: "This is not unity. It's not patriotism. It's stupor."

A year after 9/11, Nicholas Lemann wrote in the *New Yorker* that the "war on terror" was a phrase that "has entered the language so fully, and framed the way people think about how the United States is reacting to the September 11 attacks so completely, that the idea that declaring and waging war on terror was not the sole, inevitable, logical consequence of the attacks just isn't in circulation."[13] In late November 2002, a retired U.S. Army general, William Odom, told C-SPAN viewers: "Terrorism is not an enemy. It cannot be defeated. It's a tactic. It's about as sensible to say we declare war on night attacks and expect we're going to win that war. We're not going to win the war on terrorism. And it does whip up fear. Acts of terror have never brought down liberal democracies. Acts of parliament have closed a few."[14]

Problems of language and assumptions were exacerbated by the way that after September 11 the "war on terrorism" often got shortened to a "war on terror," more than a space-saver for headline writers or a syllable-saver for speakers. "Terrorism" is a word about actions. "Terror," on the other hand, is a word fraught with numerous meanings, some appreciably more ambiguous; among the subtexts of the shortened term are vague notions to the effect that we can somehow effectively wage war on our own fear, a nuance that—examined out in the open—hardly suggests an auspicious strategy.[15]

Variations on a simple dualism—we're good and people who don't like us are bad—had never been far from mainstream American politics. But 9/11 concentrated such proclivities with great intensity and narrowed the range of publicly acceptable questioning. "Inquiry into the nature of the enemy we faced, in other words, was to be interpreted as sympathy for that enemy," Didion observed. "The final allowable word on those who attacked us was to be that they were 'evildoers,' or 'wrongdoers,' peculiar constructions which served to suggest that those who used them were transmitting messages from some ultimate authority."[16] On the say-so of those in charge of the government, we were encouraged to believe that their worldviews defined the appropriate limits of discourse.

The near-paralysis of public debate gradually eased. Yet regimented thought had developed a powerful new paradigm in the concept of a nonstop, righteous siege against terrorism.

Two and a half years after September 11, in a double-page advertisement inside such magazines as the *Weekly Standard*, the American Compass book club provided this sentence to sum up one of its main new books, by Sean Hannity, a Fox News Channel host: "Hannity explores the nature of evil and offers global solutions for defeating terrorism, despotism and liberalism."[17] The book club was simply drawing from the book's title and subtitle, *Deliver Us From Evil: Defeating Terrorism, Despotism, and Liberalism.*

Two years after 9/11, Norman Mailer asked: "What does it profit us if we gain extreme security and lose our democracy? Not everyone in Iraq, after all, was getting their hands and/or their ears cut off by Saddam Hussein. In the middle of that society were hordes of Iraqis who had all the security they needed even if there was no freedom other than the full-fledged liberty offered by dictators to be free to speak with hyperbolic hosannas for the leader. So, yes, there are more important things to safeguard than security and one of them is to protect the much-beleaguered integrity of our democracy. The final question in these matters suggests itself. Can leaders who lie as a way of life protect any way of life?"[18]

Selective use of the word "terrorism" is routine. That selectivity reflects the political character of the term. Major news outlets decline to note that media coverage of terrorism is routinely subjective.[19] With an air of objectivity, journalists affix the pejorative "terrorist" label to only some acts of violence that are taking civilian lives while seeking to achieve political ends.[20]

After September 11, under the rubric of antiterrorism, battle lines hardened to justify further armed suppression. "We have built or bolstered alliances with Israel and Russia, forming a dubious global troika against terrorism, a troika that taints us in the eyes of much of the rest of the world, especially among Muslims," Chris Hedges wrote in 2003. "Suddenly all who oppose our allies and us—Palestinians, Chechens, and Afghans—are lumped into one indistinguishable mass. They are as faceless as we are for our enemies."[21] The technologies in use for killing vary widely, but the rationalizations often mirror each other with blinding light.

For the war-inclined in Washington, superpower super-righteousness offered compelling advantages after September 11, 2001. The president quickly found much to emulate in the uncompromising rhetoric and iron-fist military approach of the Israeli government. Three years after 9/11, commenting on the "insistence that all the enemy understands is force," Naomi Klein wrote: "It's not simply that Bush sees America's role as protecting Israel from a hostile Arab world. It's that he has cast the United States in the very same role in which Israel casts itself, facing the very same threat. In this narrative, the U.S. is fighting a never ending battle for its very survival against utterly irrational forces that seek nothing less than its total extermination."[22]

More than ever before, U.S. leaders were voicing great enthusiasm for a global "war on terrorism" in which the Israeli government would be a junior—but experienced and militarily powerful—partner. When House Republican leader Tom DeLay traveled to Israel in the summer of 2003, he spoke to the Knesset and underscored an outlook that had become standard for U.S. officials. Under the headline

"Israel's Fight Is Our Fight," the *Jerusalem Post* published a piece by DeLay that proclaimed: "Nations around the world have a choice, best articulated by President George W. Bush: 'You're either with us, or you're with the terrorists.'"

That was a line the Bush administration had been using in many contexts ever since the morning when the World Trade Center fell: Which side are you on? The political usefulness of such either/or statements was enormous. On message, DeLay proceeded to ratchet up the oratory to holy heights: "There is no doubt where Israel stands in our post-9/11 world. The solidarity between the U.S. and Israel is deeper than the various interests we share. It goes to the very nature of man, to the endowment of our God-given right to life, liberty and the pursuit of happiness. It is the universal solidarity of freedom. It transcends geography, culture, and generations. It is the solidarity of all people—in all times—who dream of and sacrifice for liberty. It is the solidarity of Moses and Lincoln. Of Tiananmen Square and the Prague Spring. Of Andrei Sakharov and Anne Frank. And in its name I come to you—in the midst of a great global conflict against evil—with a simple message: Be Not Afraid."[23]

Such pronouncements had no use for reflections of the kind offered a third of a century earlier by I. F. Stone.[24] In 1969 he expressed hope for "a reconstructed Palestine of Jewish and Arab states in peaceful coexistence."[25] Stone contended that "to bring it about Israel and the Jewish communities of the world must be willing to look some unpleasant truths squarely in the face."[26] He added: "One is to recognize that the Arab guerrillas are doing to us what our terrorists and saboteurs of the Irgun, Stern and Haganah did to the British. Another is to be willing to admit that their motives are as honorable as were ours. As a Jew, even as I felt revulsion against the terrorism, I felt it justified by the homelessness of the surviving Jews from the Nazi camps and the bitter scenes when refugee ships sank, or sank themselves, when refused admission to Palestine. The best of Arab youth feels the same way; they cannot forget the atrocities committed by us against villages like Deir Yassin, nor the uprooting of the Palestinian Arabs from their ancient homeland, for which they feel the same deep ties of sentiment as do so many Jews, however assimilated elsewhere."[27]

In 2005, a lot could be learned from documentation compiled by the Israeli organization B'Tselem, one of the independent human rights groups often condemning Israel for actions such as killing unarmed Palestinian civilians or demolishing their homes. But with rare exceptions the American press bypassed the kind of facts available on the organization's Web site (www.btselem.org). The journalistic avoidance continued to facilitate the momentum of with-us-or-against-us righteousness in the "war on terror."

"Most acts to which the word 'terrorism' is applied (at least in the West) are tactics of the weak, usually (although not always) against the strong. Such acts are not a tactic of choice but of last resort," lawyer John V. Whitbeck wrote in the *International Herald Tribune*. "The poor, the weak and the oppressed rarely complain about 'terrorism.' The rich, the strong and the oppressors constantly do. While most of mankind has more reason to fear the high-technology violence of the strong than the low-technology violence of the weak, the fundamental mind-trick employed by the abusers of the word 'terrorism' is essentially this: The low-technology violence of the weak is such an abomination that there are no limits on the high-technology violence of the strong that can be deployed against it. . . . Perhaps the only honest and globally workable definition of 'terrorism' is an explicitly subjective one—'violence that I don't support.' Anyone who reads both the Western and Arab press cannot help noticing that the Western press routinely characterizes as 'terrorism' virtually all Palestinian violence against Israelis (even against Israeli occupation forces within Palestine), while the Arab press routinely characterizes as 'terrorism' virtually all Israeli violence against Palestinians. Only such a formulation would accommodate both characterizations, as well as most others. . . . Every nation—and particularly the United States—must . . . recognize that in a world filled with injustice, violent outbursts by those hoping desperately for a better life—or simply seeking to strike a blow against injustice or their tormentors before they die—can never be eradicated. At best, the frequency and gravity of such outbursts can be diminished by seeking to alleviate—rather than continuing to aggravate—the injustices and humiliations that give rise to them."[28]

When there is no single standard that reliably condemns "terrorism," then the word serves as a political football rather than a term to be used with integrity. The American media condemnations are far from proportional to the cruelty or magnitude of wanton actions; a key factor is the extent to which the perpetrators are aligned with, or antagonistic toward, the United States. Basic policies tacitly distinguish between important and incidental victims—encouraging us, in effect, to ask for whom the bell tolls. The official guidance needn't be explicit to be understood or at least widely internalized by the public: Do not let too much empathy move in unauthorized directions.

Years before September 11, 2001, the activist scholar Eqbal Ahmad said: "A superpower cannot promote terror in one place and reasonably expect to discourage terrorism in another place. It won't work in this shrunken world."[29]

13

What the U.S. Government Needs Most Is Better PR

A public-relations approach lends itself to the view that solutions require improving image rather than substance. This assumption, often repeated in U.S. media (Why can't we do a better job of selling America's image to the world?, etc.), faults the government's worldwide PR outreach for not doing justice to Washington's actual policies. The message, for domestic consumption, presents the basic problem as a protracted marketing screwup. But "if we really want a genuine campaign to improve the image of the United States overseas," Nancy Snow sensibly points out, "we need to begin by changing our foreign policies—the source of much antipathy."[1] Changing those policies, of course, would be massively difficult; focusing on how to do better PR is perennially simpler—and much more suitable for progressions of wars.

While some people experience war as terror, disaster, and death, it can also be seen as a PR problem. At the Rendon Group, a public-relations firm with offices in Boston and Washington, pleasant news arrived in midautumn 2001 with a four-month contract for $397,000 to help the Pentagon look good while bombing Afghanistan. It was a job for savvy PR pros with the smarts to sound humanistic. "At the Rendon Group, we believe in people," said the company's mission statement, expressing "our admiration and respect for cultural diversity" and proclaiming a commitment to "helping people win in the global marketplace." At the Pentagon, media officer Lieutenant Colonel Kenneth McClellan explained why Rendon got the contract: "We needed a firm that could provide strategic counsel immediately.

We were interested in someone that we knew could come in quickly and help us orient to the challenge" of communicating to a "wide range of groups around the world in real time."[2]

As a public-relations outfit, Rendon moved in some powerful circles, with clients including official trade agencies of the United States, Bulgaria, Russia, and Uzbekistan. In Washington, the firm helped organize a series of conferences on "post-privatization management in the global telecommunications, electric power, oil and gas, banking and finance, and transportation sectors." Some of Rendon's clientele had been more liberal or touchy-feely: Handgun Control Inc. and the American Massage Therapy Association. And Rendon was proud to note that it provided "community and media relations counsel to the Monsanto Chemical Company in its effort to clean up several contaminated sites." Overseas, Rendon helped the Kuwait Petroleum Corporation to cope with labor strife and bad press when closing a refinery in Naples, Italy. Significantly, some clients have been quite a bit more shadowy. Rendon worked for the government of Kuwait in the early 1990s. And the firm made a lot of money by contracting with the CIA to do media work for the Iraqi National Congress, the Pentagon's favorite exile organization seeking the overthrow of Saddam Hussein.[3]

Using standard tools of the PR trade such as focus groups, Web sites, and rigorous analysis of news coverage, the Rendon Group moved ahead to spin for the war in Afghanistan by setting its sights on media content in seventy-nine countries. In the words of Defense Secretary Rumsfeld, "we need to do a better job to make sure that people are not confused as to what this is about."[4] It was typical of foreign-policy officials to claim that the biggest communication problems lay with others' faulty perceptions.[5]

On the home front, the playbook for the Pentagon's media game was a familiar one. Eugene Secunda, a professor of marketing and former senior vice president of the J. Walter Thompson public-relations firm, observed in 1991: "Operation Desert Storm allowed only one view of the battle: the one authorized by the military. Like travelers led from their buses by tour guides, the TV crews were given an opportunity to videotape the 'panoramic vista' before them, and then were whisked to the next officially authorized destination." Secunda foreshadowed coverage of the air war that bombarded Afghanistan: "In the aftermath of the [1991] war with Iraq, strategic planners, preparing for future wars, are unquestionably examining the lessons gleaned from this triumphant experience. One of the most important lessons learned is the necessity of mobilizing strong public support, through the projection of a powerful and tightly controlled PR program, with particular effort directed toward the realization of positive TV news coverage."[6] That's the kind of news that dominated television screens in the United States as bombs fell on Afghanistan; the Pentagon won its PR war at home.[7]

One morning in May 2004, I visited the Pentagon headquarters of Defense Press Operations, part of the U.S. military's huge PR apparatus. After agreeing to speak "on background," a major responded to questions in front of a tape recorder. Some excerpts:

Major: "Quite a few of us have public-relations degrees. I do, for example. And then also, before we start our career as a public-affairs officer in the military, we go to specific military training that covers all the basics of journalism, broadcast, radio, how to write a news release 101—we learn all of that before we even come on to our jobs. So it's definitely typical public relations strategies and theory that we use."

Q: "And who is your client?"

Major: "Well, that's a lot of people. We have the media, of course, is our conduit to the public. And then we also have the internal dimension, which is communicating to our employees. So we treat both the same way. It's important to let the people know what's going on in the [Defense] Department. You know, usually we like to do that before we read about it in the paper, so that they hear from their commanders what's going on."

Q: "Do you mean the 22,000 people in the [Pentagon] building?"

Major: "The whole 1.4 million."

Q: "One-point-four million in uniform."

Major: "Yes."

Q: "By the way, does that include reserves?"

Major: "No, that's another 1.3 [million]."

Q: "The 2.7 million are in that flow?"

Major: "I'd say it's everybody. . . ."

Q: "And you [the Press Operations office] are accountable to the defense secretary."

Major: "Yes."

Q: "What about, given the kind of the public-relations aspects, everybody deals with damage control—is this office here in that process?"

Major: "I would call it more crisis communications. Yes, I mean we hear about breaking news just like everybody else, and it may be something that we hadn't heard or didn't know about and we have to get spun up on it, find out what the truth is, and report on that, let the media know what the truth is."

Q: "At the professional level of the relationships [between journalists and the Pentagon press office], would you characterize them—I know we're generalizing, there's going to be exceptions, but would you characterize them as cordial, adversarial, cooperative, uncooperative, mixture?"

Major: "Cooperative. Oh, yeah, because you know we're all after the same thing. We want to get our story out and we know the only way we can do that is through the media. And once they get to know us—they have their routines throughout the day where they'll pop in every morning and say 'Hey, what's going on?' or 'Is this report gonna be released today?'—you know, you just establish that relationship. Get to trust one another. It's really not a problem."[8]

The deck of cards featuring fifty-two Iraqi villains (with Saddam Hussein as ace of spades) became one of the PR innovations of the Iraq war. When five "army intelligence specialists" who had developed the cards stepped forward to take a bow in Washington, a spokesperson for Central Command conceded that there was "no word on the cards helping find anyone."[9] Yet the Pentagon's deck had turned out to be a stroke of media genius. It tapped into the American public's appetite for fun ways to identify bad guys to be hunted down.

Even with the benefit of topflight public relations, no war can live up to advance promotion. In the longer run, the situation is bound to become much grimmer than the early PR suggested. Oversold ahead of time, a war often results in a substantial degree of buyers' remorse, especially for recruits who've experienced war up close, but also among media consumers back home. After hype has been overtaken by realities, the war's promoters must try to finesse the jarring contrasts between their sales job and the actual product.

By the start of 2004, evidence of deception by Iraq war planners had become part of the news cycle. Within a three-day period in early January:

- An establishment think tank, the Carnegie Endowment for International Peace, released a report declaring that Bush administration officials "systematically misrepresented the threat from Iraq's WMD and ballistic missile programs."[10]

- The *New York Times* reported that the Bush administration withdrew from Iraq "a 400-member military team whose job was to scour the country for military equipment. . . . The step was described by some military officials as a sign that the administration might have lowered its sights and no longer expected to uncover the caches of chemical and biological weapons that the White House cited as a principal reason for going to war."[11]

- Reporting on the results from nine months of U.S. inspections following the fall of Saddam Hussein's regime, the *Washington Post* concluded: "Investigators have found no support for the two main fears expressed in London and Washington before the war: that Iraq had a hidden arsenal of old weapons and built advanced programs for new ones. . . . Leading figures in Iraqi science and industry, supported by observations on the ground, described factories and institutes that were thoroughly beaten down by 12 years of conflict, arms embargo and strangling economic sanctions."[12]

- For good measure, at a news conference, Secretary of State Colin Powell admitted that "I have not seen smoking-gun, concrete evidence about the connection" between the Saddam Hussein regime and Al Qaeda. "But I think the possibility of such connections did exist," Powell added lamely, "and it was prudent to consider them at the time that we did."[13]

Powell began a long climb down from rhetorical heights. During his stratospheric performance at the United Nations on February 5, 2003, the secretary of state had been unequivocal about weapons of mass destruction in Iraq. And he talked of a "sinister nexus" in place "between Iraq and the Al Qaeda terrorist network, a nexus that combines classic terrorist organizations and modern methods of murder." But after the invasion, emerging facts verified long-standing charges that the Bush team had methodically run a PR hoax about phantom Iraqi weapons and nonexistent Saddam-Qaeda links. The real problem was the effectiveness—not failure—of the U.S. government's public–relations machinery.

While American soldiers continued to kill and be killed in Iraq throughout 2004, the erosion of Washington's credibility put more limits on pretense. Like some others in the upper echelons of the Bush administration, Powell felt a tactical need to retrench. He could not stick to his prewar assertions at the United Nations, such as: "There can be no doubt that Saddam Hussein has biological weapons and the capability to rapidly produce more, many more." And: "Our conservative estimate is that Iraq today has a stockpile of between 100 and 500 tons of chemical weapons agent."[14] On September 13, 2004, Powell conceded publicly: "I think it's unlikely that we will find any stockpiles."[15]

Another big PR campaign by the White House—trying to link Saddam Hussein and Al Qaeda—also ran into authoritative refutations. During 2004, Vice President Dick Cheney continued to serve as point man. "There's overwhelming evidence . . . of a connection between Al Qaeda and Iraq," he said early in the year.[16] As summer began, Cheney declared that Hussein "had long established ties with Al Qaeda."[17] But two days later, the official panel investigating 9/11 released a report that said the opposite. The commission found no evidence of a "collaborative relationship" between Hussein and Osama bin Laden.[18]

Yet deception was a big winner in the battle for public opinion. The Bush administration's media fog had blurred distinctions between the Saddam regime and those who killed thousands of people on September 11. A nationwide USA Today/CNN/Gallup poll in early 2004 asked: "Did Iraq have ties to Al Qaeda before the 2003 war?" A total of 74 percent responded "true" or "likely."[19] The PR prowess of the warmakers even persuaded many Americans of a link between Saddam and 9/11—a claim that even the Bush White House had stopped short of making. A week after the 9/11 commission reported there was "no credible evidence" that the Iraqi dictator had any role in the

September 11 attacks, *USA Today* reported that "44 percent of those surveyed say they think Saddam was personally involved in 9/11."[20]

As the Iraq war took the form of protracted occupation, some journalists ran afoul of U.S. military policies. The U.S. command frequently interfered with independent news-gathering.[21] Along the way, the military often arrested correspondents for the Al-Jazeera television network. But American journalists were not exempt from harassment. In Fallujah, when guerrillas shot down a U.S. Army helicopter in early November 2003, U.S. troops took a camera away from David Gilkey, a photographer for the *Detroit Free Press* and the Knight Ridder news service, and deleted all of his photos. During the same month, a letter to Pentagon press official Lawrence DiRita—signed by representatives of thirty news organizations from the United States and other countries—complained that they had "documented numerous examples of U.S. troops physically harassing journalists and, in some cases, confiscating or ruining equipment, digital camera discs, and videotapes."[22]

The Pentagon was in a public-relations war. Images were at stake. Overall, the Committee to Protect Journalists reported in a March 2004 document, "the conduct of U.S. troops has exacerbated the tenuous security situation for journalists in Iraq."[23] A week after release of CPJ's report, at a checkpoint in Iraq, U.S. soldiers shot a cameraman and a correspondent with the Al-Arabiya satellite TV network based in Dubai. "Arab journalists, especially if they work for the Al-Jazeera or Al-Arabiya networks, have a nasty habit of getting arrested, beaten or killed—by the Americans," the *Toronto Star* media columnist Antonia Zerbisias noted in early spring 2004. "Not that their counterparts in the U.S. media much care, as evidenced two weeks ago. That's when American journalists sat meekly in their chairs taking dictation as Secretary of State Colin Powell gave a news conference in Baghdad about 'staying the course' in Iraq. Meanwhile, thirty foreign reporters walked out in protest over the shooting deaths of two Al-Arabiya journalists."[24]

14

The Pentagon Fights Wars as Humanely as Possible

During the first several years of the Vietnam War, while stories about battlefield initiatives such as search-and-destroy missions were big news on television, there was also great emphasis on the latest technological marvels being deployed. "Next to combat stories," journalist Edward Jay Epstein found when he systematically reviewed TV news about the war, "the most prevalent form of coverage during this period featured new types of military technology—helicopter gunships, 'magic dragon' air support, Naval patrols, etc."[1]

A few weeks after arriving in Saigon at the start of 1972, *Los Angeles Times* reporter Jacques Leslie visited an aircraft carrier in the South China Sea. Aboard the USS *Constellation*—in contrast to earthbound complexities of Vietnam—"now, suddenly, I was engulfed in technology, released to a vast metallic universe where nothing grew, where doubt had no place." Decades later, he remembered: "I was on a floating American outpost, population 5,000, but I felt more like an outsider than I did in Saigon. The press officers who took turns accompanying me could tell me all about the astonishing mechanics of jet take-offs and landings, of how the pilots got graded on their bombing accuracy, but they couldn't say if the pilots thought of people below as they dropped their bombs or ever felt regret. Most of the pilots couldn't tell me either, preferring to dwell on the marvels of their flying machines."[2] Leslie recalled: "I was in the company of little boys in love with their toys. When the pilots returned after their bombing runs, they buzzed the carrier upside-down or dipped their planes' wings a few times before settling down to land: never mind the mission (or taxpayer expense), flying was fun."[3]

The following month, the same aircraft carrier hosted an ABC news crew. From the *Constellation*, network correspondent Ron Miller told viewers that the pilots "are considered the best in the world." Later in the report, he said: "It is ironic that the men who control some of the world's most destructive weapons rarely see the results of their work. Distance divorces them from ally and enemy."[4] Then there was a sound bite from a pilot: "I honestly don't like the idea of shooting a person. I don't know if I could do that. From good distances up looking down you don't have a chance to see the good you're doing. We're a tremendously effective destructive force. As far as a deep, true understanding of what the people feel, yes, you get very divorced from it. To me, that's a detriment."[5]

In the midst of the air war, the TV-like unreality was befogging. Legendary U.S. military adviser John Paul Vann invited Leslie onto a helicopter to watch a B-52 strike. Leslie put on headsets to monitor aircraft communications. "Suddenly gray clouds took shape on the ground in front of us and billowed to a height of a thousand feet or more," he recounted in a memoir. "Insulated from the explosions by earphones and helicopter vibrations, I was surprised to feel so little: no horror, no pain, just marvel at the dubious wonders of technology. Had men been killed beneath the smoke? Did they mean anything to me? I knew I should be appalled, but I felt only numbness: it was like watching people die on television."[6]

Throughout the war, the media coverage of the bombing "did not change greatly," according to Daniel Hallin. He wrote: "Controversy had surrounded the bombing since its onset in 1965. There were two major political issues. One had to do with whether the bombing was effective; the other, with civilian casualties and the moral issues these raised. But television's focus on the pilots as individuals precluded dealing seriously with either. A good deal of air war coverage simply avoided political issues, focusing exclusively on the pilots' personal experience, the technology, and so on. . . . As for the issue of civilian casualties—and the unspoken doubt that ran through the Vietnam period about technological warfare—it was usually dealt with as in the ABC report from 1972. The pilot would be asked if it didn't bother him that his bombs might kill innocent civilians, whom he could not even see. And he would say yes, it did bother him, and he did his best not to kill civilians, and meanwhile the bombing was a job that had to be done. The central theme, in other words, was again *professionalism.* The underlying message was that morally as well as technologically we—the news audience—could put our trust in the pilots: they did their jobs well and without vindictiveness, and if civilians were killed, it was not because the pilots wanted to kill them or did not care—it was just 'part of the job.'"[7]

During each war, countless news stories and features tout the extraordinary capabilities of the latest marvels in the Pentagon's arsenal. When working as designed, the technology is routinely portrayed as admirable, and the same goes for Washington's military command. The awesome weaponry is often implicit further evidence of America's greatness.

When the Gulf War's massive bombardment began, a CNN correspondent remarked on the "sweet beautiful sight" of bombers leaving runways in Saudi Arabia.[8] CBS correspondent Jim Stewart told viewers about "two days of almost picture-perfect assaults."[9] (Meanwhile, an enemy armament became anthropomorphically sinister. On NBC, reporter Arthur Kent termed the Iraqi Scud missile "an evil weapon."[10] CNN's Richard Blystone called it "a quarter-ton of concentrated hatred."[11]) After three weeks of the air war, *Newsweek* put the USA's Stealth bomber on the cover. Under the headline "The New Science of War" was a reassuring subhead, "High-Tech Hardware: How Many Lives Can It Save?"[12]

Although unfortunate deaths and injuries were understood to remain a hazard, Uncle Sam's latest weaponry signified advances in warfare. NBC anchor Tom Brokaw reported: "So far the U.S. has fought this war at arm's length with long-range missiles, high-tech weapons. This is to keep casualties down."[13] A few days into the Gulf War's air strikes, *Time* magazine explained to readers that "collateral damage" could be defined as "a term meaning dead or wounded civilians who should have picked a safer neighborhood."[14] A few weeks into the war, Senator Phil Gramm said gleefully: "When the Iraqis come out of their bunkers, whatever they come out of, your A-6 Intruder is going to welcome them to American technology."[15] Several months later, in mid-June 1991, Representative Les Aspin—one of the most powerful men on Capitol Hill when it came to military appropriations—looked back with avid satisfaction. "The F-117, with its precision-guided munitions, was one of the heroes of the Persian Gulf," he said.[16]

Seven years after the Gulf War—with anticipation running high for a new assault on Iraq during the first weeks of 1998—tidy euphemisms such as "collateral damage" returned to airwaves and print. News reports again offered assurances that America's air power would guarantee success. "The smart bombs of the Gulf War have gotten smarter, and there will be more of them," *USA Today* reported happily.[17] The news was filled with footage and descriptions of cruise missiles, F-117 Stealth bombers, F-16CJ jets, and other ultramodern aircraft, in detail. The same could not be said about coverage of what would happen to people when the warheads detonated.

In a *Morning Edition* broadcast that aired on NPR close to Thanksgiving in 2001, while U.S. bombing of Afghanistan was in its second month, the program's longtime host interviewed a twelve-year-old boy about a new line of trading cards marketed "to teach children about the war on terrorism" by "featuring photographs and information about the war effort." The elder male was enthusiastic as he compared cards. "I've got an air force F-16," Bob Edwards said. "The picture's taken from the bottom so you can see the whole payload there, all the bombs lined up." After the boy replied with a bland "yeah," Edwards went on: "That's pretty cool."[18]

A year later, with another war on the near horizon, a *USA Today* news feature described the B-2 as "a technological marvel" that cost $1.5 billion each and "can drop 16 of the one-ton satellite-guided bombs in a single mission." The story explained that the bombers "can also carry eight 5,000-pound 'bunker buster' bombs"; the 5,000-pound warhead was "known in Air Force lingo as 'the crowd pleaser.'" Implying that somehow only one tyrannical individual would be the target of all that weaponry, the article reported that the Pentagon was publicizing "the lethal firepower that it will deploy against Saddam in case of war."[19]

This is common: Media outlets often echo White House efforts to interpret a U.S. military assault as a blow against one despotic individual. In 1991, after the end of the Gulf War led to an ill-fated Shiite uprising, ABC correspondent Ann Compton reported: "If there is any use of chemical weapons [against the Shiites], it will bring more air attacks down on Saddam Hussein's head."[20] Yet the preceding massive air bombardment, while killing tens of thousands of Iraqis, had apparently not harmed a hair on Saddam Hussein's head. Midway through 1991, President George H. W. Bush repeated the refrain that the Iraqis who had died during the war were not U.S. targets—that the target had been a lone man. "Before the war started," Bush said, "I made it very clear over and over again that our argument was not with the people of Iraq, it wasn't even with the regime in Iraq. It was with Saddam Hussein."[21]

There's nothing new about claiming to send a righteous message with bullets or bombs. As a war reporter, Chris Hedges saw such communications up close: "Corpses in wartime often deliver messages. The death squads in El Salvador dumped three bodies in the parking lot of the Camino Real Hotel in San Salvador, where the journalists were based, early one morning. Death threats against us were stuffed in the mouths of the bodies." Hedges added: "And, on a larger scale, Washington uses murder and corpses to transmit its wrath. We delivered such incendiary messages in Vietnam, Iraq, Serbia, and Afghanistan. Osama bin Laden has learned to speak the language of modern industrial warfare. It was Robert McNamara, the American Secretary of Defense in the summer of 1965, who defined the bombing raids that would eventually leave hundreds of thousands of civilians north of Saigon dead as a means of communication to the Communist regime in Hanoi."[22]

During four days of missile attacks in December 1998, there was much media enthusiasm for the line that the assault would "send a message" to Saddam Hussein; the bombs did send the clear message that the U.S. government viewed civilian lives as expendable.[23] Several years later, in a major speech just before the launch of war in March 2003, President George W. Bush said: "Many Iraqis can hear me tonight in a translated radio broadcast, and I have a message for them: If we must begin a military campaign, it will be directed against the lawless men who rule your country and not against you."[24]

The day after that preinvasion speech by the president, journalist Christopher Hitchens came out with an essay providing similar cozy assurances. He wrote that "the Defense Department has evolved highly selective and accurate munitions that can sharply reduce the need to take or receive casualties. The predictions of widespread mayhem turned out to be false last time—when the weapons [in the Gulf War] were nothing like so accurate." Hitchens went on to proclaim "it can now be proposed as a practical matter that one is able to fight against a regime and not a people or a nation."[25] *As a practical matter*, such words ended up providing zero comfort to people killed or maimed by two-thousand-pound bombs, cruise missiles, and more pedestrian weapons.

"A week of airstrikes, including the most concentrated precision hits in U.S. military history, has left tons of rubble and deep craters at hundreds of government buildings and military facilities around Iraq but has yielded little sign of a weakening in the regime's will to resist," the *Washington Post* reported on March 26, 2003. Shrewd tactics and superlative technology were supposed to do the grisly trick. But military difficulties during the invasion's first days set off U.S. media alarm bells. In contrast, humanitarian calamities were often reported as PR problems, whether the subject was the cutoff of water in Basra or the missiles that killed noncombatants in Baghdad; the main concern appeared to be that extensive suffering and death among civilians would make "the coalition of the willing" look bad.

Meanwhile, as the war proceeded, most U.S. news outlets paid tribute to the nation's high-tech arsenal. The *Washington Post* printed a large color diagram under the headline "A Rugged Bird."[26] Unrelated to ornithology, the diagram annotated key features of the AH-64 Apache—a helicopter excelling as a killing machine.[27]

In the capital city of the world's only superpower, the *Post* was cheering. "Ultimately the monument that matters will be victory and a sustained commitment to a rebuilt Iraq," the newspaper concluded. Its assessment came in an editorial that mentioned the pain—but not the anger—of family members grieving the loss of Kendall D. Waters-Bey, a Marine from Baltimore who died soon after the war began. The *Post*'s editorial quoted the bereaved father as saying that "the word 'sorrow' cannot fill my pain."[28] But the editorial did not include a word of the response from the dead man's oldest sister, Michelle Waters, who faulted the U.S. government for starting the war and said: "It's all for nothing. That war could have been prevented. Now, we're out of a brother. Bush is not out of a brother. We are." The *Baltimore Sun* reported that Michelle Waters spoke those words "in the living room of the family home, tears running down her cheeks."[29]

Iraqi tears were less visible in U.S. media coverage. As bombs exploded in Baghdad, "for all the noisy triumphalism from both sides, what resounded was the silence of the dead," said the *Guardian*'s book about the war. "On the outskirts of Baghdad, desolation and adversity pitted the faces of ordinary Iraqis. Conflict was a curse and there was little sign, as American bombers took wing above, that it would be lifted soon." The war was really "untold stories" that news coverage bypassed. "Far from rhetoric and the real-time television coverage, people were dying unnoticed and uncared for. One strike on the edge of Baghdad in early April destroyed two homes of an extended family of 12 people."[30] *Guardian* reporter Suzanne Goldenberg went to the village of Sueb, twenty-two miles from the center of Baghdad, populated by poor Shias with the misfortune of living near a military zone drawing heavy American bombardment. "Tragedy struck Sueb when U.S. missiles killed six members of one family and five others living in the same road. Twelve houses were destroyed in the blast, hastily built one-storey structures crumpled into the earth. Taliya Ali Mohammed, whose house was strewn with shattered glass, said: 'The people living in this area are the very poorest people. It really is so cruel that we are being hit.' The children in Sueb cried themselves to sleep. And the missiles still rained down."[31]

Adulation for the Pentagon's arsenal becomes a permanent aspect of the American war story. Several months into the occupation of Iraq, for instance, at the top of the front page of the *New York Times*, a color photo showed a gunner aiming his formidable weapon downward from a Black Hawk helicopter, airborne over Baghdad. Underneath the picture was an article lamenting the recent setbacks in Iraq for such U.S. military aircraft. "In two weeks," the article said, "the Black Hawks and Chinooks and Apaches that once zoomed overhead with such grace and panache have suddenly become vulnerable."[32] Referring to machinery of death in a reportorial voice, the words "grace" and "panache" were attributed to no one; they hovered as objective characterizations by a newspaper widely seen as epitomizing the highest journalistic standards.

The headline had a vaguely foreshadowing quality: "A Full Range of Technology Is Applied to Bomb Fallujah." During the U.S. military's fourteenth month of fighting in Iraq, the *New York Times* led off the news story by reporting that "the airstrikes in Fallujah in the past three days by American warplanes and helicopter gunships have been the most intense aerial bombardment in Iraq since major combat ended nearly a year ago." What followed were a score of paragraphs that conveyed a military on the leading edge, with a steady flow of numbing terminology: "Air Force F-15E and F-16 warplanes, and carrier-based F-14 and F-18 fighter-bombers, have dropped about three dozen 500-

pound laser-guided bombs . . . AH-1W Super Cobra helicopters have hovered over the city, launching Hellfire missiles . . . lumbering AC-130 gunships have pounded trucks and cars ferrying fighters with the distinctive thump-thump of 105-millimeter howitzers. British Tornado ground-attack planes are also flying missions . . . and remotely piloted Predator reconnaissance aircraft prowl the skies . . . the air campaign's weapons of choice—500-pound GBU-12 laser-guided bombs . . . the Air Force has also dropped 1,000-pound and 2,000-pound laser-guided bombs, and Maverick missiles . . . a Global Hawk reconnaissance aircraft is to arrive next week."[33]

For the reader, such verbiage could provide some affirmation that the "full range of technology" mentioned in the headline was always at the ready to get things under control, whether for the current war or the next one. And the closing paragraph quoted an unnamed pilot with a perspective from on high: "The good guys were closing in one side, and suddenly we saw Iraqis shooting their own guys in the back, trying to push them forward. So we left those soldiers in front alone and I said, 'Let's get the really bad guys.' We trained our firepower on them. We could see all that from above, and could separate the bad guys from the really bad guys." This article, as it happened, had a Washington dateline.[34]

Summarizing military actions on a given day, news reports over time have ways of coming to sound not much more lifelike than weather data or ball scores. Here's a typical summary that millions of CBS viewers heard from anchor Walter Cronkite on the last day of October 1967: "In the war, U.S. and South Vietnamese troops smashed the second Communist attempt in three days to capture the district capital of Loc Ninh, some 72 miles north of Saigon. The allies killed more than 110 VC, boosting the enemy death toll since Sunday to 365. American losses were reported at 4 dead and 11 wounded."[35]

The subject of civilian deaths in Southeast Asia was a low priority for American news media, and it was carefully avoided by U.S. officials. Daniel Ellsberg remembers asking Henry Kissinger a pointed question during a public conference at MIT in late January 1971: "You have said that the White House is not a place for moral philosophizing. But in fact the White House does educate the people by everything that it does and everything it says and does not say. Specifically, tonight you *are* expressing moral values when you tell us that the war is trending down and will continue to trend down, and then in that connection you mention only U.S. troop presence and U.S. casualties. You failed to mention Indochinese casualties, or refugees, or bombing tonnages, which in fact are trending *up*. By your omission, you are telling the American people that they need not and ought not care about our impact on the Indochinese people, and you encourage them to support decisions that ignore that impact."[36] Ellsberg went on: "So I have one question for you. What is your best estimate of the number of Indochinese that we will kill, pursuing your policy in the next 12 months?"

Kissinger declined to answer the question.[37]

Nine months passed after the December 1989 invasion of Panama before the CBS program *60 Minutes* reported that hundreds of civilians were killed—many incinerated as they slept—in the early hours of the U.S. attack.[38] Within days of the invasion, the story had been told throughout Latin America and elsewhere. When it finally got onto *60 Minutes*, it was news to viewers.

In early 2002, several months into war in Afghanistan, the Pentagon deputy director of operations, Admiral John Stufflebeem, told reporters at a Washington briefing that "there were a lot of Taliban, a lot of Al Qaeda in this country." He added: "We don't do body counts, nor actually do we do head counts, but we know we haven't gotten them all."[39] Six weeks later, interviewed on *CBS Evening News*, the defense secretary used the same charged phrase, perhaps to reinforce the idea that a new kind of approach to war had taken hold. "I don't do body counts," Donald Rumsfeld said. "This country tried that in Vietnam and it didn't work."[40]

The war victims whom commanders are least interested in talking about—civilians—are the most prevalent. "In the wars of the 1990s," says the 2003 book *What Every Person Should Know About War*, "civilian deaths constituted between 75 and 90 percent of all war deaths."[41] Such figures are recent indicators of a century-long trend that has turned warriors into a steadily dwindling proportion of war's dead.[42]

Civilian anonymity cuts against accountability.[43] "If we do not count the bodies, this atrocity will never have a face," *Boston Globe* columnist Derrick Z. Jackson wrote eight months after the invasion of

Iraq. He added that "just one Iraqi civilian death is horrible blood on our hands given that the attack on Iraq appears to have been based on a lie."[44]

Even the more liberal newspapers are often inclined to treat the American fatalities as the sum of a war's fatalities worth noting. In early May 2004, when the *San Francisco Chronicle* printed a sidebar reporting that "as of Monday, 751 U.S. service members had died since the beginning of military operations in Iraq last year," the headline said simply: "Death Toll in Iraq."[45] In mid-June the lead story on the *USA Today* front page, reporting on persistent strife in Fallujah, recalled "three weeks of combat in April that killed 600 to 700 insurgents and 10 Marines."[46] The several hundred civilians who died in that Iraqi city went unmentioned. Months later, the standard headline over *New York Times* news items listing American soldiers who died in Iraq was "Names of the Dead."[47] For American media outlets and domestic politics back home, the stats that really mattered were the casualty figures for American troops.

Meanwhile, the toll among civilians in Iraq continued to receive much less coverage. "The only comprehensive estimate comes from Iraqbodycount.net, a consortium of researchers working from media reports," *National Journal* told readers in spring 2004. "The researchers say that between 9,153 and 11,010 Iraqis had died through the end of April; only 692 of the names of the dead are known."[48] (Of course the names of all the dead were known to their loved ones.) Other estimates of civilian deaths went much higher. On October 29, 2004, the *Lancet* medical journal released a study by researchers from Johns Hopkins and Columbia universities indicating that about 100,000 Iraqi deaths had occured over an eighteen-month period as a result of the invasion and occupation. More than half of those who died were women and children killed in the air strikes, the study reported.[49]

When television seems to be some kind of ultimate reference point to comprehend war, the illusion of coming to terms with war by watching it on TV is helpful to a wartime president who would prefer that public perceptions be superficial. "Look, nobody likes to see dead people on their television screens," President Bush said at a news conference in 2004. "I don't. It's a tough time for the American people to see that. It's gut-wrenching."[50] Yet TV news coverage is apt to convey the notion that most people dying at the hands of the American military deserve to die. Such assumptions are encouraged by Pentagon media spinners whose default position is that civilian casualties are very low compared to those of the enemy fighters.

In early April 2004, with a sudden upsurge of combat in a number of cities, Fallujah residents were in a merciless war zone. "Iraqi casualties were heavy: locals said hundreds of civilians have been killed, though the U.S. says most of the dead are insurgents," *Time* reported.[51] A day after that edition of the magazine came out, the Associated Press was reporting: "A hospital official said over 600 Iraqis were killed in Fallujah alone—mostly women, children and the elderly."[52] Hours later, during a news conference defending the Iraq war, President Bush denounced "the merciless horror inflicted upon thousands of innocent men and women and children on September the 11th, 2001."[53] He did not decry the horror experienced by innocent men and women and children in Fallujah during recent days.

Meanwhile, author Rahul Mahajan wrote: "During the course of roughly four hours at a small clinic in Fallujah, I saw perhaps a dozen wounded brought in. Among them was a young woman, 18 years old, shot in the head. She was having a seizure and foaming at the mouth when they brought her in; doctors did not expect her to survive the night. Another likely terminal case was a young boy with massive internal bleeding. . . . Makki al-Nazzal, a lifelong Fallujah resident who works for the humanitarian NGO InterSOS, had been pressed into service as the manager of the clinic, since all doctors were busy, working around the clock with minimal sleep. . . . He told us about ambulances being hit by snipers, women and children being shot. Describing the horror that the siege of Fallujah had become, he said: 'I have been a fool for 47 years. I used to believe in European and American civilization.' . . . Nothing could have been easier than gaining the goodwill of the people of Fallujah had the Americans not been so brutal in their dealings. People I interviewed vehemently denied that they were Saddam supporters and expressed immense anger and disappointment at American conduct."[54]

But the combination of official U.S. spin and the tendencies of mainstream American journalism routinely precludes much sustained media attention to the human dimensions of the killing and wounding by Uncle Sam. Even in ostensibly sophisticated media venues, the discourse is commonly black-hat and white-hat. In the midst of an occupation hyped as an effort to help ordinary Iraqis, the U.S. Marine Corps' retired general Bernard Trainor—a repeat wartime guest on the PBS *NewsHour with Jim Lehrer*—told national TV viewers that the Marines were facing difficult challenges. "They're fighting an irregular organization that does not wear uniforms, that does not subscribe to the laws of war and are mixed in with the population," he said. "And this makes it rather difficult in distinguishing good people from bad people."[55]

The occupying troops, who had made themselves unwelcome to a large proportion of the population, were—naturally enough—likely to be confused as to exactly who to shoot. A few days after Trainor's comment, *Time* published a spread of articles promoted on a cover declaring, "As rebellion flares up across Iraq, the U.S. faces its toughest test yet." (That Iraq also was facing a tough—and far more calamitous—test appeared to be a subordinate matter.) A story inside the magazine reported that American intuition was left to fend for itself: "In some neighborhoods, the Marines say, anyone they spot in the streets is considered a 'bad guy.' Says Marine Major Larry Kaifesh: 'It is hard to differentiate between people who are insurgents or civilians. You just have to go with your gut feeling.' U.S. commanders say many residents of the town haven't declared their allegiance to either the coalition or the insurgents and are waiting to see who prevails. But the Marines sensed that, no matter how the battle turns out, winning hearts and minds in Fallujah after so much destruction may be impossible."[56]

Whether the explanations were coming from a retired general in a TV studio or an active-duty major in the line of fire, once the rationales were stripped away, the remaining approach sometimes was not much more discerning than *kill 'em and let God sort 'em out*. Satiric words in a Vietnam-era song by Country Joe and the Fish could seem all too resonant as the Pentagon's firepower blasted urban Iraqi neighborhoods: "And you know that peace can only be won / When we've blown 'em all to kingdom come."[57]

In U.S. media coverage, the civilians in Iraq who mattered most were from the United States. It was apt to be very big news when death came to American contractors, who could in some cases be described as hired guns or quasi-paramilitaries. By the fourth paragraph of a front-page *New York Times* piece—headlined "U.S. Workers, Lured by Money and Idealism, Face Iraqi Reality"—the word "civilians" was evidently used to mean *American* civilians: "There are no concrete figures on the number of civilians who have been killed or wounded in Iraq, but Halliburton has acknowledged that 30 of its employees and contractors have died since the war began last year."[58]

While it would be unfair to claim that U.S. news media did not cover heartbreaking stories of Iraqi civilians, such coverage often appeared within a peculiarly lacquered news frame—as if the Iraqi suffering was most significant in the context of the occupiers' image. The same edition of the *Times* published a sizable and terribly poignant photo of a wide-eyed little boy, showing an arm with a bandaged stump instead of a hand, over the caption: "Nasser Fadil, right, watched over his four-year-old son, Ali, yesterday in the Medical City hospital in Baghdad. The boy, who was wounded during recent violence in Fallujah, lost his left hand and left leg." The headline over the accompanying story, however, indicated what was most pressing on the minds of editors back in New York: "News Reports on Arab TV Stir Up Iraqis Against U.S."[59]

The empire was inclined to strike back and blame the messenger for horrific images inflaming Arab sentiments against the United States. On the day after that headline appeared, during a Pentagon news briefing, Defense Secretary Rumsfeld went on the media offense.

> *Rumsfeld*: "I can definitively say that what Al-Jazeera is doing is vicious, inaccurate, and inexcusable."
>
> *Reporter*: "Do you have a civilian casualty count?"
>
> *Rumsfeld*: "Of course not, we're not in the city [Fallujah]. But you know what our forces do; they don't go around killing hundreds of civilians. That's just outrageous nonsense! It's disgraceful what that station is doing."[60]

Four days later, while noting Rumsfeld's disparagement of Al-Jazeera for its focus on civilian deaths, the London-based *Guardian* reported that "the accounts of witnesses in Fallujah and nearby villages suggest many have been injured and killed."[61] The *Guardian*'s reporting on the matter was in keeping with other news stories. But Al-Jazeera was in the U.S. government's media crosshairs. The week after Rumsfeld's blast at the Arabic-language network, Secretary of State Colin Powell was putting renewed pressure on Al-Jazeera's sponsor, the government of Qatar, to rein in the news channel.

Qatar had become a key U.S. ally in the Persian Gulf region. Its support for Al-Jazeera had made possible the launch of one of the only major media outlets in the Arab world to exercise independence. Officials in Washington grew fond of saying that they were eager to encourage democratization in the Middle East, but the Bush administration's moves to throttle Al-Jazeera indicated otherwise. Yet there were ways that the U.S. government could legitimately reduce the negative coverage it got on Al-Jazeera; for instance, if President Bush wanted Al-Jazeera to stop airing grisly footage of dead Iraqi civilians, as commander in chief he could order U.S. troops to stop killing them. But instead, the squeeze was on. At the end of April 2004, the *Washington Post* reported that Powell said he'd had "very intense" and blunt discussions about Al-Jazeera that week with Qatar foreign minister Hamad Bin Jasim Thani. Another Qatari official visiting Washington said in an interview that a "reevaluation commission" had been assigned by Al-Jazeera's board of directors, and the *Post* added: "He also suggested that government funding for the station was about to end."[62] More direct ways for Qatar's undemocratic government to pressure the Al-Jazeera management were also available.

Al-Jazeera was in the habit of putting American officials on the air for extended segments. And if its coverage was inflammatory, it was arguably no more so than the standard fare on Fox News Channel, an outlet not known to have received any sort of rebuke from the Bush administration. What was obvious to Arab observers was obscure or pernicious as far as officials in Washington were concerned: while the U.S. media's perspective was mostly from the vantage point of where the missiles were fired from, Al-Jazeera's was focused mostly on where they landed.

So, while hundreds of deaths in Fallujah provoked the hearts and stoked the wrath of many Arabs in the spring of 2004, there was an abstract quality to much of the U.S. media coverage. Some American journalists worried aloud that those deaths might inflame Iraqis and make the occupiers' tasks more difficult. On the last day of April, at the top of a *New York Times* news page, a heading summarized the fixations of coverage below: "The Struggle for Iraq: Fallujah as a Military and Political Headache."

When ABC's *Nightline* scheduled a program to recite the names and show the photos of each U.S. soldier killed in Iraq, the company that owned eight ABC affiliate TV stations preempted that broadcast;

the strongly prowar management of the Sinclair Broadcast Group charged that *Nightline* was seeking to promulgate an antiwar message. Anchor Ted Koppel responded by asserting that he was merely honoring the fallen troops and documenting the war's "human cost."[63] Senator John McCain quickly issued a statement that lauded the program for providing viewers with "an opportunity to be reminded of war's terrible costs, in all their heartbreaking detail."[64] But it was a media controversy about war coverage that tightly circumscribed the scope of the war's human dimensions; in that case, as in so many others, the defenders of the media treatment (as well as the most publicized critics) seemed unconcerned about failure to shed light on civilian deaths—which, as usual, were far more numerous than the deaths among U.S. troops. When McCain proclaimed that the television show's tribute was a way of reminding people about "war's terrible costs, in all their heartbreaking detail," the Iraqis killed were completely out of the picture. And the controversy about *Nightline* showing the American war dead was quite mild compared to the uproar that would have accompanied a similar showcasing of Iraqi civilians killed by American firepower. But, of course, no such show was to be contemplated by *Nightline* or by, say, the PBS *NewsHour with Jim Lehrer*, which routinely aired the photos and names of fallen American soldiers at the end of the program ("our honor roll") once the deaths had been announced by the Pentagon.

A warhead with the technical name CBU-87/B functioned properly in Yugoslavia, as promised by the manufacturer, which called it an "all-purpose, air-delivered cluster weapons system." The Pentagon categorized it as a "combined effects munition." One of its memorable performances came at about noon on a Friday in the city of Nis, where people were shopping at a vegetable market.

A news dispatch reported that "the bombs struck next to the hospital complex and near the market, bringing death and destruction, peppering the streets of Serbia's third-largest city with shrapnel and littering the courtyards with yellow bomb casings." It was one of the cluster bombs' few moments in the U.S. media limelight. "In a street leading from the market, dismembered bodies were strewn among carrots and other vegetables in pools of blood. A dead woman, her body covered with a sheet, was still clutching a shopping bag filled with carrots."[65] Reporting from Belgrade, the BBC correspondent

John Simpson wrote a commentary that appeared in the *Sunday Telegraph* in London: "In Novi Sad and Nis, and several other places across Serbia and Kosovo where there are no foreign journalists, heavier bombing has brought more accidents." Simpson noted that cluster bombs "explode in the air and hurl shards of shrapnel over a wide radius." He went on: "Used against human beings, cluster bombs are some of the most savage weapons of modern warfare."[66]

If cluster bombs had been used by Yugoslav army troops, of course, a huge outcry would have occurred in the American media.

The cluster warhead utilized in Yugoslavia that spring was a one-thousand-pound marvel with an ingenious design.[67] When it went off, a couple of hundred "bomblets" shot out in all directions, aided by little parachutes that slowed down the descent of the bomblets and dispersed them. After each bomblet broke into about three hundred pieces of jagged steel shrapnel, they hit a lot of what the weapon's maker described as "soft targets." The fact that its use in Yugoslavia during spring 1999 received scant U.S. media attention smoothed the way for the Defense Department to drop cluster bombs in Afghanistan during the autumn of 2001 and then to fire cluster munitions in Iraq during the spring of 2003.

Soon after the fall of Saddam's regime, researchers at FAIR pointed out that American news outlets "have been quick to declare the U.S. war against Iraq a success, but in-depth investigative reporting about the war's likely health and environmental consequences has been scarce."[68] During the war the U.S. Army had fired thousands of cluster munitions. As in other countries where cluster weaponry had been used, unexploded cluster bomblets continued to detonate, sometimes in the hands of children. In addition, as had occurred during the Gulf War, the U.S. government again fortified some armaments with depleted uranium, leaving behind fine-particle radioactive dust of the sort that researchers have linked to cancer and birth defects.

Those important stories—about cluster weaponry and depleted uranium—became known to many news watchers on several continents. But not in the United States. More than six weeks after the invasion began, FAIR examined the comprehensive Nexis media database through May 5 and found that "there have been no in-depth reports about cluster bombs" on the major U.S. broadcast TV networks' nightly news shows since the start of the war.[69]

But stories continued to be well worth telling. "On April 19,

2003, a little girl walked out of a crowd in Baghdad carrying a steel gray canister attached to a white ribbon," *National Journal* reporter Corine Hegland wrote thirteen months later. "U.S. troops had left the canister behind in her part of town, and she was trying to return it to the American soldiers then on patrol. Sgt. Troy Jenkins, 25, a big man with blue eyes, recognized the child's gift as a cluster bomblet, one of the hundreds of thousands left dotting the country, and he threw himself onto it as the explosion began. When the dying was done, a family in California had lost its father and a family in Iraq had lost its daughter."[70]

What was unusual about this event was not that it occurred but that some readers were to run across a vivid description of it in a mainstream American publication. Citing a Human Rights Watch report that during the invasion a U.S. Army cluster-munitions attack in the town of Hilla had resulted in more than five hundred civilian injuries, Hegland added: "And the danger lingered after the major combat phase of the war was over. Not all of the bombs went off. Most of the Army's cluster munitions have an official 'dud' rate of 16 percent, but the actual rate is much higher; in Kosovo, some estimates put it as high as 25 percent. Over the course of the invasion period in Iraq, more than 2 million bomblets were released. Even at the official rate, that leaves about 300,000 tiny bombs waiting in fields, trees, roofs, or yards, for a child, a farmer, or even a patrolling soldier to nudge the wrong way."[71] The U.S. military's commanders had chosen to use these weapons. If most Americans were aware of the human consequences, the war might have lost some of its moral stature and public support.

The war effort in Afghanistan during autumn 2001 was often touted as humanitarian, laced with references to airborne food drops. Details were sketchy, but television became a free-fire zone for self-congratulation on waging an extraordinarily humane war. On *Larry King Live*, a bipartisan panel of senators affirmed their loyalty to the president. Senator John Warner, a former secretary of the navy, spoke as the ranking GOP member of the Senate Armed Services Committee when he said: "This, I think, is the first time in contemporary military history where a military operation is being conducted against the government of a country, and simultaneously, with the troops carrying out their mission, other troops are trying to take care of the innocent

victims who all too often are caught in harm's way."[72] Yet hours after
Warner's explanation, the United Nations World Food Program
halted its convoys of emergency aid to Afghanistan because of the
bombing campaign. Private relief workers voiced escalating alarm.
The president of the humanitarian aid organization Conscience International, Jim Jennings, warned: "Food drops from high altitudes
alone absolutely cannot provide sufficient and effective relief that is
urgently necessary to prevent mass starvation."[73]

To underscore the life-affirming function of the war, the Pentagon
emphasized its air drops of food parcels from two C-17 planes, and
President Bush made a plea for American children to aid Afghan kids
with dollar bills. Many U.S. news outlets ate it all up. A *New York
Times* editorial proclaimed that "Mr. Bush has wisely made providing
humanitarian assistance to the Afghan people an integral part of
American strategy."[74] Four days later, on October 12, the same newspaper offered additional praise: "His reaffirmation of the need for
humanitarian aid to the people of Afghanistan—including donations
from American children—seemed heartfelt." While thousands of kids
across the United States stuffed dollar bills into envelopes and mailed
them to the White House, the U.S. government kept bombing.
Jonathan Patrick, an official with the humanitarian aid group Concern, minced no words from Islamabad. Calling the food drops
"absolute nonsense," Patrick said: "What we need is 20-ton trucks in
huge convoys going across the border all the time."[75]

In tandem with the intensive bombing, the U.S. government maintained a PR blitz about its food-from-the-sky effort. But the Nobel
Peace Prize–winning French organization Doctors Without Borders
charged that the gambit was "virtually useless and may even be dangerous."[76] One aid group after another echoed the assessment. The
United States was dropping thirty-seven thousand meals a day on a
country where many Afghans had reason to fear starvation. Some of
the food, inevitably, was landing on minefields.

15

Our Soldiers Are Heroes, Theirs Are Inhuman

The bad soldiers in Vietnam lacked human qualities as far as mainstream U.S. news outlets were concerned. "Television painted an almost perfectly one-dimensional image of the North Vietnamese and Vietcong as cruel, ruthless, and fanatical—clearly beyond the bounds of Legitimate Controversy," writes Daniel Hallin. "Just as television journalists often waived the strictures of objectivity to celebrate what was seen at the beginning of the war as a national consensus behind it, they also, much more consistently, waived them to denounce the enemies of that consensus—the inhabitants of the Sphere of Deviance—both in Vietnam and . . . at home as well."[1] Hallin concluded: "Like most 20th-century war propaganda, television coverage of Vietnam dehumanized the enemy, drained him of all recognizable emotions and motives and thus banished him not only from the political sphere, but from human society itself. The North Vietnamese and Vietcong were 'fanatical,' 'suicidal,' 'savage,' 'halfcrazed.' They were lower than mere criminals . . . they were vermin. Television reports routinely referred to areas controlled by the NLF as 'Communist infested' or 'Vietcong infested.'"[2]

Old wartime media themes would sound familiar to Americans who never saw news coverage of Vietnam. The technologies of waging wars—and reporting on them—have shifted markedly over the decades, but some boilerplate psychological mechanisms seem frozen in time. As the Iraq war raged during its second year, many news accounts exuded the kinds of moods and messages embodied in an NBC television report from An Lao, Vietnam, that aired in February 1966.

"Brave men need leaders," correspondent Dean Brelis reported.

"This is a leader of brave men. His name is Hal Moore. He comes from Bardstown, Kentucky. He is married and the father of five children."

After commenting on tactics, Moore talked about the men under his command: "They are the greatest soldiers in the world. In fact, they're the greatest men in the world. They're well trained, they're well disciplined, their morale is outstanding. Their motivation is tremendous. They came over here to win."[3]

Another network was also eager to trumpet Moore's battlefield leadership. A day later, a young CBS reporter named Dan Rather identified the thirty-three-year-old "Lightning" Hal Moore as "one of the youngest full colonels in the army, hero of the Ia Drang Valley in November, and itching for another head-on clash." Rather asked the colonel: "What do you hope to accomplish?"

The reply: "We hope to clear out this entire valley, get the VC out of here and let the people come back and live a normal life."[4]

After U.S. soldiers massacred about three hundred Vietnamese civilians at My Lai in March 1968, nearly a dozen major print and TV outlets suppressed the evidence and photos of the bloodbath for well over a year—until a small, independent news service released the information. "Reporting of My Lai and other war crimes cases . . . was extensive in the last few years of the war," Daniel Hallin noted, adding: "Stories of these incidents of course focused attention on civilian victims of the war, and no doubt contributed to some weakening of the moral dichotomy television had set up between Americans and the enemy. . . . But My Lai coverage was usually cautious and dispassionate, a great deal of it focused on legal issues in the trial of Lieutenant Calley, rather than on the massacre itself, which of course became an 'alleged massacre' once charges were filed. So it may be that for much of the viewing public, My Lai was less an atrocity, comparable to those they had heard about on the other side, than confirmation that American morale was on the decline. Many Americans, incidentally, did not believe the news of the My Lai massacre."[5]

As war drags on, the media coverage is likely to become more downbeat. But the emphasis on human consequences is typically quite skewed. Overall, "it was the costs of the war to Americans that was stressed more heavily in the later years," Hallin found, "more than its costs to the Vietnamese. There was a considerable increase in the sheer volume of reporting on ARVN [South Vietnam's army] casualties as Vietnamization put the South Vietnamese army in the news. But the special effort to humanize the casualties of war applied primarily to Americans. Coverage of North Vietnamese and NLF casualties remained mostly statistical."[6] Throughout the war, the much smaller numbers of U.S. deaths and injuries gained much more U.S. media attention than the toll for Vietnamese people.[7]

Media emphasis on American suffering was a factor in the attitude expressed by Jimmy Carter when, two months into his presidency—explaining why the U.S. government had no responsibility to provide aid to Vietnam—he said that "the destruction was mutual."[8] The claim was in harmony with an American media chorus that had little use for guilt or self-reproach.

During the Iraq war, American networks uncritically relayed a non-stop barrage of statements from U.S. officials portraying deadly Iraqi actions as heinous and deadly American actions as positive. *They* had death squads and *we* had noble troops. Their bullets and bombs were odious; ours were remedies for tyranny. "It looks and feels like terrorism," a Pentagon official said on national television after several American soldiers died at the hands of an Iraqi suicide bomber.[9]

"While we venerate and mourn our own dead we are curiously indifferent about those we kill," Chris Hedges wrote in *War Is a Force That Gives Us Meaning*. "Thus killing is done in our name, killing that concerns us little, while those who kill our own are seen as having crawled out of the deepest recesses of the earth, lacking our own humanity and goodness."[10]

The frequent media adulation for "our" soldiers could hardly be more different than the media treatment of "theirs." News coverage that actually depicts fighters on the other side in human terms is apt to be conspicuous—a rare departure from the baseline of omissions, stereotypes, and bloodless references. Overwhelmingly, in U.S. media contexts, those killed by American firepower might as well be cardboard cutouts on a shooting range, with no hint of humanity behind the images and the numbers.

Pentagon boosters rocketed Jessica Lynch into the news stratosphere, but the first publicity about her came in a run-of-the-media-mill story on the Associated Press wire. "A West Virginia woman who joined the Army because there were few jobs in her hometown is among a dozen soldiers reported missing after a supply convoy was ambushed in southern Iraq, her father said." The date was Monday, March 24, 2003.

Amid the profuse gravity of war coverage, the Lynch story quickly gained altitude. On Tuesday, a *Washington Post* story—about GIs in the 507th Maintenance Company who'd been "killed or captured near the southern Iraqi city of Nasiriyah"—devoted several sentences to Private First Class Jessica Lynch.[11] Her name was prominent in a front-page *New York Times* article headlined "TV Images Confirm Fears of Prisoners' Kin."[12]

The ink on those newspapers was hardly dry before the TV networks plunged in. An ABC News correspondent interviewed Lynch's kindergarten teacher and high school softball coach on *Good Morning America*. Meanwhile, the Associated Press began to churn out more pieces from picturesque rolling hills in West Virginia. "Jessica Lynch is known for her smile, her laugh and for loving children so much that she wants to be a teacher," one AP story began.[13] Another had this lead: "Both floral shops in this rural West Virginia town scrambled Tuesday to get more red, white, blue and yellow ribbons after residents transformed every scrap into huge bows to show support for one of their own who is missing in action in Iraq."[14]

News stories about Lynch swiftly approached flood stage. On Wednesday, the *Baltimore Sun* devoted more than a thousand words to Lynch in a page-one article datelined from her hometown of Palestine.[15] The next morning, National Public Radio did its bit by interviewing Lynch's kindergarten teacher, and correspondent Wade Goodwyn closed his report by declaring: "For the family and friends of those who are held prisoner or who are missing in action, the advance of the American Army toward Baghdad cannot go fast enough."[16] By then, TV networks were transfixed with the Jessica Lynch story.

On Thursday, NBC's Katie Couric interviewed the missing soldier's father, Greg Lynch, on the *Today* show. *CBS Evening News* interviewed him on Friday, and the network followed up with a more extensive segment on *48 Hours* Saturday night featuring Jessica Lynch's father, her "best friend," her kindergarten teacher, and others. Jessica Lynch was famous. But Jessica mania was just getting started.

Days later, when NBC anchor Tom Brokaw reported her rescue, he proclaimed it to be "one of the most dramatic moments of this war."[17] A network correspondent in Iraq provided viewers with the basic plot line: "The rescue operation began with a fierce barrage from the 2nd

Battalion, 1st Marines, firing on Baath party headquarters to draw out Iraqi soldiers, that diversion providing cover so special operations forces could drop in to Saddam Hospital. . . . Inside, the U.S. forces found the Army private first class wounded, a gunshot to her leg."[18]

In the United States, the news media—from tabloids to the most widely respected daily newspapers—went wild, relying on Pentagon sources and pumping out reportage that later turned out to be nonsense. Typical was a big story put together by *Los Angeles Times* reporters in Doha, Qatar, with help from the newspaper's Washington bureau. Hailing the rescue as "a triumphant moment for U.S. forces," the front-paged April 3 article reported that special operations troops "landed a Black Hawk helicopter in the courtyard of the hospital, shot their way into the building under heavy fire and moved to the room where Lynch lay. . . . Once inside, the U.S. forces grabbed Lynch, strapped her to a stretcher and—again, under fire—carted her to the waiting chopper." On the same day, the *Washington Post* preferred to lead with an entirely false set of pseudo revelations about her capture. The *Post* account claimed that Lynch "fought fiercely and shot several enemy soldiers" during the ambush, "continued firing at the Iraqis even after she sustained multiple gunshot wounds," and "was also stabbed when Iraqi forces closed in on her position."

On May 1, the same day that President Bush issued his top-gun proclamation that the war was basically finished, a column in the *Philadelphia Inquirer* began with this observation: "Television's most heavily reported story of the Iraq war focused on a single person, Jessica Lynch. Although her rescue illuminated the daring and ingenuity of the U.S. military, it did not affect the conduct or outcome of the war. But it was the perfect story for what should be called The TV War, a production that demonstrated without question that when the nation's two biggest exports, aerospace equipment and show business, come together, useful and informative news gets left behind."

That column was by the *Inquirer*'s television critic, Jonathan Storm. The rescue of Jessica Lynch, he wrote insightfully, "demonstrated the principle that the Pentagon expected would apply when it allowed reporters to tag along with the troops: The thirst for visceral storytelling would overwhelm the higher journalistic goal of in-depth, and possibly unflattering, coverage. And, as in most aspects of the war, the Pentagon was right. Television could not resist using breathless, scattershot dispatches from 'embedded' reporters to produce

The TV War. It was a show that sanitized the horror and death of combat, invited savvy veterans to provide commentary, and produced an entertaining combination of sports-style action and drama. . . . All is quiet on the tube now, as President Bush prepares to stand on an aircraft carrier tonight—no chance for TV imagery is wasted on this administration—and tell the nation that the major combat is over."

The Pentagon's captivating story about Jessica Lynch had served its purposes. Only later did contrary facts emerge to illuminate what BBC News called "one of the most stunning pieces of news management ever conceived."[19]

The unraveling of the official Jessica Lynch saga began many weeks after she became a household name. Various news outlets started to question some fundamentals. A report by BBC News, airing on May 18, shredded numerous Pentagon claims about what happened to her. When *Los Angeles Times* columnist Robert Scheer cited the emerging information, the Pentagon went ballistic, branding his assertions "outrageous, patently false and unsupported by the facts."[20] But the high-dudgeon salvo from officialdom was a desperate attempt at damage control as news accounts finally revealed that U.S. officials had eagerly concocted all sorts of story lines—such as the tall tale that Lynch had suffered gunshot wounds but kept firing weapons until her ammunition ran out, "fighting to the death" at the time of her capture.[21]

Also bogus was the Pentagon's account of the rescue. "Some brave souls put their lives on the line to make this happen," said spokesman General Vincent Brooks, who assured the media that "it was a classic joint operation, done by some of our nation's finest warriors, who are dedicated to never leaving a comrade behind."[22] But as the BBC reported, witnesses said the U.S. special forces "knew that the Iraqi military had fled a day before they swooped on the hospital." And the widely televised video of her rescue, supplied by the Defense Department, was shot as a work of dramatic artifice. "It was like a Hollywood film," said Anmar Uday, a doctor who worked at the hospital. "They cried 'go, go, go,' with guns and blanks without bullets, blanks and the sound of explosions. They made a show for the American attack on the hospital—action movies like Sylvester Stallone or Jackie Chan."[23]

The BBC explained that "the American strategy was to ensure the right television footage by using embedded reporters and images from their own cameras, editing the film themselves. The Pentagon had been influenced by Hollywood producers of reality TV and action movies, notably the man behind *Black Hawk Down*, Jerry Bruckheimer." He had been an adviser to the Pentagon for a prime-time TV series about American troops in Afghanistan. "That approach was taken on and developed on the field of battle in Iraq."[24]

Truth could have supplied a truly moving narrative, though not the kind of tale favored in Washington. "What is particularly sad in all of this," Scheer wrote, "is that a wonderfully hopeful story was available to the Pentagon to sell to the eager media: one in which besieged Iraqi doctors and nurses bravely cared for—and supplied their own blood to—a similarly brave young American woman in a time of madness and violence. Instead, eager to turn the war into a morality play between good and evil, the military used—if not abused—Lynch to put a heroic spin on an otherwise sorry tale of unjustified invasion."[25]

But ultimately, Jessica Lynch spoke for herself. In November, appearing on ABC's *Primetime Live* program, she criticized the Pentagon for putting out fanciful stories about her.[26] Yet Lynch's most significant statement was still to come.

Near the end of *I Am a Soldier, Too*, the book quotes the famous hero at a reflective moment, sitting in her mother's kitchen. "We went and we did our job, and that was to go to the war," Jessica Lynch said, "but I wish I hadn't done it—I wish it had never happened. I wish we hadn't been there, none of us."[27]

16

America Needs the Resolve to Kick the "Vietnam Syndrome"

The specter of Vietnam has been buried forever in the desert sands of the Arabian peninsula," President George H. W. Bush said of the Gulf War victory in early 1991.[1] He told a gathering of state legislators, "It's a proud day for America—and, by God, we've kicked the Vietnam syndrome once and for all."[2] Many politicians and pundits have spoken of a Vietnam syndrome as though it were a virulent political ailment.[3]

Often discussed by news media, the "Vietnam syndrome" usually has a negative connotation, implying knee-jerk opposition to military involvement. Yet public backing for a war has much to do with duration and justification. A year after the invasion of Iraq began, Noam Chomsky observed in an interview: "Polls have demonstrated time and time again that Americans are willing to accept a high death toll—although they don't like it, they're willing to accept it—if they think it's a just cause. There's never been anything like the so-called Vietnam syndrome: it's mostly a fabrication. And in this case too if they thought it was a just cause, the 500 or so [American] deaths would be mourned, but not considered a dominant reason for not continuing. No, the problem is the justice of the cause."[4] Overall, if history is any guide, most Americans are inclined to favor just about any war after it starts—in the short run—but if the war drags on and the rationales for it lose credibility in the public mind, support is apt to plummet. "World War II support levels never fell below 77 percent,

despite the prolonged and damaging nature of the conflict," according
to Chris Hedges. In contrast, "the Korean and Vietnam Wars ended
with support levels near 30 percent."[5]

Those words appeared in Hedges' book *What Every Person Should
Know About War*, published in June 2003. If it had gone to the printer
a year later, the book could have noted that the American public's initially high levels of support for the Iraq war fell sharply as bloodshed
continued and Washington's prewar lies became more apparent.

Facing a war's negative political consequences at home, presidents like
to emphasize more palatable outcomes. Thirty-five years before President George W. Bush assured the American public that like-minded
Iraqis would take up the burdens of fighting and dying as the occupation of their country wore on, President Richard Nixon unveiled a
doctrine envisioning that more soldiers of Asian allies would die in
place of American troops.

During a visit to Guam in July 1969, Nixon announced that the
U.S. government "would furnish military and economic assistance
when requested in accordance with our treaty commitments. But we
shall look to the nation directly threatened to assume the primary
responsibility for its defense."[6] A year after Nixon proclaimed his bal-
lyhooed doctrine, amounting to let's-you-and-them-fight, I. F. Stone
wrote astutely: "White House briefers speak of abandoning our world
policeman role, but the alternative they offer is not a revitalized U.N.
but the so-called Guam Doctrine. This is imperialism by proxy. We
may be on the verge of imposing quotas against the Orient's low-wage
textiles but we are eager to buy its low-wage soldier-power. The
Guam Doctrine will be seen in Asia as a rich white man's idea of fighting a war: we handle the elite airpower while coolies do the killing on
the ground."[7]

To ease stateside worries about U.S. troops being entangled in continuing warfare, the White House is eager to convey that the military
burden will increasingly rest on the broadening shoulders of the people who live in the country at stake. Yet Stone's July 1970 essay concluded presciently: "Not enough Asians are going to fight Asians for
us even if the price is right."[8] Despite the best-laid and most Machi-
avellian of plans, whether under the rubric of "Vietnamization" or
"Iraqization," the recruitment and retention of native surrogates
effectively loyal to the United States is a dicey thing.

A third of a century after Stone's prediction, an observer of the war in Iraq would have a strong basis to forecast that "not enough Arabs are going to fight Arabs for us." After disbanding Saddam Hussein's army, the Pentagon tried to build a new one, but a year into the occupation the recruit numbers were low—just 10 percent of the 40,000 target level. After half of the initial battalion quit in December 2003, a pay raise helped in retaining soldiers. Nevertheless, the occupying authorities were let down the following spring, as the *Wall Street Journal* reported: "When the second battalion was pressed last week to fight Sunni insurgents alongside Marines . . . in Fallujah, soldiers refused, saying they had signed up to defend Iraq from foreign threats, not fight fellow Iraqis."[9] Nor was the Pentagon's quest to replace its own troops with reliable Iraqi fighters doing better in the heavily Shiite region. "In the south, a number of units, both in the police force and also in the [Iraqi Civil Defense Corps], did not stand up to the intimidators of the forces of Sadr's militia, and that was a great disappointment to us," said General John Abizaid, commander of all U.S. troops in the Middle East.[10]

Proclaimed doctrines of replacing American soldiers with natives are apt to be real crowd-pleasers in the United States. When a war becomes unpopular, moving to reduce U.S. casualties while shifting the death burden onto other combatants is a big presidential goal. But measures such as Vietnamization or Iraqization do not necessarily mean that fewer people will be dying. Three years after Nixon's mid-1969 pronouncement, the U.S. troop levels in Vietnam had fallen to sixty-nine thousand. Yet during that three-year exodus of nearly half a million American soldiers, the tonnage rate of U.S. bombs falling on Vietnam actually increased.[11]

In effect, condemnations of "the Vietnam syndrome" are efforts to promote the legitimacy of at least two wars at once—the past one in Vietnam and the war that's currently under way (and/or on the horizon). To boosters of U.S. military intervention, the United States will triumph if only it is willing to show enough resolve. But the U.S. government's problems in Iraq after the invasion, as in Vietnam, were far from extrinsic to the basic realities—and the actual merits—of the war itself. The eagerness of so many supposed beneficiaries of American intervention to eject the occupiers was pivotal, not coincidental; it corresponded to the weakness of the U.S. warmakers' position in multiple, concentric ways. The spiraling problems encountered by the outsiders—whether manifested as military adversity or hostile propaganda in the occupied country—revolved around an absence of legitimacy. At the core of the war's long-term lack of viability (or "winnability") was the hollowness of Washington's claims, not the least of which were the pretensions of benevolence and zeal to foster a new democratic government for the benighted land. In short, good puppets were hard to find—and local people were so difficult to train as reliable military proxies to lift the burdens of the stymied U.S. troops—because the entire war project rested on a collapsible platform of falsehoods.

Rhetoric aside, democracy in Iraq would run counter to U.S. policy priorities. "From the start," the *Wall Street Journal* noted, "the effort to build a government was marked by unresolved tension between political leaders who are palatable to the U.S. but have little public support in Iraq, and religious figures who have the biggest popular followings but also hold religious views that alarm American policy makers."[12] Stated another way, it was a classic imperial problem, with the occupiers seeking to retain control of an Iraqi government, while most people in the country had very different ideas about who they wanted their leaders to be.[13]

"When popular resolve among the Vietnamese disappointed Washington, U.S. strategists would change the government in Saigon," William Greider recalled. "The U.S. proconsul in Baghdad, Paul Bremer, fired the interior minister in charge of the Iraqi police we trained to maintain civil order, because they fled the police stations rather than shoot it out with their countrymen." A journalist with several professional decades behind him by 2004, Greider saw a recurring motif: "To my eyes, the insurrection under way in Iraq looks like 'little Tet'—a smaller version of the original Tet offensive the Vietcong staged in 1968. It shocks Americans in much the same way. Iraq is a 'little war' compared with Vietnam, but Americans are learning, once again, that the indigenous people we 'liberated' do not love us. Many want our occupying army to withdraw."[14]

In mid-spring 2004, *USA Today* readers encountered this front-page story: "Only a third of the Iraqi people now believe that the American-led occupation of their country is doing more good than harm, and a solid majority support an immediate military pullout even though they fear that could put them in greater danger, according to a new *USA Today*/CNN/Gallup Poll. The nationwide survey, the most comprehensive look at Iraqi attitudes toward the occupation, was conducted in late March and early April. It reached nearly 3,500 Iraqis of every religious and ethnic group. The poll shows that most continue to say the hardships suffered to depose Saddam Hussein were worth it. Half say they and their families are better off than they were under Saddam. And a strong majority say they are more free to worship and to speak. But while they acknowledge benefits from dumping Saddam a year ago, Iraqis no longer see the presence of the American-led military as a plus. Asked whether they view the U.S.-led coalition as 'liberators' or 'occupiers,' 71 percent of all respondents say 'occupiers.' . . . In the multiethnic Baghdad area, where a Gallup Poll [in summer 2003] of 1,178 residents permits a valid comparison, only 13 percent of the people now say the invasion of Iraq was morally justifiable. In the 2003 poll, more than twice that number saw it as the right thing to do."[15]

A year after a Saddam statue dramatically fell in Baghdad,[16] some of the tyrant's bitterest enemies were firing rocket-propelled grenades at American troops. The turn of events—the launch of a fierce Shiite insurrection against the occupiers—undermined many of the basic claims from administration officials who had been preening themselves as liberators. Damage Control 101 called for downplaying the scope and significance of the uprising.

As the president and appointees tried to paper over the vast disconnects between Washington's narrative and emerging realities in Iraq, the rhetoric was familiar stuff, the foreign-policy rough equivalent of whistling past graveyards. A *New York Times* front-page story with an alarming headline—"7 U.S. Soldiers Die in Iraq as a Shiite Militia Rises Up"—quoted a spokesman for the American in charge of the occupation, Paul Bremer, saying merely: "We have isolated pockets where we are encountering problems." Meanwhile, the article said, an unnamed "senior American officer" in Baghdad was "using the insistently understated language that the American command has used at every juncture of the war."[17]

Yet there was less understatement and much candor two days later in George Will's influential column. Appearing in the *Washington Post* under the headline "A War President's Job," the piece cut to the chase with a revised logic for the occupation. "In the war against the militias," Will wrote, "every door American troops crash through, every civilian bystander shot—there will be many—will make matters worse, for a while. Nevertheless, the first task of the occupation remains the first task of government: to establish a monopoly on violence."[18]

True to time-honored form, the president certainly knew how to keep ordering the use of violence on a massive scale. Despite all the belated media exposure of the Bush administration's prewar deceptions about Iraq, the public was seeing a familiar limited spectrum of responses in mainstream U.S. media—many liberals wringing their hands, many conservatives rubbing their hands—at the sight of military escalation. In almost ritualistic fashion, numerous commentators reacted by criticizing the president for policy flaws. The tactical critiques were profuse, as when a *New York Times* editorial lamented that Washington "and its occupation partners" were by then "in real danger of handing over a meaningless badge of sovereignty to a government that is divided internally, is regarded as illegitimate by the people and has no means other than foreign armies in Iraq to enforce its authority."[19] Such careful language was notable for what it emphatically refused to say: *Get U.S. troops out of Iraq.*

To fight a counterinsurgency war under such circumstances—with increasingly unwelcome occupiers provoking indigenous rage—was a setup for extreme polarization in Iraq. No amount of fast talk could outrun the shadows of fallacies that loomed so large and seemed so convoluted. On his way to confirmation as U.S. ambassador to Iraq in the spring of 2004, Washington's then ambassador to the United Nations, John Negroponte, twisted language into pretzels at a Capitol Hill hearing when Senator Chuck Hagel inquired as to whether "the sovereign Iraqi government of July 1 would not have veto authority over military involvement" by U.S. forces. The senator asked: "If they have sovereignty, Mr. Ambassador, what does that mean?"[20]

Negroponte's reply was facile enough: "That is why I use the term 'exercise of sovereignty.' I think in the case of military activity, their forces will come under the unified command of the multinational force. That is the plan." In other words, the new Iraqi government would be praised as the embodiment of Iraqi sovereignty while the U.S. military would continue to do whatever Washington wanted it to do in Iraq—including order the Iraqi government's military around. In the period leading up to the ostensible handover of sovereignty midway through 2004, methodical gibberish streamed from U.S. officials. At his Senate confirmation hearing, Negroponte could rattle off explanations about how Iraqi power to make decisions would be "a work in progress" and "evolutionary." He talked about "real dialogue between our military commanders, the new Iraqi government and, I think, the United States mission as well." Ultimately, he said, the American military "is going to have the freedom to act in their self-defense, and they're going to be free to operate in Iraq as they best see fit."[21] The meaning of sovereignty would be quite ambiguous.[22]

Part of the process was for major U.S. news media to simultaneously acknowledge and deny fundamental contradictions between the Bush administration's rhetoric about democracy and its actual policies. In his novel *1984*, George Orwell wrote about a process that "in short, means protective stupidity"—an approach that involves "holding two contradictory beliefs in one's mind simultaneously, and accepting both of them." Among the semiconscious maneuvers are "to forget any fact that has become inconvenient, and then, when it becomes necessary again, to draw it back from oblivion for just so long as it is needed, to deny the existence of objective reality and all the while to take account of the reality which one denies—all this is indispensably necessary."[23] And so it was, as the much-hyped deadline of June 30, 2004, drew near, a benchmark at once farcical and very useful for White House strategists bent on perception management.

When the *New York Times* published an article on April 24 about its interview with "the top United States commander in the Middle East," the second sentence explained: "The commander, General John P. Abizaid, said the security situation was liable to worsen as June 30 approached, and with it the return of self-rule to Iraq." Lovely as it may have sounded in the news story, "the return of self-rule to Iraq" was no more scheduled for June 30 than the splashdown of a million-pound asteroid in the Tigris River. The editors of the *New York Times* did not need to be clairvoyant to adduce the evidence to that effect. On the day before the story appeared about the impending self-rule, all those editors needed to do was read the front page of their own newspaper—an article reporting that "the Bush administration's plans for a new caretaker government in Iraq would place severe limits on its sovereignty, including only partial command over its armed forces and no authority to enact new laws."[24]

For that matter, "partial command" was enough of a stretch to be an oxymoron, since—in effect—the U.S. government was insisting on the right to pretty much tell any Iraqi government what to do and not do with its own military. "Asked whether the new Iraqi government would have a chance to approve military operations led by American commanders, who would be in charge of both foreign and Iraqi forces, a senior official said Americans would have the final say," the *Times* reported in the same story, adding that an undersecretary of state, Marc Grossman, said "American commanders will 'have the right, and the power, and the obligation' to decide."[25]

The planet's only superpower was straining to tighten a grip on Iraq while turning concepts of national autonomy into national abnegation.[26] Not coincidentally, the same *New York Times* story that pegged "self-rule" for Iraq to June 30 appeared under the headline "General Says He May Ask for More Troops."[27]

During the 1960s, the ask-for-more-troops shuffle was a morbid art form in Washington as President Lyndon Johnson, General William Westmoreland, and the Joint Chiefs of Staff steadily upped the numbers of soldiers being packed off to Vietnam. During the spring and early summer of 1965, Johnson considered—and then decided to okay—a request from the Joint Chiefs of Staff to add 100,000 more troops to supplement the 75,000 already in some stage of Vietnam deployment. But at a news conference on July 28, Johnson dissembled and merely announced a decision to send an additional 50,000 soldiers. Nor did he disclose that deploying a total of approximately 400,000 troops in Vietnam was under serious consideration.

LBJ was heeding advice from something called a "Special National Security Estimate"—a secret document issued days earlier about the already-approved new deployment, urging that "in order to mitigate somewhat the crisis atmosphere that would result from this major U.S. action . . . announcements about it be made piecemeal with no more high-level emphasis than necessary."[28] Translation: Avoid upsetting the American public more than unavoidable.

Along with already choosing to escalate the troop levels to go appreciably higher than he was disclosing publicly, the president had decided to cross a policy Rubicon by committing the United States military to the goal of defeating the Communist Vietnamese forces in

South Vietnam. But at his July 28 press conference in 1965, Johnson denied that the new troop deployment he was announcing represented a significant shift. "It does not imply any change of policy whatever," he lied. "It does not imply any change of objective."[29]

History would record the spring of 2004 as a time when the Bush administration was not forthcoming about the outlook for American troop deployments in Iraq. Overall, the earmarks were plentiful for evasion on the subject, along the lines of the internal government recommendation four decades earlier about striving to "mitigate somewhat the crisis atmosphere" with low-key public statements. "We're going to make sure we have the right forces in place to do the job that needs to be done," General Abizaid told the *New York Times*. Promising "we'll see this thing through," he added: "We'll adjust to a combination of U.S. force levels, Iraqi readiness and steadiness, and coalition forces."[30]

Midway through 2003, the *Los Angeles Times* reported that top Pentagon officials "are studying the lessons of Iraq closely—to ensure that the next U.S. takeover of a foreign country goes more smoothly."[31] A high-ranking assistant to Defense Secretary Rumsfeld was upbeat. "We're going to get better over time," said Lawrence DiRita. "We've always thought of post-hostilities as a phase" apart from combat, but "the future of war is that these things are going to be much more of a continuum. . . . We'll get better as we do it more often."[32]

At about the same time, shortly before he was promoted to the job of *New York Times* executive editor, Bill Keller had this to say in an essay about the intelligence debacle on Iraq: "The truth is that the information-gathering machine designed to guide our leaders in matters of war and peace shows signs of being corrupted. To my mind, this is a worrisome problem, but not because it invalidates the war we won. It is a problem because it weakens us for the wars we still face."[33]

17

Withdrawal Would Cripple U.S. Credibility

Obsession with seeming unequivocal and immovable has been frequent in the Oval Office. During the Vietnam War, such fixations were indifferent to the fact that the war was losing the U.S. government moral credibility around the world. Yet from the outset, Lyndon Johnson invoked credibility as an argument for staying the course. "If we are driven from the field in Vietnam, then no nation can ever again have the same confidence in American promises, or in American protection," President Johnson said on July 28, 1965. Early the next year, when the Senate Foreign Relations Committee heard testimony from a legendary foreign-policy savant, there was this exchange with a senator from Iowa:

> *Senator Bourke Hickenlooper*: "Now, there are problems facing us and others. . . . How we disengage ourselves without losing a tremendous amount of face or position in various areas of the world."

> *George Kennan*: "Senator, I think precisely the question, the consideration that you have just raised is the central one that we have to think about; and it seems to me, as I have said here, that a precipitate, sudden, and unilateral withdrawal would not be warranted by circumstances now."[1]

Thirty-eight years later, in a *Time* cover story headlined "No Easy Options," the magazine noted that "calls for a pullout could increase" and then swiftly put its editorial foot down in the penultimate paragraph: "Foreign policy luminaries from both parties say a precipitous U.S. withdrawal would cripple American credibility, doom reform in the Arab world and turn Iraq into a playground for terrorists and the armies of neighboring states like Iran and Syria." The consensus range of alternatives would need to stay within the bounds of plunging deeper into a bloody vortex of war. For its several million readers, the nation's largest-circulation newsmagazine summed up with a question and a ready answer: "So when can the U.S. walk away? After last week's eruptions, the most this administration—or, should Kerry win in November, the next one—can hope for is that some kind of elected Iraqi government will eventually emerge from the wreckage, at which point the U.S. could conceivably reduce the number of its troops significantly. But getting there requires a commitment of at least several more months of American blood and treasure."[2]

Hedge words were plentiful: "the most" that could be hoped for was that "some kind" of elected Iraqi government would "eventually emerge," at which time the United States "could conceivably" manage to "reduce" its troop level in Iraq "significantly," although even that vague hope necessitated a commitment of "at least several more months" of Americans killing and dying. But in several more months, predictably, there would still be no end in sight—just another blank check for more "blood and treasure," on the installment plan.[3]

"Quagmire" is a word made famous during the Vietnam War. The invasion of Iraq and the subsequent occupation came out of a very different history, but there were some chilling parallels. One of them was that the editorial positions of major U.S. newspapers had an echo like a dirge.

At one end of the limited spectrum, the *Wall Street Journal* could not abide any doubts. Its editorials explained, tirelessly, that the Iraq invasion was Good and the occupation was Good—and those who doubted were fools and knaves (the rough modern equivalent of LBJ's "Nervous Nellies"). In 2004 the *Journal* editorial writers were fervently promoting a "war on terrorism" version of what used to be called the domino theory. Ultimately disproved by actual events, that theory—put forward as a momentous fact by supporters of the Vietnam War during the 1960s and early '70s—insisted that a U.S. defeat in Vietnam would set the dominos falling through Southeast Asia until the entire region and beyond went Communist. The day after the United Nations' Baghdad headquarters blew up in August 2003, the *Wall Street Journal* closed its latest gung-ho editorial by touting a quote from General John Abizaid: "If we can't be successful here, then we won't be successful in the global war on terror. It is going to be hard. It is going to be long and sometimes bloody, but we just have to stick with it."[4]

On the same day, the lead editorial of the *New York Times* insisted: "The Bush administration has to commit sufficient additional resources, and, if necessary, additional troops." The *Times* went on to describe efforts in Iraq as "now the most important American foreign policy endeavor."[5] In other words, the occupation that resulted from an entirely illegitimate invasion should be seen as entirely legitimate.

During the late 1960s, concerns about a "quagmire" grew at powerful media institutions. Following several years of assurances from the Johnson administration about the Vietnam War, rosy scenarios for military success were in disrepute. But here's a revealing fact: In early 1968, the *Boston Globe* conducted a survey of thirty-nine major U.S. daily newspapers and found that not a single one had editorialized in favor of U.S. withdrawal from Vietnam.[6] While millions of Americans were demanding an immediate pullout, such a concept was still viewed as extremely unrealistic by the editorial boards of big daily papers—including the liberal *New York Times* and *Washington Post*.

After more than a year of U.S. occupation warfare in Iraq, the editorial positions of major dailies were much more conformist than the American public. In midspring 2004, a *Wall Street Journal*/NBC poll was showing that "one in four Americans say troops should leave Iraq as soon as possible and another 30 percent say they should come home within 18 months."[7] But as usual, when it came to rejection of the latest war, the media establishment lagged way behind the populace. Despite sometimes-withering media criticism of the Bush administration's foreign policy, all of the sizable newspapers steered clear of urging withdrawal. Many favored sending in even more troops. On May 7, 2004, *Editor & Publisher* headlined a column by the magazine's editor this way: "When Will the First Major Newspaper Call for a Pullout in Iraq?"[8]

In September 2003, trying to justify Washington's refusal to let go of the occupation of Iraq, Colin Powell had used the language of a venture capitalist: "Since the United States and its coalition partners have invested a great deal of political capital, as well as financial resources, as well as the lives of our young men and women—and we have a large force there now—we can't be expected to suddenly just step aside."[9]

Over a span of thirteen months, there was a doubling of the number of Americans who viewed the Iraq war as a "mistake"—24 percent when the invasion began, 48 percent in April 2004.[10] In late June, a *USA Today*/CNN/Gallup poll found that 54 percent said so. "It is the first time since Vietnam that a majority of Americans has called a major deployment of U.S. forces a mistake," *USA Today* reported.[11] Given the swing of public sentiment against the war, the media's shortage of high-profile policy advocates calling for swift withdrawal of U.S. troops was notable.[12]

In effect, the war had to go on because the war had to go on—widely promoted as the least bad option, in contrast to the taboo of withdrawal. Meanwhile, a prerequisite for any Baghdad government to exist would be that it sufficiently satisfied the administration in Washington.

The fact that John Negroponte's diplomatic résumé included a stint in Vietnam got a positive spin at his confirmation hearing to be ambassador to the new U.S.-assembled Iraq government. "Senator after senator praised Mr. Negroponte for his willingness to take on a tough assignment after a long career that began as a junior Foreign Service officer in Saigon during the Vietnam War, a posting many said might prepare him for Iraq," the *New York Times* recounted.[13] He had gone on to be the U.S. ambassador to Honduras from 1981 to 1985. When Negroponte took the oath for his new post in late June 2004, Larry Birns at the Council on Hemispheric Affairs commented: "Rather than heading for Iraq, Ambassador Negroponte should be facing proceedings concerning his sanctioning of Honduran death squads, payoffs to venal Honduran military officials, violations of environmental procedures relating to a supply road construction project he was supervising, and a cover-up of the full scale of human rights violations that occurred in Honduras during his watch."[14] But Negroponte flew off to Baghdad unimpeded by his record in Tegucigalpa.

Pretense and realism were at war. Washington was preparing to hand over power to Iraqis while steadfastly refusing to do so; putting an Iraqi "face" on authority in Iraq while retaining ultimate authority in Iraq; striving for Iraqis to take up the burden of their country's national security while insisting that military control must remain in Uncle Sam's hands.

To some readers, the headline across the top of *USA Today*'s front page one day in June 2004 must have been reassuring: "New Leader Asks U.S. to Stay." The banner headline was a classic of occupation puppetry and media gimmickry. Iraq's "new leader" Iyad Allawi—selected and installed as prime minister by the U.S. government—had shown distinct reliability over the years. The *USA Today* story made only fleeting reference to Allawi's longtime U.S. entanglement, identifying him as "a Shiite close to the CIA."[15] The contradiction did not seem to trouble American media outlets, though they sometimes openly fretted that Iraqis might not be so accepting. Allawi "is the secretary general of the Iraqi National Accord, an exile group that has received funds from the Central Intelligence Agency," the *New York Times* reported. "His ties with the CIA and his closeness to the United States could become an issue in a country where public opinion has grown almost universally hostile to the Americans."[16] A separate *Times* article noted that Allawi "lived abroad for 30 years and is not well known in Iraq."[17] All in all, by Washington's lights, the man was eminently qualified to be Iraq's "new leader." And his superb judgment was immediately apparent: New leader asks U.S. to stay!

Major U.S. news media and politicians refused to challenge the Iraq war along the lines that activist historian Howard Zinn explored in 1967: "The only way we can stop the mass killing of civilians—of women and children—is to stop the war itself. We have grown accustomed to the distinction between 'ordinary' acts of war and 'atrocities,' and so came a whole host of international conventions setting up rules for mass slaughter. It was a gigantic fraud, enabling the normal horror of war to be accepted if unaccompanied by 'atrocities.' The Vietnam War, by its nature, does not permit this distinction. In Vietnam, the war *itself* is an atrocity. Since the killing of civilians is inevitable in our military actions in Vietnam, it cannot be called an 'accident' on the ground that nobody *intends* to kill civilians. The B-52 crews, the Marines and GIs moving through the villages, don't *plan* to kill civilians, but when bombs are dropped on fishing villages and sampans, when grenades are dropped down tunnels, when artillery is poured into a hamlet, when no one can tell the difference between a farmer and a Vietcong and the verdict is guilty until proved innocent, then the mass killing of civilians is inevitable. It is not deliberate. But neither is it an accident. It is not *part* of the war and so discardable. It *is* the war."[18]

In the midst of a deepening counterinsurgency war, with the Vietnamese population largely hostile to the U.S. military presence, the White House and editorialists insisted that withdrawal of soldiers from Vietnam was an irresponsible notion, a bumper-sticker idea lacking in realism. From the start, the pullout option was stigmatized as beyond reasonable discussion. Uncounted numbers of erudite commentators made fervent declarations very much like what *New York Times* columnist C. L. Sulzberger wrote in January 1963: "Come what may, we cannot afford to be driven ignominiously from Vietnam, where we have committed so much prestige, interest and treasure and are beginning tangibly to commit our blood."[19] Two years later, moderate accommodation to more war was passing for opposition: "In its editorials and in the opinions of its major columnists," Daniel Hallin writes, "the *Times* broke sharply with the administration early in 1965, calling for negotiation rather than escalation and decrying the secrecy that surrounded administration policy. But it never broke with the assumption that the cause of the war was Communist aggression and that—to quote [James] Reston—'the political and strategic consequences of defeat would [be] serious for the free world all over Asia.' The debate of 1965 . . . was a debate over tactics: there were some who favored escalation, some who favored negotiation, but very few in Congress, the press, the administration, and the 'establishment' generally who doubted that the United States had, in one way or another, to preserve South Vietnam as an outpost of the Free World."[20]

"Antiwar" politicians had ways of being circumspect. "We must face the fact that there is no quick or easy answer to Vietnam," Senator Robert F. Kennedy said on April 27, 1966;[21] even when he ran for president in the spring of 1968, RFK did not support quick withdrawal of U.S. troops from Vietnam.

The mainstream press went with the war flow. Countercurrents were mild. In August 1966, the owner of the *Washington Post* huddled with a writer in line to take charge of the newspaper's editorial page: "We agreed that the *Post* ought to work its way out of the very supportive editorial position it had taken, but that we couldn't be precipitate; we had to move away gradually from where we had been," Katharine Graham was to write (unapologetically) in her autobiography.[22] Many years of horrendous tragedies resulted from such unwillingness to "be precipitate." During the late '60s, after several years of assurances from the Johnson administration about the Vietnam War, rosy scenarios for military success were wilting. But the public emphasis was on developing a winnable strategy—not ending the war. Pull out the U.S. troops? The idea was unthinkable.

"Thus far," Zinn wrote in 1967, "almost all of the nationally known critics of our Vietnam policy—perceptive as they are—have been reluctant to call for the withdrawal of the United States from Vietnam." He believed that frequently "it is because these critics consider total military withdrawal, while logical and right, 'too extreme' as a tactical position, and therefore unpalatable to the public and unlikely to be adopted as national policy." The dynamic included journalists, politicians, and academics. "Scholars, who pride themselves on speaking their minds, often engage in a form of self-censorship which is called 'realism.' To be 'realistic' in dealing with a problem is to work only among the alternatives which the most powerful in society put forth. It is as if we are all confined to a, b, c, or d in a multiple-choice test, when we know there is another possible answer. American society, although it has more freedom of expression than most societies in the world, thus sets limits beyond which respectable people are not supposed to think or speak. So far, too much of the debate on Vietnam has observed these limits."[23]

With the Iraq war in its second year, the option of withdrawal was often derided with the pejorative "cut and run." The phrase had currency among a cross section of the war's supporters. Terry Anderson, the former Associated Press reporter who'd endured a six-year ordeal as a hostage in Lebanon until 1991, wrote an op-ed piece in spring 2004 declaring that the United States was duty-bound to stay in Iraq: "We cannot cut and run, as we did in Lebanon, Somalia, Sudan and Vietnam."[24] The reference to Vietnam was remarkable. The U.S. war there lasted a dozen years, causing fifty-eight thousand American deaths in Vietnam and upward of two million Vietnamese deaths. The magnitude of the bombardment was beyond comprehension. "Before we finished in Vietnam," according to author Ronald Bruce St. John, who was a U.S. serviceman in the war, "we had dropped more bombs on Indochina than had been dropped on the remainder of the world in all the wars to that time."[25] It's difficult to imagine what more Anderson wished the U.S. government had done to Vietnam in order to avoid the retrospective accusation that it had "cut and run."

When Anderson's essay appeared in the *Wall Street Journal*, the cover story of the latest *Newsweek* was "Crisis in Iraq: The Vietnam Factor." Near the top of the lead article, assistant managing editor Evan Thomas wrote that the president "did surprise reporters by appearing before them after meeting with the family of Army infantryman Chris Hill, killed by a bomb in the Iraq town of Fallujah. 'We've got to stay the course and we will stay the course,' said Bush, who appeared teary-eyed." The rest of the paragraph also spun ahead like a war press agent's dream: "Hill's father-in-law, Douglas Cope, had not been eager for the meeting with the president because, he told *Newsweek*, he was concerned that the encounter would be 'political.' But Cope reported that Bush was emotional and that the president told the dead soldier's family, 'I promise this job will be finished over there.' Cope added: 'That really was what I wanted to hear. We cannot leave this like Vietnam.'"[26]

Newsweek's Thomas wrote: "Not a quagmire, not yet. But the atmospherics have a distinctly familiar feel. At a recent Washington dinner party attended by some famous names from the foreign-policy establishment and the media elite, the conversation went something like this." The article proceeded to paraphrase the discourse:

Former Senior Administration Official: I had real doubts about going in there . . .

Echoes around the Table: Me too, me too, but . . .

Chorus: But we have to stay the course. We can't cut and run.

Lone Voice (who has imbibed one more, or perhaps one less, glass of wine than the others): Why not?

Chorus: American credibility!

"The exact same conversation," the article added, "could have been heard in a dozen Georgetown salons on almost any given weekend night from about 1966 to the winter of 1968, when the establishment decided that it was time to get out, one way or the other."[27]

While mocking the lemming-like trudge for war, the *Newsweek* spread also participated in it. And there was an unnoted irony in the article's claim that "the establishment decided that it was time to get out" of Vietnam in the winter of 1968; after all, the Vietnam War

went on for several years after that while the United States continued
to make war in Southeast Asia. As would be the case in 2004 with
U.S. forces in Iraq, the calcified wisdom of politics and media insisted
that withdrawal was not practical. Even when "the establishment
decided that it was time to get out," the elites were determined to take
their time; much more carnage would have to ensue. A key technique
for keeping the war going was to blast those who suggested otherwise
as less-than-honorable people eager to abandon sacred obligations. At
the start of what turned out to be his last spring as president, Lyndon
Johnson traveled to Minneapolis and delivered a speech that accused
war opponents of wanting to "tuck our tail and violate our commitments." Advocates of withdrawal from Vietnam, the president
declared, would "cut and run."[28]

For *Newsweek* in 2004, the way to close the main story of a
twenty-three-page "Vietnam Factor" spread was to quote the father
of a U.S. Army captain killed a year earlier in Iraq—"If my son
were here today, and I wasn't disabled, we'd both put our uniforms on
and say, 'Where to?'"—and then the dead man's mother. Her final
words: "I don't think you can go into a place and start something so
significant and just walk out. . . . As family members of soldiers
serving in wartime, we have to have faith. It's not blind faith, but it's
a deep faith."

That set up one last paragraph, from *Newsweek*'s reportorial
voice, telling readers what it all meant with a generalization that
winked at the further war to come in Iraq: "It is such faith that
sustains Americans and drives them forward. We do best when we
defend freedom without trampling it, defeat tyranny without becoming tyrannical, and understand what is worth the blood of our children and what is not. That is the true lesson of Vietnam."[29]

In fact, any number of "true lessons" of Vietnam could be cited—
including many diametrically opposed to each other. For Americans,
the Rorschach qualities of the U.S. experience in Vietnam made it sus-
ceptible to all kinds of conclusions. If the "lessons" were about trying
to make war better next time, then those who had drawn those particular conclusions were inclined to support letting others suffer the
consequences. When it became evident during the first few months of
2004 that the American troops in Iraq were fighting a counterinsurgency war against forces gaining strength, polls showed the U.S. public roughly split—the exact numbers, of course, varied depending on

how questions were phrased—about whether the continuing war was worthwhile. A month into the spring, assessing a new *Washington Post*–ABC News poll and a Gallup poll, the *Wall Street Journal* noted: "Both surveys found there is significant support for sending more troops to Iraq—a sentiment that the Gallup poll found actually has grown as the problems have gotten worse."[30] A confluence of political tendencies, including many conservative and liberal commentators, saw increasing the troop levels in Iraq as the least bad option; thus it seemed that the biggest "lesson of Vietnam" might be that no crucial lesson had been learned.[31]

As for what was actually going on in Iraq, a U.S. media focus on the trials and tribulations of the occupiers had the continuing effect of keeping at a psychological distance the people living and dying in their own country. Seen through the lenses of American media and politics, Iraq's big problem was that it was a problem for America.

"Regime change, occupation, nation-building—in a word, empire— are a bloody business," George Will wrote. "Now Americans must steel themselves for administering the violence necessary to disarm or defeat Iraq's urban militias, which replicate the problem of modern terrorism—violence that has slipped the leash of states."[32]

For the horrors that continued to result from unleashing the Pentagon's violence, the rationales were inexhaustible. "There are thugs and terrorists in Iraq who are trying to shake our will," presidential spokesman Scott McClellan told reporters. "And the president is firmly committed to showing resolve and strength."[33] With many Iraqis, liberated by the Americans, now taking up arms to liberate themselves *from* the Americans, the major players of the administration in Washington were on message. A day later, the man running the Pentagon echoed the White House. "We're facing a test of will," Donald Rumsfeld said, "and we will meet that test." The declaration was newsworthy enough for the main headline in the *New York Times*: "Iraqi Uprising Spreads; Rumsfeld Sees It as 'Test of Will.'"[34]

Donning the royal "we" mantle of the "civilized world," President Bush told a televised news conference: "Now is the time, and Iraq is the place, in which the enemies of the civilized world are testing the will of the civilized world. We must not waver." The crucial need was to not back down: "It's the intentions of the enemy to shake our will. That's what they want to do. They want us to leave. And we're not going to leave. We're going to do the job."[35] *New York Times* columnist Paul Krugman commented: "One of the real motives for the invasion of Iraq was to give the world a demonstration of American power. It's a measure of how badly things have gone that now we're told we can't leave because that would be a demonstration of American weakness."[36]

The writer James Baldwin challenged our desire to deny responsibility—what he called "the fraudulent and expedient nature of the American innocence which has always been able to persuade itself that it does not know what it knows too well."[37] Do we really not know that bombs financed by our tax dollars are turning life into death? Aren't we at least dimly aware that—no matter how smooth and easy the news media and elected officials try to make it for us—in faraway places there are people not so different than us who are being destroyed by what journalists and politicians glibly depict as necessary war?

Afterword

Red and swollen tears tumble from her eyes
While cold silver birds who came to cruise the skies
Send death down to bend and twist her tiny hands
And then proceed to target "B" in keeping with their plans
Khaki priests of Christendom interpreters of love
Ride a stone Leviathan across a sea of blood
And pound their feet into the sand of shores they've never seen
Delegates from the western land to join the death machine
And we send cards and letters.

The oxen lie beside the road their bodies baked in mud
And fat flies chew out their eyes then bathe themselves in blood
And super heroes fill the skies, tally sheets in hand
Yes, keeping score in times of war takes a superman
The junk crawls past hidden death its cargo shakes inside
And soldier children hold their breath and kill them as they hide
And those who took so long to learn the subtle ways of death
Lie and bleed in paddy mud with questions on their breath
And we send prayers and praises.[1]

—Joe McDonald, 1968

'Tis the time's plague when madmen lead the blind.[2]

—Gloucester in *King Lear*

Why, of course, the *people* don't want war. . . . But, after all,
it is the *leaders* of the country who determine the policy and
it is always a simple matter to drag the people along, whether it
is a democracy or a fascist dictatorship or a Parliament or a

Communist dictatorship. . . . [V]oice or no voice, the people can always be brought to the bidding of the leaders. That is easy. All you have to do is tell them they are being attacked and denounce the pacifists for lack of patriotism and exposing the country to danger. It works the same way in any country.[3]

—Hermann Goering, 1946

We have again been lied into war, a war as hopeless, unnecessary, and wrongful, as potentially endless and disastrous, as Vietnam. Again, almost surely, hundreds of officials who saw what was happening in just those terms, and who had a chance to avert it by informing Congress and the public of what they knew, with documents, chose not to do so. They kept their mouths shut, or repeated official lies, out of misguided loyalty to their bosses, to the president, to their agency and party—and to their own careers—over loyalty to the Constitution and their fellow citizens. If we're ever to escape from the deadly trap we're in, those values and that behavior must change, soon.[4]

—Daniel Ellsberg, 2004

On February 27, 1968, I sat in a small room on Capitol Hill. Around a long table, the Senate Foreign Relations Committee was in session, taking testimony from an administration official. Most of all, I remember a man with a push-broom mustache and a voice like sandpaper, raspy and urgent. Wayne Morse did not resort to euphemism. He spoke of "tyranny that American boys are being killed in South Vietnam to maintain in power." Moments before the hearing adjourned, the senior senator from Oregon said that he did not "intend to put the blood of this war on my hands." And Morse offered clarity that was prophetic: "We're going to become guilty, in my judgment, of being the greatest threat to the peace of the world. It's an ugly reality, and we Americans don't like to face up to it."

Near the end of the 1960s, drawing on a careful reading of secret documents and a reappraisal of firsthand observations, Daniel Ellsberg came to a breakthrough realization: "On the basis of the record ever since 1946, 'telling truth to presidents' privately, confidentially—what I and my colleagues regarded as the highest calling and greatest opportunity we could imagine to serve our country—looked entirely unpromising as a way to end our war in and on Vietnam. That conclusion challenged the premises that had guided my entire professional career. To read the continuous record of intelligence assessments and forecasts for Vietnam from 1946 on was finally to lose the delusion that informing the Executive Branch better was the key to ending the war—or to fulfilling one's responsibilities as a citizen. It appeared that only if power were brought to bear upon the Executive Branch from outside it, with the important secondary effect of sharing responsibility for later events more broadly, might the presidential preference for endless, escalating stalemate rather than 'failure' in Vietnam be overruled."[5]

It was not very tough to invade and quickly dominate a small country like Grenada or Panama, where resistance could be flattened with military might and subsequent goodies in exchange for elite collaboration. Except for some unlucky combatants and their loved ones, the American people tended to view such wars as easy. In the mid-1980s, Daniel Hallin commented that "the fear of repeating the Vietnam experience showed signs of giving way to a desire to relive it in an idealized form."[6] Whatever the circumstances, in the shadow of Vietnam, every subsequent U.S. war seemed to offer the opportunity to do it right, with less muss, less fuss, and more ease. Early in the 1990s, the Gulf War was, for the U.S. forces and the folks back home, mostly a war of air power. And near the end of the decade, the protracted bombing of Yugoslavia was the high-tech archetype of a very good American war waged overwhelmingly from the skies.

Yet the horrific and continuous air-war component of the Vietnam War had not sufficed to spare American troops the tactical need to fight on the ground, nor did it bring victory. And Americans expect to win—which is a key reason why President George W. Bush had some difficulty with Iraq as a campaign issue in 2004. The stream of revelations about prewar lies, turning into a flood with political impacts after the invasion phase of the war, would have counted for relatively little if not for (to use Paul Krugman's phrase) "how badly things have gone."[7] Failure to "win the peace" is failure to really triumph. For the White House and its domestic allies in the realms of government, media, think tanks, and the like, the political problem of war undergoes a shift after the Pentagon goes into action in earnest. Beforehand, it's about making the war seem necessary and practical; if the war does not come to a quick, satisfactory resolution, the challenge becomes more managerial so that continuation of the war will seem easier or at least wiser than cutting the blood-soaked Gordian knot.

Advocates for humanitarian causes might see the United States as a place where "madmen lead the blind." But that's a harsh way to describe the situation. Our lack of vision is in the context of a media system that mostly keeps us in the dark.

"We took space back quickly, expensively, with total panic and close to maximum brutality," war correspondent Michael Herr recalled about the U.S. military in Vietnam. "Our machine was devastating. And versatile. It could do everything but stop."[8]

War coverage becomes routine. Missiles fly, bombs fall. Live briefings—with talkative officers, colorful charts, and gray videos—appear on cable television, sometimes like clockwork, sometimes with sudden drama. The war is right in front of the American public and very far away.

When a country—particularly a democracy—goes to war, the tacit consent of the governed lubricates the machinery. Silence is a key form of cooperation, but the warmaking system does not insist on quietude or agreement. Mere self-restraint will suffice.

Post-9/11 fears that respond more affirmatively to calls for military attacks are understandable. Yet fear is not a viable long-term foundation for building democratic structures or finding alternatives to future wars. Despite news media refusals to be sufficiently independent, many options remain to invigorate the First Amendment while challenging falsehoods, demagoguery, and manipulations.

While going to war may seem easy, any sense of ease is a result of distance, privilege, and illusion. The United States has the potential to set aside the habitual patterns that have made war a frequent endeavor in American life.

There remains a kind of spectator relationship to military actions being implemented in our names. We're apt to crave the insulation that news outlets offer. We tell ourselves that our personal lives are difficult enough without getting too upset about world events. And the conventional war wisdom of American political life has made it predictable that most journalists and politicians cannot resist accommodating themselves to expediency by the time the first missiles are fired. Conformist behavior—in sharp contrast to authentic conscience—is notably plastic.

"Anyone who has the power to make you believe absurdities has the power to make you commit injustices," Voltaire wrote. The quotation is sometimes rendered with different wording: "As long as people believe in absurdities they will continue to commit atrocities."[9]

Either way, a quarter of a millennium later, Voltaire's statement is all too relevant to this moment. As an astute cliché says, truth is the first casualty of war. But another early casualty is conscience.

When the huge news outlets swing behind warfare, the dissent propelled by conscience is not deemed to be very newsworthy. The mass media are filled with bright lights and sizzle, with high production values and lower human values, boosting the war effort. And for many Americans, the gap between what they believe and what's on their TV sets is the distance between their truer selves and their fearful passivity.

Conscience is not on the military's radar screen, and it's not on our television screen. But government officials and media messages do not define the limits and possibilities of conscience. We do.

Notes

Prologue: Building Agendas for War

1. General Bruce Palmer Jr., who was commander of U.S. forces in the Dominican Republic during the invasion, wrote in his 1989 book *Intervention in the Caribbean* (Lexington: University Press of Kentucky, 1989) that U.S. ambassador William Tapley Bennett had rushed back to the Dominican Republic after cutting short a visit to his sick mother in the United States. "Bennett told me later how deeply and personally he felt affronted by the PRD's [the Bosch party's] coup attempt in his absence, and that . . . he was not about to let the PRD wiggle out of its self-inflicted predicament," recalled Palmer, who added that the ambassador "was under direct, urgent, and personal presidential instructions to take no chances" on the risk of "a Communist takeover." (p. 25) Former Colombian diplomat Clara Nieto wrote in her book *Masters of War* (New York: Seven Stories Press, 2003) that Bennett "had sent a hysterical communiqué to the State Department alleging that the lives of United States citizens were in danger and requesting that troops be sent to insure their evacuation." (p. 100)

2. Richard Goodwin, *New York Times*, February 8, 2004.

3. Alan McPherson, *Latin American Research Review*, University of Texas Press, June 1, 2003.

4. Johnson-Mann phone conversation, 9:35 A.M., April 26, 1965, quoted in Alan McPherson, *Latin American Research Review*, June 1, 2003. (According to McPherson, in the book *Reaching for Glory* presidential scholar Michael Beschloss erroneously dated this conversation as April 24.)

5. In the words of Patrick Breslin, a former foreign-policy research director at the Carnegie Endowment for International Peace, the pro-Bosch insurgents briefly faltered in Santo Domingo because "the officers they'd counted on to swing key bases behind them vacillated. Initiative swung to their enemies, who still controlled more men, all the tanks and planes in the country, and the navy. A merciless bombardment of the city began, softening it for the final blow, a tank-led sweep by a powerful infantry force across the Duarte Bridge. The coup's leaders threw in the towel, sought asylum in embassies. Only a couple remained, resigned to a pointless but honorable death among the leaderless soldiers and civilians being massacred at the Duarte Bridge. But at the bridge they found a population in arms, bottling up the army's tanks in narrow streets, resisting every foot of the advance. The attack stalled. At dusk on April 27, the army fled back across the bridge. For the first time in their history, the Dominican people had won. Their freedom lasted barely 24 hours." (Breslin's description appeared in his review of *The Dominican Crisis*, authored by Piero Gleijeses, in the *Washington Post Book World*, January 21, 1979.)

6. U.S. embassy cable quoted in Patrick Breslin, *Washington Post Book World*, January 21, 1979. Breslin noted that "Lyndon Johnson, who had represented the U.S. at Bosch's inauguration, gave the orders that crushed the revolt seeking to restore him to office."

7. McPherson, *Latin American Research Review*, June 1, 2003.

8. Jan Glidewell, *St. Petersburg Times*, September 16, 1994.

9. President Lyndon Johnson, April 30, 1965, quoted in McPherson, *Latin American Research Review*, June 1, 2003.

10. Johnson, May 2, 1965, quoted in McPherson, *Latin American Research Review*, June 1, 2003.

11. McPherson, *Latin American Research Review*, June 1, 2003.

12. John Bartlow Martin quoted in McPherson, *Latin American Research Review*, June 1, 2003.

13. Johnson-Martin phone conversation, 3:42 P.M., May 2, 1965, quoted in McPherson, *Latin American Research Review*, June 1, 2003.

14. John Quigley, *The Ruses for War* (New York: Prometheus Books, 1992), p. 136.

15. Johnson quoted by Murrey Marder, *Washington Post*, October 30, 1983.

16. Marder, *Washington Post*, October 30, 1983.

17. Assistant Secretary of State Thomas Mann quoted in Murrey Marder, *Washington Post*, October 30, 1983.

18. "After the military coup against João Goulart" in 1964, Clara Nieto wrote, "Brazil became a center for experimentation with sophisticated torture techniques taught by American agents. These methods were later applied in other countries." (Nieto, *Masters of War*, p. 155)

19. Juleyka Lantigua, Knight Ridder/Tribune News Service, April 29, 2000.

20. Nieto, *Masters of War*, p. 101.

21. Ibid.

22. In June 1966, Balaguer defeated Bosch and became president—a position he was to hold, on and off, for decades. "The Constitutionalists attributed their leader's defeat to a reign of terror against their followers," Sidney Lens wrote, "and Bosch's failure to leave his home to conduct an active campaign, for fear of being assassinated." (Sidney Lens, *The Forging of the American Empire* [Sterling, Va.: Pluto Press, 2003], p. 419) The Balaguer-Bosch rivalry continued; Bosch was never able to regain the presidency. Observing the 1990 election in the Dominican Republic, former president Jimmy Carter ignored fraud that resulted in the paper-thin "victory" margin for incumbent president Balaguer in a rematch with Bosch. Announcing that Balaguer's bogus win was valid, Carter used his prestige to give international legitimacy to the election.

23. *New York Times*, May 1, 1985. Five years later, when a news story in the same paper appeared under the headline "One Last Round for 2 Old Dominican Rivals" (*New York Times*, May 8, 1990), political analyst Noam Chomsky noticed some journalistic problems: "Reporting the Bosch-Balaguer 1990 election campaign in the Dominican Republic, [*Times* correspondent] Howard French tells us that Juan Bosch, 'a lifelong Marxist,' 'was removed from office in a military coup shortly after winning the country's first free elections, in 1963 [sic],' and that his rival, Joaquin Balaguer, defeated Bosch in the 1966 presiden-

tial election. Omitted are a few pertinent facts, among them: that there had been no prior free elections because of repeated U.S. interventions, including long support for the murderer and torturer Trujillo until he began to interfere with U.S. interests; that the 'lifelong Marxist' advocated policies similar to those of the Kennedy Democrats; that the U.S. was instrumental in undermining him and quickly backed the new military regime; that when the populace arose to restore constitutional rule in 1965, the U.S. sent 23,000 troops on utterly fraudulent pretexts to avert the threat of democracy, establishing the standard regime of death squads, torture, repression, slave labor conditions, increase in poverty and malnutrition, vast emigration, and wonderful opportunities for its own investors, and tolerating the 'free election' of 1966 only when the playing field had been leveled by ample terror." (Noam Chomsky, *Deterring Democracy* [New York: Hill and Wang, 1992], p. 72)

24. Associated Press, April 28, 1997.

25. Stephen J. Randall, *Latin American Research Review*, University of Texas Press, June 1, 2003.

26. Lantigua, Knight Ridder/Tribune News Service, April 29, 2000.

27. Associated Press, May 18, 2004.

28. During his presidential campaign in 1960, John F. Kennedy made claims that contrasted sharply with actual U.S. policies in many Western Hemisphere countries. For instance, his book *The Strategy of Peace* (New York: Popular Library, 1961) included the text of a speech to a dinner audience in Puerto Rico on December 15, 1958, when he stated: "I realize that it will always be a cardinal tenet of American foreign policy not to intervene in the internal affairs of other nations—and that this is particularly true in Latin America." (John F. Kennedy, *The Strategy of Peace*, p. 172) On March 16, 1964, scarcely a year before ordering the invasion of the Dominican Republic, President Lyndon Johnson declared: "Here, despite occasional conflict, we have peacefully shared our hemisphere to a degree unmatched by any nation, anywhere." Whatever the rationales or results, military intervention against small Caribbean countries boosted the measurable domestic popularity of U.S. presidents even at times when there might seem to be reasons to expect downturns in polling numbers. "After the April 1961 failure of the Bay of Pigs, John Kennedy's approval rating was four points higher than it had been in March," wrote Joan Didion. "After the 1965 intervention in the Dominican Republic, Lyndon Johnson's approval rating rose six points. After the 1983 invasion of Grenada, Ronald Reagan's approval rating rose four points, and what was that winter referred to in Washington as 'Lebanon'—the sending of American marines into Beirut, the killing of 241, and the subsequent pullout—was, in the afterglow of this certified success in the Caribbean, largely forgotten." (Joan Didion, *Fixed Ideas: America Since 9.11* [New York: New York Review of Books, 2003], pp. 33–34)

29. If there was a hiatus spanning several decades during which large numbers of U.S. military boots did not march into war in Latin America and the Caribbean, that was largely because other means were sufficient to get Washington enough of what it wanted—including acceptable economic relations and efficacious covert operations, whether involving bribes, disinformation campaigns, well-placed military aid, or counterinsurgency training. And there were

continuing benefits from the installation of dictators (often long-lived) with the help of U.S. military forces, especially when successors maintained or adapted a dynasty's ruthless grip. "Like the Somozas in Nicaragua, Trujillo [in the Dominican Republic] had come to power courtesy of an army created, trained, and equipped by the United States, left behind after a Marine Corps occupation in the 1920s," Patrick Breslin noted. (*Washington Post Book World*, January 21, 1979)

30. In 1988, George H. W. Bush was bedeviled by what media outlets called "the wimp factor." After eight years as vice president, Bush was making a run for the Oval Office. But quite a few journalists kept asking whether he was a tough enough man for the job. *Newsweek* even headlined the "wimp" epithet in a cover story about him. But the image problem faded in December 1989, when the U.S. invasion of Panama caused a familiar upward spike of war-driven acclaim for President George H. W. Bush. As commander in chief, he drew blood—proving to some journalists that he had the right stuff. A seasoned *New York Times* reporter, R. W. Apple, wrote that the assault on Panama was Bush's "presidential initiation rite"—as though initiating a war was mandatory evidence of leadership mettle. In contrast, the director of the Council on Hemispheric Affairs, Larry Birns, was wry instead of fawning: "The military action has more to do with White House fears of 'wimpdom' than any realistic threat to U.S. national security." (*Guardian*, December 21, 1989) Even later, while still ensconced in the White House, the senior Bush remained notably stung by the epithet. He couldn't always keep the pain of it under wraps. "You're talking to the 'wimp,'" President Bush commented on June 16, 1991. "You're talking to the guy that had a cover of a national magazine, that I'll never forgive, put that label on me."

31. *New York Times*, December 27, 1989.

32. Ibid.

33. Noam Chomsky's book *What Uncle Sam Really Wants* (Berkeley, Calif.: Odonian Press, 1993) includes these observations: "The U.S. government knew that Noriega was involved in drug trafficking since at least 1972, when the Nixon administration considered assassinating him. But he stayed on the CIA payroll. In 1983, a U.S. Senate committee concluded that Panama was a major center for the laundering of drug funds and drug trafficking. The U.S. government continued to value Noriega's services. . . . And yet, when Noriega was finally indicted in Miami in 1988, all the charges except one were related to activities that took place *before* 1984—back when he was our boy, helping with the U.S. war against Nicaragua, stealing elections with U.S. approval and generally serving U.S. interests satisfactorily. It had nothing to do with suddenly discovering that he was a gangster and a drug-peddler—that was known all along." (p. 51) Chomsky added: "It's all quite predictable, as study after study shows. A brutal tyrant crosses the line from admirable friend to 'villain' and 'scum' when he commits the crime of independence. One common mistake is to go beyond robbing the poor—which is just fine—and to start interfering with the privileged, eliciting opposition from business leaders. By the mid-1980s, Noriega was guilty of these crimes. Among other things, he seems to have been dragging his feet about helping the U.S. in the contra war. . . . Since we could no longer trust Noriega to do our bidding, he had to go. Washington imposed economic sanctions that virtually

destroyed the economy, the main burden falling on the poor nonwhite majority. They too came to hate Noriega, not least because he was responsible for the economic warfare (which was illegal, if anyone cares) that was causing their children to starve." (pp. 51–52)

34. Norman Bailey quoted in Haynes Johnson column, *Washington Post*, December 22, 1989. The "clear and incontrovertible evidence was, at best, ignored," Bailey testified, "and, at worst, hidden and denied by many different agencies and departments of the government of the United States in such a way as to provide cover and protection for [Noriega's] activities while, at the same time, assuring that they did the maximum damage to those very interests that the officials involved were sworn to uphold and defend."

35. John C. Lawn quoted in Alexander Cockburn, *St. Louis Post-Dispatch*, January 2, 1990. Cockburn's article first appeared on the editorial page of the *Wall Street Journal*, December 28, 1989. Lawn's letter was dated May 8, 1986.

36. Associated Press, June 19, 1986.

37. *Los Angeles Times*, June 14, 1986.

38. The Knight-Ridder news service reported: "When Noriega did not respond to a direct request from then-national security adviser Vice Admiral John Poindexter that he resign, the United States cut off aid to Panama, then leaked damaging classified documents about Noriega to the *New York Times* and NBC News." The U.S. move against Noriega was part of "a secret campaign of threats and intimidation" during 1985 and 1986 "against five Latin American governments in an effort to scuttle Central American peace talks and win support for the contras." (*Chicago Tribune*, May 10, 1987) Poindexter's demand for Noriega's resignation reportedly occurred in December 1985.

39. Noriega apparently mucked up some efforts to arm the Nicaraguan Contras. "Associates of retired Air Force Major General Richard Secord tried to buy Nicaraguan rebels $1.5 million worth of Soviet-bloc weapons originally purchased by the Peruvian navy, according to a published report," said an Associated Press dispatch (May 14, 1987). "However, the deal fell through because Panama decided to seize the shipment in retaliation for political pressure the Reagan administration was putting on that country to support pro-contra policies, according to an interview with an arms dealer published today in the *Miami Herald*."

40. Haynes Johnson, *Washington Post*, December 22, 1989. Johnson added: "During that period, Noriega had also worked out a secret partnership with Colombian drug lords. In time, he transformed Panama into a vast, secure base for drug smuggling. U.S. officials knew about these activities and cynically ignored them."

41. Judd Rose, *Nightline*, ABC, May 8, 1989.

42. United Press International, May 15, 1989.

43. Lawrence Eagleburger, United Press International, August 24, 1989.

44. United Press International, August 24, 1989.

45. *Boston Globe*, August 26, 1989.

46. Representative Dan Burton quoted in *Washington Times*, October 25, 1989.

47. Senator David Boren quoted in Associated Press, October 9, 1989.

48. *Washington Times*, December 19, 1989.

49. Quigley, *The Ruses for War*, p. 249. The National Assembly's "state of war" resolution on December 15, 1989, "was not Panama's first reference to a 'state of war' with the United States," Quigley wrote. Four months earlier, in August, "Panama's government declared that our military maneuvers created 'a state of imminent war,' although Bush did not make much of this statement. The December 15 resolution was, according to the *Christian Science Monitor* [December 20, 1989], more a statement that the United States had initiated an economic war than one of Panamanian intent to initiate a shooting war." (pp. 248–249)

50. *Washington Times*, December 19, 1989.

51. Peter Jennings, *World News Tonight*, ABC, December 20, 1989. In the same segment, correspondent John Martin reported: "Today's action marked the thirteenth time the United States has intervened in Panama in this century."

52. *Boston Globe*, December 21, 1989.

53. *El Pais*, December 25, 1989; translation in Quigley, *The Ruses for War*, p. 252. To the extent that the Panama Canal hung in the balance, the threat was not an immediate short-term danger but long-term and political. Shortly after the invasion, Noam Chomsky commented: "On January 1, 1990, most of the administration of the Canal was due to go over to Panama—in the year 2000, it goes completely to them. We had to make sure that Panama was in the hands of people we could control before that date." (*What Uncle Sam Really Wants*, p. 52)

54. Quigley, *The Ruses for War*, p. 252.

55. Bill Richardson, *World News Tonight*, ABC, December 20, 1989.

56. Senator George Mitchell quoted in *Los Angeles Times*, December 21, 1989.

57. Nicholas Mavroules quoted in *Boston Globe*, December 20, 1989.

58. Ron Dellums quoted in States News Service, December 20, 1989.

59. Representative Don Edwards quoted in *Los Angeles Times*, December 21, 1989.

60. Edward Rollins quoted in *Washington Post*, December 22, 1989.

61. United Press International, December 21, 1989.

62. Ibid.

63. Elias Canetti wrote several decades ago: "It is the first death which infects everyone with the feeling of being threatened. It is impossible to overrate the part played by the first dead man in the kindling of wars. Rulers who want to unleash war know very well that they must procure or invent a first victim. It need not be anyone of particular importance, and can even be someone quite unknown. Nothing matters except his death; and it must be believed that the enemy is responsible for this. Every possible cause of his death is suppressed except one: his membership of the group to which one belongs oneself." (Canetti quoted in Chris Hedges, *War Is a Force That Gives Us Meaning* [New York: Anchor Books, 2003], p. 145)

64. President George H. W. Bush, December 21, 1989.

65. Very few pundits with access to mainstream ink called attention to the U.S. president's contortions in chivalry. An exception was Alexander Cockburn, who wrote: "What insights does this give us into the actual range of Bush's sym-

pathies for outraged American womanhood? On November 2 [1989], Sister Diana Ortiz, a U.S. nun in the Ursuline Order, was kidnapped at gunpoint from the garden of the Belen Retreat House in Antigua, Guatemala. She was taken to a house guarded by policemen in Guatemala City and there beaten, sexually molested, and burned 111 times on her back with cigarettes while being asked about photographs her interrogators placed before her. Finally she was released, with the apology that she had been mistaken for someone else. Patti McSherry, reporting for the weekly *In These Times*, was told by the State Department on November 20 that the United States had filed no protest against this abduction and torture of a U.S. citizen because the case fell under Guatemalan jurisdiction." (*St. Louis Post-Dispatch*, January 2, 1990; reprinted from *Wall Street Journal*, December 28, 1989)

66. Associated Press, December 22, 1989.

67. *Washington Post*, December 23, 1989.

68. Ibid.

69. Associated Press in *Los Angeles Times*, December 22, 1989.

70. George H. W. Bush quoted in Associated Press, December 22, 1989.

71. *Washington Post*, December 23, 1989.

72. Colonel Mike Snell quoted in ibid.

73. Ibid.

74. General Maxwell Thurman, Associated Press, December 23, 1989.

75. *Boston Globe*, December 23, 1989.

76. *St. Louis Post-Dispatch*, December 23, 1989.

77. Ibid.

78. *Boston Globe*, December 23, 1989.

79. *Washington Times*, December 25, 1989.

80. *Jerusalem Post*, December 27, 1989.

81. *Times* (London), December 24, 1989.

82. Associated Press, December 24, 1989.

83. Cockburn, *St. Louis Post-Dispatch*, January 2, 1990; reprinted from *Wall Street Journal*, December 28, 1989.

84. *Toronto Globe & Mail*, January 8, 1990; cited in Chomsky, *Deterring Democracy*, p. 157.

85. *Christian Science Monitor*, December 29, 1989; cited in Chomsky, *Deterring Democracy*, p. 157.

86. Snell quoted in *St. Louis Post-Dispatch*, December 23, 1989.

87. *Boston Globe*, December 23, 1989.

88. Associated Press, January 23, 1990. The tamales were made out of farina, cornmeal, and lard. "Asked their street value, a [Pentagon] spokesman referred reporters to the Agriculture Department." (*Washington Post*, January 31, 1990)

89. *Nation*, February 12, 1990.

90. *New York Times*, June 7, 2004.

91. *New York Times*, October 27, 1983. The newspaper noted that eighteen years earlier, "when President Johnson sent Marines into the Dominican Republic, there was press coverage from the beginning."

92. *New York Times*, October 27, 1983.

93. Howard Simons quoted in *New York Times*, October 27, 1983.

94. President Reagan, October 25, 1983. Speaking to journalists, Reagan said that "American lives are at stake" and emphasized them: "Let me repeat, the United States objectives are clear: to protect our own citizens, to facilitate the evacuation of those who want to leave, and to help in the restoration of democratic institutions in Grenada."

95. See Didion, *Fixed Ideas*, p. 34.

96. Palmer, *Intervention in the Caribbean*, p. 190.

97. Quigley, *The Ruses for War*, pp. 136–137.

98. Ibid., pp. 204–210.

99. Ibid., pp. 249–250. The quote from Fred Hoffman appeared in *Newsweek*, June 25, 1990.

100. Ken Adelman, *Washington Post*, February 13, 2002. The op-ed piece was headlined "Cakewalk in Iraq."

101. Ken Adelman, *Washington Post*, April 10, 2003. The blurb at the end of Adelman's piece included a plug for a current entrepreneurial effort: "He now co-hosts TechCentralStation.com."

102. Days before their son ordered the start of the Iraq invasion, when a *Good Morning America* correspondent interviewed former President George H. W. Bush and Barbara Bush and asked about TV-watching habits, Mrs. Bush concluded her answer this way: "But why should we hear about body bags, and deaths, and how many, what day it's gonna happen, and how many this or what do you suppose? . . . It's not relevant. So why should I waste my beautiful mind on something like that? And watch him suffer." (ABC, March 18, 2003)

103. Nancy Snow, *Information War* (New York: Seven Stories Press, 2003), p. 22.

104. David Ogilvy, *Confessions of an Advertising Man* (New York: Ballantine, 1963), p. 79.

105. Colin Powell quoted in *Washington Post*, December 31, 2001. Powell knew Beers from the previous decade—they'd been on the corporate board of Gulfstream Aerospace together—and her reputation as an advertising genius obsessed with promoting brands was in sync with Powell's goals as secretary of state. He had been clear in testimony to the House Budget Committee a few weeks after George W. Bush became president: "I'm going to be bringing in people into the public diplomacy function of the [State] department who are going to change from just selling us in the old USIA way to really branding foreign policy, branding the department, marketing the department, marketing American values to the world and not just putting out pamphlets." (Testimony on March 15, 2001; quoted in Snow, *Information War*, pp. 84–85) In theory, for the most part, the agencies behind "public diplomacy" are not supposed to target U.S. citizens back home, but as a practical matter the public-relations efforts reach a domestic audience on a regular basis. American news media frequently report on U.S. "public diplomacy" efforts overseas, including the endeavors of taxpayer-financed TV and radio stations; the architects of such projects, widely interviewed and quoted in U.S. media, find their way to many platforms for conveying strong messages to Americans.

106. Charlotte Beers quoted in *Wall Street Journal*, October 15, 2001.

107. Alfred McClung Lee quoted in Snow, *Information War*, p. 25.

Chapter 1: America Is a Fair and Noble Superpower

1. Charles Krauthammer, *Time*, December 27, 1999.

2. *Fortune*, December 20, 1999.

3. Harold Evans, *Sunday Morning*, CBS News, December 26, 1999.

4. Krauthammer, *Weekly Standard*, June 4, 2001.

5. "A Year After Iraq War," Summary of Findings, Pew Research Center for the People & the Press, March 16, 2004.

6. Ibid. Survey data on responses to the Iraq war were indicative: "Americans have a far different view of the war's impact—on the war on terrorism and the global standing of the U.S.—than do people in the other surveyed countries. Generally, Americans think the war helped in the fight against terrorism, illustrated the power of the U.S. military, and revealed America to be trustworthy and supportive of democracy around the world. These notions are not shared elsewhere."

7. "A Year After Iraq War," Summary of Findings, Pew Research Center for the People & the Press, March 16, 2004. Meanwhile, at the same time that 31 percent of Americans and 41 percent of Brits said they thought the war was based on lies, the totals were much bigger in other nations: "Large majorities in almost every country surveyed think that American and British leaders lied when they claimed, prior to the Iraq war, that Saddam Hussein's regime had weapons of mass destruction."

8. Krauthammer, *Weekly Standard*, June 4, 2001.

9. Michael Ignatieff, *New York Times Magazine*, January 5, 2003.

10. Howard Zinn, foreword to *The Forging of the American Empire* by Sidney Lens (Sterling, Va.: Pluto Press, 2003), p. xii. Zinn coauthored *A People's History of the United States* (New York: Harper & Row, 1980).

11. *New York Times*, January 8, 1999.

12. For details on U.S. media avoidance of reporting on Washington's improper use of U.N. inspectors for spying, see *Target Iraq: What the News Media Didn't Tell You* by Norman Solomon and Reese Erlich (New York: Context Books, 2003), pp. 29–31 and pp. 75–76.

13. *Times* (London), March 5, 2003.

14. The *Washington Post* printed a 514-word article on a back page with the headline "Spying Report No Shock to U.N." Meanwhile, the *Los Angeles Times* published a longer piece, emphasizing from the outset that U.S. spy activities at the United Nations were "long-standing." For good measure, the piece reported "some experts suspected that it could be a forgery"—and "several former top intelligence officials said they were skeptical of the memo's authenticity." Within days, any doubt about the memo's "authenticity" was gone. The British press reported that the U.K. government had arrested an unnamed female employee at a British intelligence agency in connection with the leak. By then, however, the spotty coverage in the mainstream U.S. press had disappeared. In fact—except for a high-quality detailed news story by a pair of *Baltimore Sun* reporters that appeared in that newspaper on March 4, 2003—there isn't an example of mainstream U.S. news reporting on the story at the time that was worthy of any pride. The U.S. media treatment contrasted sharply with coverage on other continents. "While some have taken a ho-hum attitude in the U.S., many around the world are furious," said Ed Vulliamy, one of the *Observer* reporters who broke the

story. "Still, almost all governments are extremely reluctant to speak up against the espionage. This further illustrates their vulnerability to the U.S. government." (News release, Institute for Public Accuracy, March 4, 2003) The *Observer*'s exposé, headlined "Revealed: U.S. Dirty Tricks to Win Vote on Iraq War," came eighteen days before the invasion of Iraq began. By unveiling a top-secret U.S. National Security Agency memo, the newspaper provided key information when it counted most: before the war began.

For fifty-one weeks—from the day that the *Observer* broke the news about spying at the United Nations until the moment that British prosecutors dropped charges against whistle-blower Katharine Gun—major news outlets in the United States almost completely ignored the story. Even though—or perhaps especially because—the memo was from the U.S. government and showed that Washington was spying on U.N. diplomats, the American media showed scant interest. In mid-November, for the first time, Katharine Gun's name became public when the British press reported that she'd been formally charged with violating the draconian Official Secrets Act. Appearing briefly at court proceedings, she was a beacon of moral clarity. Disclosure of the NSA memo, Gun said, was "necessary to prevent an illegal war in which thousands of Iraqi civilians and British soldiers would be killed or maimed." And: "I have only ever followed my conscience." A search of the comprehensive LexisNexis database finds that for nearly three months after her name was first reported in the British media, U.S. news stories mentioning her scarcely existed. Again, with the notable exception of the *Baltimore Sun* (which ran an in-depth news article about Gun and Daniel Ellsberg on February 1, 2004), the best and the brightest—as well as the worst and the dimmest—mainstream U.S. news departments simply proceeded as though Katharine Gun were a nonperson and the U.N. spying a nonstory. Until charges were dropped in late February 2004, when her name did appear in U.S. dailies it was almost always on an opinion page. The *Baltimore Sun* printed an op-ed piece that I wrote about her case on December 14, 2003 (and the article appeared days later in the *Boston Globe* and a few other papers). The *New York Times* printed a very fine opinion piece about her, by columnist Bob Herbert (January 19, 2004), and syndicated columnist Molly Ivins wrote an uplifting essay about Gun (*Fort Worth Star-Telegram*, February 15, 2004). Belatedly and laudably, NPR's *Morning Edition* aired an eloquent commentary by Ellsberg on February 25, 2004, the same day charges were dropped against her. It could be safely assumed that Adolfo Aguilar Zinser, a former Mexican ambassador to the United Nations, did not speak lightly when he made a strong statement that appeared in an Associated Press dispatch from Mexico City on February 12, 2004: "They are violating the U.N. headquarters covenant." He was referring to officials of the U.S. government.

Chapter 2: Our Leaders Will Do Everything They Can to Avoid War

1. George H. W. Bush, *New York Times*, August 19, 1988. Bush was giving his acceptance speech to the Republican National Convention.

2. George H. W. Bush, *Washington Post*, August 9, 1990.

3. Part of Jesse Jackson's statement was quoted in *Regardie's Magazine*, December 1990. Full quote is in Norman Solomon, *The Power of Babble* (New York: Dell, 1992), pp. 214–215.

4. General William Westmoreland, *Nightline*, ABC News, October 19, 1990.

5. Daniel Ellsberg quoted in Norman Solomon and Jeff Cohen, *Wizards of Media Oz: Behind the Curtain of Mainstream News* (Monroe, Maine: Common Courage Press, 1997), p. 197. The book added (p. 198): "Ironically, Ellsberg singled out two of the worst 1990 offenders: the *New York Times* and the *Washington Post*"—the first two newspapers to publish the Pentagon Papers in 1971.

6. President Lyndon Johnson, August 10, 1964.

7. Vice President Hubert Humphrey, February 17, 1965.

8. Johnson, May 17, 1966.

9. Humphrey, March 1967.

10. Johnson, January 17, 1968.

11. I. F. Stone, *Polemics and Prophecies, 1967–1970* (New York: Vintage Books, 1972), p. 120.

12. Ibid.

13. President Richard Nixon, November 3, 1969.

14. H. R. Haldeman, Oval Office tapes, June 14, 1971; quoted in Daniel Ellsberg, *Secrets: A Memoir of Vietnam and the Pentagon Papers* (New York: Viking, 2002), p. 413. Haldeman's comment attributed the point to Donald Rumsfeld, then a young staffer at the White House.

15. Ellsberg, *Secrets*, pp. 415–416.

16. Nixon, Ziegler, Kissinger, White House tapes, April 25, 1972; quoted in ibid., p. 418.

17. Nixon, Oval Office tapes, May 4, 1972; quoted in Ellsberg, *Secrets*, p. 419.

18. Nixon, November 3, 1969.

19. Leslie added: "For the first time in my Vietnam tour, the daily news briefings, labeled 'the four o'clock follies,' got interesting, though certainly no more informative. One reporter asked an Air Force briefer if he was 'ashamed' of hiding the truth from the American people; it was a bold question even though its premise was dubious, since it implied that the Air Force normally conveyed truth." (Jacques Leslie, *The Mark: A Memoir of Vietnam* [New York: Four Walls Eight Windows, 1995], p. 111)

20. Ellsberg, *Secrets*, p. 420.

21. Leslie, *The Mark*, p. 123.

22. In late January 1973, with the war officially about done, "Saigon again swelled with a thousand journalists, gorging on the agreement's complications and willing to pretend that the war was truly ending," Leslie wrote. "*Newsweek* had jumped the gun, having run a 'Goodbye Vietnam' cover . . . two months earlier; now all the newspapers carried their special Vietnam supplements and war histories. It was ethnocentrism, nothing more: Americans perceived the war as over because Americans would no longer fight it." (*The Mark*, p. 128) Though U.S. taxpayers continued to finance a war that was to go on for over two more years, they saw a drastic shift in media coverage. "As anticipated, the most significant change set in motion by the ceasefire was to remove American soldiers from direct involvement, but without them, combat continued to flourish; indeed, casualties among Communist and ARVN troops were significantly higher during the first two months of the ceasefire than during the comparable period of

the previous year, when no ceasefire was in effect. This fact appeared to matter little to the news editors of America, who reasoned that if Americans weren't fighting, the war wasn't worth covering, or at least not to the same extent, anyway." (*The Mark*, pp. 173–174) Among the American POWs released from captivity in North Vietnam, many had been badly treated and some had been tortured. Yet Jacques Leslie was one of the few American journalists who did not share the enthusiasm for the massive coverage that their repatriation was accorded in the U.S. media: "The first prisoner story I covered provoked Pavlovian drools of anticipation in most American journalists, but it left me indifferent: the POWs were coming home. I hated being a cog in the POW publicity machine, for it seemed to me that their welfare had taken precedence over the greater suffering of the Vietnamese. The POWs were the props on which American policy was based; we'd traded in the war for them. They were 500 men on one side of an equation that on the other side comprised hundreds of thousands of lives, all expended so that they could be freed. They were said to have suffered horribly, to have been tortured, but so many of the stories I read about them confused Vietnamese torture with American culture shock, with the American incapacity to believe that fish and rice was the diet of a significant portion of the world's people, not just of POWs, that I was skeptical of the claims. Anyway, weren't the POWs military men who accepted capture as a risk of their profession, weren't most of them officers caught bombing the North? What did they expect? They were the American fig leaf, obscuring our lack of purpose in Vietnam." (*The Mark*, p. 157) In diametrical contrast to the huge American media attention to the POWs released by the North Vietnamese, there was scant coverage of the conditions endured by Vietnamese prisoners being held by Thieu's regime, based in Saigon. "Most stories on political prisoners—people imprisoned for their political beliefs rather than for the commission of a crime—focused on whether there were hundreds of thousands of them, as Thieu's opponents extravagantly claimed, or none, as Thieu just as preposterously asserted," Leslie wrote. "I gathered that 40,000 to 70,000 was a reasonable estimate, but I found the debate unilluminating, as if accountants had defined its terms. The Thieu government unquestionably held thousands of people without trials or sentences, and, according to some claims, tortured many of them." (*The Mark*, p. 160) Leslie got into a hospital prison ward in Quang Ngai province, and he was deeply troubled to find that prisoners were routinely subjected to horrible, sadistic treatment by the United States–backed South Vietnamese government: "In the name of freedom the United States gave license to torture, a fact which surely many Americans were not prepared to face." (*The Mark*, p. 164)

23. On May 19, 2003, President Bush denounced "killers who can't stand peace." In that particular instance, Bush was referring to people who had engaged in deadly attacks that took the lives of Israeli civilians. But a similar description could be applied to Israeli government leaders who ordered attacks that predictably took the lives of Palestinian civilians. And while Bush had become fond of denouncing "killers"—using the word righteously—the same word could be applied to him and other top officials in Washington. Such a harsh assessment would undoubtedly come from thousands of Iraqi people who lost their loved ones to the U.S. invasion and the occupation that followed.

24. Karl von Clausewitz, *On War*, quoted in George Seldes, ed., *The Great Quotations*, p. 161. Clausewitz wrote that "war is an instrument of policy; it must necessarily bear the character of policy; it must measure with policy's measure." (*On War* [New York: Modern Library, 1943], p. 601)

25. Rambouillet text, "Appendix B: Status of Multi-National Military Implementation Force," archived at United States Institute of Peace library, Peace Agreements Digital Collection: Kosovo.

26. Ibid.

27. The April 16, 1999, news release from the Institute for Public Accuracy also noted: "Some have said that the Serbian parliament 'voted to be bombed' because it refused NATO troops as outlined in Rambouillet. But the *New York Times* has reported (April 8) that 'just before the bombing, when [the Serbian parliament] rejected NATO troops in Kosovo, it also supported the idea of a United Nations force to monitor a political settlement there.' Did the administration start bombing because it rejected the idea of a U.N. force and insisted on a NATO one? Has that insistence blocked the recent German peace plan?"

28. For details on what occurred when Amy Goodman and Jeremy Scahill declined their citation from the Overseas Press Club, see article by Norman Solomon, "American Media Dropping Ball as U.S. Is Dropping Bombs," *Palm Beach Post*, May 9, 1999. Though some attending journalists left the event under the impression that Richard Holbrooke would be answering questions from Goodman and Scahill privately later that evening, a recording of the postevent encounter documented that he did not do so.

29. The dual discourse about the United Nations alternately involves surface deference and underlying contempt, which right-wing U.S. administrations are more inclined to vent publicly. President Ronald Reagan spoke frankly the day after the U.N. General Assembly rebuked the U.S. government for invading Grenada. The vote was 108 to 9 in favor of a resolution "deeply deploring" the military intervention. Reagan responded: "One hundred nations in the United Nations have not agreed with us on just about everything that's come before them where we're involved, and it didn't upset my breakfast at all." (*Washington Post*, November 4, 1983) Two decades later, the same President George W. Bush who had made a major production out of seeking U.N. Security Council support for invading Iraq was pleased to tell the American public that he would never wait for a "permission slip" from foreigners before going to war. Generally, the outlooks of top officials and most pundits in Washington are predictable: U.N. resolutions approved by the Security Council are very important if the White House says so. Otherwise, the resolutions have little or no significance, and they certainly can't be allowed to interfere with the flow of American economic, military, and diplomatic support to any of Washington's allies. And the United Nations can be extremely "relevant" or "irrelevant," depending on the circumstances; when the United Nations serves as a useful instrument of U.S. foreign policy, it is a vital world body taking responsibility for the future and reaffirming its transcendent institutional vision; but when the United Nations balks at serving as a useful instrument of U.S. foreign policy, its irrelevance is so obvious that it risks collapsing into the dustbin of history. (See Norman Solomon and Reese Erlich, *Target Iraq: What the News Media Didn't Tell You* [New York: Context

Books, 2003], pp. 73–74) Rage is audible in Washington when the United Nations fails to assist with some major goals of U.S. foreign policy. Frustrated at a lack of bloodshed after disputes between the United States and Iraq, columnist Charles Krauthammer was apoplectic in a November 1998 essay, deriding U.N. Secretary-General Kofi Annan as "the head of a toothless bureaucracy that commands no army, wields no power and begs for revenue." What's worse, Annan's diplomacy stalled the U.S. war machine. "It is perfectly fine for an American president to mouth the usual pieties about international consensus and some such," Krauthammer wrote. "But when he starts believing them, he turns the Oval Office over to Kofi Annan and friends." (*Time*, November 30, 1998)

It's a notable setback when the U.S. government doesn't get its way in the balloting at the Security Council of the United Nations. Customarily, if the White House is determined to win a "good warmaking seal of approval" from the Security Council, the U.S. diplomatic apparatus hands out sizable goodies and brandishes hefty threats. There are plenty of economic and political favors that Washington can do—and foreign aid can be withdrawn when a U.N. ambassador votes the wrong way. The independent British journalist John Pilger wrote about an episode at the Security Council shortly before the Gulf War began in January 1991: "Minutes after Yemen voted against the resolution to attack Iraq, a senior American diplomat told the Yemeni ambassador: 'That was the most expensive No vote you ever cast.' Within three days, a U.S. aid program of $70 million to one of the world's poorest countries was stopped. Yemen suddenly had problems with the World Bank and the IMF; and 800,000 Yemeni workers were expelled from Saudi Arabia. . . . When the United States sought another resolution to blockade Iraq, two new members of the Security Council were duly coerced. Ecuador was warned by the U.S. ambassador in Quito about the 'devastating economic consequences' of a No vote. Zimbabwe was threatened with new IMF conditions for its debt." (*New Statesman*, September 23, 2002) After the Security Council adopted its Iraq resolution of November 8, 2002, U.N. analyst Phyllis Bennis wrote that "the impoverished nation of Mauritius emerged as the latest poster child for U.S. pressure at the U.N. The ambassador, Jagdish Koonjul, was recalled by his government for failing to support the original U.S. draft resolution on Iraq. Why? Because Mauritius receives significant U.S. aid, and the African Growth and Opportunity Act requires that a recipient of U.S. assistance 'does not engage in activities that undermine U.S. national security or foreign policy interests.'" (*Nation*, December 2, 2002)

30. Fareed Zakaria, *Newsweek*, September 2, 2002.

31. *Washington Post*, January 21, 2003.

32. For an assessment of Powell's February 5, 2003, presentation to the U.N. Security Council and the media coverage it generated, see Michael Massing, *Now They Tell Us: The American Press and Iraq* (New York: New York Review of Books, 2004), pp. 56–60.

33. FAIR, "Media Advisory: Bush Uranium Lie Is Tip of the Iceberg," July 18, 2003.

34. Ambassador Adlai Stevenson quoted in Stone, *Polemics and Prophecies*, p. 308.

35. American journalists didn't confront Powell with basic questions like: (1)

You cite Iraq's violations of U.N. Security Council resolutions to justify the U.S. launching a war. But you're well aware that American allies such as Turkey, Israel, and Morocco continue to violate dozens of Security Council resolutions. Why couldn't other nations claim the right to militarily "enforce" the Security Council's resolutions against countries they'd prefer to bomb? (2) You insist that Iraq is a grave threat to the other nations of the Middle East. But, with the exception of Israel, no country in the region has made such a claim or expressed any enthusiasm for a war on Iraq. If Iraq is a serious threat to the region, why doesn't the region feel threatened? (3) You say that the Iraqi regime is committed to aggression. Yet Iraq hasn't attacked any country for more than twelve years. And just eight days before Iraq's invasion of Kuwait on August 2, 1990, the U.S. envoy to Baghdad gave what appeared to be a green light for the invasion when she met with Saddam Hussein. An Iraqi transcript of the meeting quotes Ambassador April Glaspie: "We have no opinion on your Arab-Arab conflicts, such as your dispute with Kuwait. Secretary [of State James] Baker has directed me to emphasize the instruction . . . that Kuwait is not associated with America." Mr. Powell, why don't you ever mention such information? (4) Washington tilted in favor of Iraq during its war with Iran in the 1980s. Like other U.S. officials, you emphasize that Saddam Hussein "gassed his own people" and used chemical weapons against Iran, but you don't talk about the intelligence data and other forms of assistance that the United States provided to help Iraq do such things. If the history of Baghdad's evil deeds is relevant, why aren't facts about U.S. complicity also relevant? (5) When you warn that the U.N. Security Council "places itself in danger of irrelevance" if it fails to endorse a U.S.-led war on Iraq, aren't you really proclaiming that the United Nations is "relevant" only to the extent that it does what the U.S. government wants? . . . If Colin Powell had faced such questions on a regular basis, his media halo might have become tarnished before the Iraq invasion started. But tacit erasure of inconvenient history—including his own—was integral to the warm relationship between Powell and U.S. news media. There was a lot to erase. For instance, in January 1986, serving as a top aide to Pentagon chief Caspar Weinberger, he supervised the transfer of 4,508 TOW missiles to the CIA, then sought to hide the transaction from Congress and the public. No wonder: Almost half of those missiles had become part of the Iran-Contra scandal's arms-for-hostages deal. As President Reagan's national security adviser, Powell worked diligently on behalf of the Contra guerrillas who were terrorizing and killing civilians in Nicaragua.

36. Randeep Ramesh, ed., *The War We Could Not Stop: The Real Story of the Battle for Iraq* (London: Faber & Faber, 2003), p. 34.

37. Mary McGrory, *Washington Post*, February 6, 2003.

38. Richard Cohen, *Washington Post*, February 6, 2003.

39. Jim Hoagland, *Washington Post*, February 6, 2003. Fifteen months later, Hoagland wrote: "The administration's original case for invading and occupying Iraq has been dismantled almost piece by piece. The large stockpiles of weapons of mass destruction that were presumed to be there have not been found." (*Washington Post*, May 20, 2004)

40. Editorial, *Washington Post*, February 6, 2003.

41. Editorial, *New York Times*, February 6, 2003.

42. President Bill Clinton quoted by United Press International, November 15, 1998.

43. George Will, Charles Krauthammer, and Richard Cohen, *Washington Post*, November 17, 1998.

44. *New York Times*, November 16, 1998.

45. James R. Schlesinger quoted in *New York Times*, July 30, 2002.

46. Once set, a disastrous course is apt to be maintained for a very long time. A year after the invasion, there was nothing unusual about the way President Bush closed his high-profile news conference on April 13, 2004, in the midst of escalating carnage in Iraq. "One thing is for certain, though, about me," he said, "and the world has learned this: When I say something, I mean it. And the credibility of the United States is incredibly important for keeping world peace and freedom." Maintaining a resolute image of determination becomes an end in itself, no matter how false the claims or horrific the consequences. "A free Iraq will confirm to a watching world that America's word, once given, can be relied upon, even in the toughest times," Bush said at the same news conference. Reacting to such comments, *Slate*'s chief political correspondent, William Saletan, wrote: "To Bush, credibility means that you keep saying today what you said yesterday, and that you do today what you promised yesterday. . . . The only words and deeds that have to match are his. No correspondence to reality is required. Bush can say today what he said yesterday, and do today what he promised yesterday, even if nothing he believes about the rest of the world is true." (*Slate*, April 14, 2004)

47. John Bolton quoted in *Observer*, August 4, 2002.

48. *Wall Street Journal*, July 26, 2002. The headline: "No Declaration of War Needed."

49. *USA Today*, August 6, 2002; *New York Times*, August 6, 2002.

50. *New York Times*, August 6, 2002.

51. *USA Today*, August 6, 2002.

52. Scott Ritter, news release, Institute for Public Accuracy, July 29, 2002.

53. Scott Ritter, *Newsday*, July 30, 2002.

54. Richard Butler, Senate Foreign Relations Committee hearing, July 31, 2002, FDCH transcripts.

55. Andrew Card quoted in *New York Times*, September 7, 2002.

56. *Columbia Journalism Review*, July/August 2003, p. 26.

57. The president had strong domestic political incentives to keep "wagging the puppy" while floating a variety of unsubstantiated claims—like references to wispy dots that implausibly connected the Iraqi dictatorship and Al Qaeda. Propelled with countless semi-assertions, insinuations, and subsequently discredited "evidence" from administration officials and some media outlets, the groundless belief in a link between the Saddam Hussein regime and Al Qaeda was to persist. A year after the fall of Saddam, according to a poll conducted by the University of Maryland's Program on International Policy Attitudes, 57 percent of Americans said that Saddam's regime had provided "substantial support" to Al Qaeda or believed the Baghdad government had direct involvement in 9/11. (*Washington Post*, April 25, 2004) Two months later, despite the just-released findings by the official 9/11 commission that "no credible evidence" linked Saddam Hussein to the September 11 attacks, *USA Today* (June 25, 2004) reported that "44 per-

cent of those surveyed say they think Saddam was personally involved in 9/11."

58. George Shultz, *Washington Post*, September 6, 2002. Eighteen months later, Shultz filled most of the *Wall Street Journal*'s editorial page with the essay "An Essential War," which never acknowledged the falsity of the unequivocal prewar claims he and so many others had joined the Bush administration in making about weapons of mass destruction. "The question of Iraq's presumed stockpile of weapons will be answered," Shultz wrote obliquely, "but that answer, however it comes out, will not affect the fully justifiable and necessary action that the coalition has undertaken to bring an end to Saddam Hussein's rule over Iraq." (March 29, 2004)

59. For a detailed analysis of key U.S. newspapers' editorials during the early 2003 run-up to the Iraq invasion, see Chris Mooney, "The Editorial Pages and the Case for War," *Columbia Journalism Review*, March/April 2004.

60. The *Wall Street Journal*'s dismissive comment was later quoted in the March/April 2004 issue of the *Columbia Journalism Review* (p. 31), which noted that the denial "now appears to have been the truth."

61. Christopher Hitchens, *A Long Short War* (New York: Plume, 2003), p. 67. The essay first appeared on February 13, 2003.

62. Senator John Kerry, *Hardball*, MSNBC, October 2, 2002.

63. "No more Vietnams!" exclaimed Representative Rod Chandler on January 11, 1991, just before voting to authorize the U.S. government to lead a coalition into launching the Gulf War. Former secretary of state Alexander M. Haig has said that the U.S. policy in Vietnam "was bad because if we decided to shed one drop of American blood, it should be under a formula in which we had intended to take all of the actions necessary to win—and win decisively and promptly." (January 30, 1988)

64. George W. Bush, March 17, 2003.

Chapter 3: Our Leaders Would Never Tell Us Outright Lies

1. Daniel Ellsberg, *Secrets: A Memoir of Vietnam and the Pentagon Papers* (New York: Viking, 2002), p. 41. Ellsberg, who began working as special assistant to Assistant Secretary of Defense McNaughton in early August 1964, added: "The lies themselves didn't bother me, but there were several cases that year when I thought a false story was so likely to be found out that it made me nervous. My worry was nearly always misplaced; the cover story held surprisingly long." When Secretary of Defense Robert McNamara visited Vietnam for the first time, in May 1962, he came back saying that he'd seen "nothing but progress and hopeful indications of further progress in the future." (Howard Zinn, *Vietnam: The Logic of Withdrawal* [Cambridge, Mass.: South End Press, 2002], p. 41) In October 1966, McNamara held a press conference at Andrews Air Force Base after returning from a trip to Vietnam; he spoke of the progress he had seen there—a presentation that, according to Ellsberg, occurred "minutes after telling me that everything was much worse than the year before." (*Secrets*, photo caption) Such duplicity, with a relentlessly upbeat public face, is routine from the president on down. A few weeks after the Gulf of Tonkin Resolution, campaigning to remain president, Lyndon B. Johnson proclaimed on September 16, 1964: "Somehow or other, optimist that I am, I just believe that peace is coming nearer." The following spring,

LBJ ordered massive escalation of the war. Two years later, in early 1967, with warfare going full throttle, Johnson declared from a podium in Omaha: "Peace is more within our reach than at any time in this century." (I. F. Stone, *Polemics and Prophecies, 1967–1970* [New York: Vintage Books, 1972], p. 79) Giving new meaning to the term "happy warrior," Vice President Hubert Humphrey talked about the Vietnam War to the U.S. embassy staff during a visit to Saigon: "This is our great adventure, and a wonderful one it is." (United Press International, October 31, 1967) In early April 2004, while an insurrection raged in numerous Iraqi cities, a spokesman for the U.S. chief administrator in Iraq told reporters: "We have isolated pockets where we are encountering problems." (*New York Times*, April 5, 2004; Dan Senor was speaking for L. Paul Bremer III) President George W. Bush was also straining to minimize: "It's not a popular uprising. Most of Iraq is relatively stable. Most Iraqis by far reject violence and oppose dictatorship." (April 13, 2004) With the occupation of Iraq entering its second year, the need to replenish public support for the war was as strong as—and more desperate than—ever. Such agenda-building is a continuous process, from the first trial balloon until the last shot is fired.

2. George W. Bush, Associated Press, February 25, 2002.

3. Donald Rumsfeld, *Washington Post*, February 27, 2002.

4. Donald Shepperd quoted in *St. Louis Post-Dispatch*, February 27, 2002.

5. Ellis Henican, *Newsday*, February 27, 2002.

6. Maureen Dowd, *New York Times*, February 20, 2002.

7. Lucy Dalglish quoted in *Chicago Tribune*, February 27, 2002.

8. Lieutenant Colonel Karen Kwiatkowski, *Hijacking Catastrophe* film, 2004.

9. Quoted in Martin A. Lee and Norman Solomon, *Unreliable Sources: A Guide to Detecting Bias in News Media* paperback edition (New York: Carol Publishing Group, 1991), p. xviii.

10. Tariq Aziz quote was transcribed from author's tape recording.

11. A few months later, when U.S. forces took Tariq Aziz into custody, the *Houston Chronicle* quoted two sentences from me in an April 27, 2003, editorial: "Aziz epitomized the urbanity of evil. He was articulate and deft at rationalizing government actions that caused enormous suffering." But the daily newspaper's editorial did not quote the next sentence of my statement, which had appeared in a news release from the Institute for Public Accuracy: "His similarities to top U.S. officials are much greater than we're comfortable acknowledging." That sort of point was pretty much taboo in U.S. mass media coverage, which sometimes included vehement tactical arguments about the Bush administration's war—but not about the prerogatives of Washington to intervene militarily around the world. A basic media assumption is that leaders in the United States are cut from entirely different cloth than the likes of Tariq Aziz. But in some respects, the terrible compromises made by Aziz seem more explainable than the ones that are routine in U.S. politics. Aziz had good reason to fear for his life—and the lives of loved ones—if he ran afoul of Hussein. In contrast, many politicians and appointed officials in Washington have gone along with lethal policies merely because of fear that dissent might cost them reelection, prestige, or power.

12. On July 1, 2004, prisoner Tariq Aziz appeared before an Iraqi judge in a courtroom on a U.S. military base near the Baghdad airport. Aziz said: "What I

want to know is, are these charges personal? Is it Tariq Aziz carrying out these killings? If I am a member of a government that makes the mistake of killing someone, then there can't justifiably be an accusation against me personally. Where there is a crime committed by the leadership, the moral responsibility rests there, and there shouldn't be a personal case just because somebody belongs to the leadership." And Aziz added: "I never killed anybody, by the acts of my own hand." (*New York Times*, July 2, 2004)

13. News releases that debunked Bush administration WMD claims at the time they were made are archived on the Web site of the Institute for Public Accuracy, www.accuracy.org.

14. The U.S. media failure on the subject of WMDs and Iraq went beyond factual matters to encompass basic attitudes. The Washington press corps implicitly accepted as proper a U.S. government stance of extreme hypocrisy. Nuclear weapons were a case in point, as noted in *Target Iraq: What the News Media Didn't Tell You* (Norman Solomon and Reese Erlich, New York: Context Books, 2003): "When chief U.N. inspector Hans Blix arrived in Baghdad on November 18, 2002, his comments included expressing hope for 'a zone free of weapons of mass destruction in the Middle East as a whole.' That's not a concept that gets much news coverage in the United States, and this instance was no exception; a search of all the major U.S. daily papers in the Nexis database found Blix's statement quoted only by the *Washington Post* (and paraphrased by the *Atlanta Journal-Constitution*). Yet, as the *Scotsman* newspaper reported the same day, Blix was referring to 'the Security Council's original measures in the wake of the Gulf War of 1991, which in theory outlined a nuclear-free zone to cover Iraq's neighbors Iran and particularly Israel.'" One of Blix's predecessors as the U.N. chief weapons inspector, Richard Butler, made some critical statements about the superpower's approach to nuclear weapons in the early fall of 2002 after returning home to Australia: "My attempts to have Americans enter into discussions about double standards have been an abject failure even with highly educated and engaged people. . . . Amongst my toughest moments in Baghdad were when the Iraqis demanded that I explain why they should be hounded for their weapons of mass destruction when, just down the road, Israel was not, even though it was known to possess some 200 nuclear weapons." (*Target Iraq*, pp. 53–54)

15. Author interview with John Barry, February 25, 2003.

16. *Newsweek*, March 3, 2003.

17. Reuters, February 24, 2003; *Birmingham Post*, February 25, 2003.

18. Author interview with Seth Ackerman, February 26, 2003; also, FAIR, "Media Advisory: Star Witness on Iraq Said Weapons Were Destroyed," February 27, 2003.

19. Vice President Dick Cheney quoted in *National Review*, August 27, 2002.

20. It was routine for major U.S. media outlets to misrepresent the December 1998 departure of U.N. weapons inspectors from Iraq by erroneously reporting that the Iraqi government had ejected them. (Prominent distortion of the historical record continued well past the invasion, thanks to many political figures and journalists. Midway through July 2003—even while *Time*'s latest cover was asking "Untruth & Consequences: How Flawed Was the Case for Going to War Against Saddam?"—the president told reporters: "The fundamental question is,

did Saddam Hussein have a weapons program? And the answer is, absolutely. And we gave him a chance to allow the inspectors in, and he wouldn't let them in. And, therefore, after a reasonable request, we decided to remove him from power." (July 14, 2003) Bush's assertion about Hussein and the inspectors—that he "wouldn't let them in"—was out of touch with historic reality. Some journalists gingerly noted that the statement was false. But the media response was mild. The president openly uttering significant falsehoods was no big deal. Likewise, there was no stir when the main anchor of CBS's *60 Minutes* made a similar false statement on June 20, 2004. In a voice-over for footage that accompanied an interview with Bill Clinton tied to his memoirs, Dan Rather told viewers: "President Clinton points out that when Saddam Hussein kicked U.N. weapons inspectors out of Iraq in 1998, he ordered a four-day bombing raid, but was unable to find out how many, if any, chemical and biological weapons were destroyed in those attacks.") Actually, the inspectors left Iraq in December 1998 under orders from UNSCOM head Richard Butler just before the days of U.S. bombing dubbed Operation Desert Fox. But later, with notable disregard for historical facts, many reporters at leading news organizations flatly asserted that Saddam Hussein had "expelled" or "kicked out" the U.N. inspectors at that time. Among the purveyors of that misinformation during the last months of 2002 were Daniel Schorr of National Public Radio (August 3), John Diamond of *USA Today* (August 8), John McWethy of *ABC World News Tonight* (August 12), John King of CNN (August 18), John L. Lumpkin of the Associated Press (September 7), Randall Pinkston of *CBS Evening News* (November 9), Betsy Pisik of the *Washington Times* (November 14), and Bob Woodward of the *Washington Post* (November 17). An editorial in the *Washington Post* (August 4, 2002) declared: "Since 1998, when U.N. inspectors were expelled, Iraq has almost certainly been working to build more chemical and biological weapons."

21. Kenneth Pollack, *Weekend All Things Considered*, NPR News, November 10, 2002.

22. Bill Keller memo quoted in *Editor & Publisher*, May 26, 2004.

23. Ibid.

24. FAIR memo, May 27, 2004.

25. Faith in Ahmad Chalabi was hardly confined to *New York Times* correspondents or to other staff reporters at mainstream outlets. Independent journalist Christopher Hitchens, in contrast to his image of feisty skepticism, was so enthralled that he dedicated his book about the Iraq invasion to Chalabi, along with three others; Hitchens included Chalabi among those he called "comrades in a just struggle and friends for life." (*A Long Short War* [New York: Plume, 2003], p. vi) Given Chalabi's record of dishonesty, Hitchens could have chosen his friends—and sources—more carefully.

26. For an in-depth look at Ahmad Chalabi as a consummate dissembler, see Jane Mayer's article "The Manipulator" in the *New Yorker*, June 7, 2004.

27. *New York Times*, May 26, 2004.

Chapter 4: This Guy Is a Modern-Day Hitler

1. President Lyndon Johnson, July 28, 1965, quoted partially in Daniel Ellsberg, *Secrets: A Memoir of Vietnam and the Pentagon Papers* (New York:

Viking, 2002), p. 94, and in Daniel C. Hallin, *The "Uncensored War": The Media and Vietnam* (Berkeley: University of California Press, 1989), p. 60.

2. Silber quoted by Associated Press, March 2, 1984.

3. President George H. W. Bush quoted in *New York Times*, August 16, 1990.

4. William Pfaff, *Chicago Tribune*, August 15, 1990.

5. "In a *New York Times*/CBS News poll conducted August 16–19 [1990], 77 percent of those interviewed supported the decision to deploy troops, planes and ships to the Persian Gulf." (*St. Petersburg Times*, September 1, 1990)

6. *St. Petersburg Times*, September 1, 1990.

7. Charles Osgood, *CBS This Morning*, October 16, 1990.

8. George H. W. Bush, Burlington, Vermont, October 23, 1990.

9. George H. W. Bush, ABC News, October 23, 1990.

10. General William Westmoreland, *Nightline*, ABC News, October 19, 1990.

11. The April 27, 1987, edition of the *New Republic* published an article by Daniel Pipes and Laurie Mylroie titled "Back Iraq: It's Time for a U.S. Tilt." The writers contended that Washington should lean even more favorably toward Iraq in its war with Iran, arguing that "Iraq is now the de facto protector of the regional status quo." And they declared: "If our tilt toward Iraq is reciprocated, moreover, it could lay the basis for a fruitful relationship in the longer term."

12. Mary McGrory, *Seattle Post-Intelligencer*, January 15, 1992.

13. David Nyhan, *Boston Globe*, January 20, 1999.

14. Sylvia Poggioli, *Nieman Reports*, Fall 1993.

15. Misha Glenny, *The Fall of Yugoslavia*, 3rd rev. ed. (New York: Penguin Books, 1996), p. 123.

16. Ibid., pp. 284–285.

17. Carl Bildt quoted in Misha Glenny, *The Fall of Yugoslavia*, p. 285.

18. President Bill Clinton quoted in column by Charles Krauthammer, *Pittsburgh Post-Gazette*, March 27, 1999.

19. *Washington Post*, March 25, 1999.

20. Marlin Fitzwater quoted in *Washington Post*, March 27, 1999.

21. Ibid.

22. Jim Hoagland, *Washington Post*, March 28, 1999. The column made some observations that should have given pause to enthusiasts. "The technology, skill and strategy that protect NATO pilots in Kosovo stoke the Serb-ignited fires of destruction that claim the lives and homes of the province's rebellious Albanian majority," he wrote. "The initial costs of NATO's air intervention in Kosovo's civil war now include the indiscriminate massacre of Kosovar Albanians by Serb forces."

23. *Newsday*, March 28, 1999.

24. Associated Press, April 1, 1999.

25. Ibid.

26. "This is the repetition of the acts of Hitler in World War II," said Sam Gejdenson, a member of Congress from Connecticut. (Associated Press, April 26, 1999)

27. Christopher Matthews, *Albany (N.Y.) Times Union*, April 2, 1999.

28. *Providence Journal-Bulletin*, April 7, 1999.

29. Ibid.

30. Clarence Page, *Chicago Tribune*, April 14, 1999.

31. David Nyhan, *Boston Globe*, April 23, 1999.

32. Page, *Chicago Tribune*, April 14, 1999.

33. Michael Dobbs, *Washington Post*, May 16, 1999. Dobbs added: "Over-simplistic comparisons between Kosovo and Bosnia or Milosevic and Hitler have helped transform what would otherwise have been a Balkan crisis into a global crisis, the ramifications of which are being felt from Moscow to Beijing. Administration officials claim that they acted to forestall a new round of ethnic cleansing by Milosevic against Kosovo Albanians. Yet, even if their worst fears were realized, it is hard to see how they could be any more nightmarish than what has already come to pass: nearly 800,000 refugees; another 500,000 people internally displaced within Kosovo; thousands, possibly tens of thousands, murdered; Macedonia destabilized; relations with Russia and China severely strained."

34. *New York Daily News*, June 22, 1999.

35. After the 2003 invasion, on the day news broke about the capture of Saddam Hussein (December 14, 2003), CBS's Lesley Stahl and ABC's Peter Jennings each interviewed Secretary of Defense Donald Rumsfeld. In step with their mainstream media colleagues, both failed to ask about Rumsfeld's cordial 1983 meeting with Hussein in Baghdad on behalf of the Reagan administration that opened up strong diplomatic and military ties between the U.S. government and the dictator, ties that lasted through seven years of his worst brutality.

36. Representative Christopher Shays, *The Abrams Report*, MSNBC, October 2, 2002.

37. Like quite a few of his colleagues, Shays could not resist making Hitler references part of his standard sound bites. A few weeks before he voted for the war resolution, the *Hartford Courant* (September 24, 2002) reported that in Shays's southwestern Connecticut district "the calls continue to be overwhelmingly against strong military action." But the congressman was on the war train: "Remember the 1930s, Shays said. Leaving Hussein alone would be akin to 'saying let Hitler have Czechoslovakia,' the appeasement strategy of the pre–World War II era that did not work." The fact that Saddam's Iraq had not invaded any country in a dozen years—and showed no sign of doing so—was beside the rhetorical point.

38. Tom Lantos, October 2, 2002. While many American politicians resorted to Hitler analogies, very few had the added punch that Lantos brought to bear. An Associated Press article (April 26, 1999) identified him as "a Hungarian Jew who is the only Holocaust survivor in Congress."

39. Jay Garner, United Press International, July 18, 2003.

40. Norman Mailer, "The White Man Unburdened," *New York Review of Books*, July 17, 2003.

Chapter 5: This Is about Human Rights

1. During the first week of the bombing of Yugoslavia in spring 1999, the U.S.-based Committee to Protect Journalists released its annual report, "Attacks on the Press." The committee disclosed that "for the fifth consecutive year, Turkey held more journalists in prison than any other country." Among the twenty-seven Turk-

ish journalists behind bars as the year began, "most are victims of the government's continued criminalization of reporting on the 14-year-old conflict with Kurdish insurgents in Turkey's southeast." That conflict involved what could be called "ethnic cleansing," the charge that was the key rationale for the United States–led NATO bombardment of Kosovo and Serbia. In fact, the government of Turkey— lauded by Washington as an important member of NATO—had engaged in torture and murder for many years. Of course, rationalizations for such actions were always available, whether in Ankara or Belgrade. By almost any measure, the crimes of the Turkish government in its treatment of Kurds were even more terrible and widespread than those of Serbs in Kosovo. But the missiles were exploding in Belgrade, not in Ankara. To depart from their own propaganda functions, major U.S. media outlets could have insisted on pursuing tough questions, such as: If humanitarian concerns were so high on Washington's agenda, why drop bombs on Yugoslavia and provide assistance to Turkey's government?

2. Irene Khan, Amnesty International annual report, May 28, 2003.

3. Khan quoted in Agence France Presse, May 26, 2004.

4. Noam Chomsky, *The Chomsky Reader* (New York: Pantheon Books, 1987), p. 306.

5. *New York Times*, May 17, 1998.

6. Ibid., June 2, 1998.

7. Ibid., May 16, 1998.

8. Ibid., May 17, 1998.

9. President Jimmy Carter quoted in *Washington Post*, December 7, 1978.

10. *Wall Street Journal*, February 10, 1982.

11. *Newsweek*, November 2, 1992; *Newsday*, February 16, 1993.

12. *New York Times*, September 15, 1988.

13. In news coverage of El Salvador, the phrase "human rights abuses on both sides" appeared, for instance, in stories by the *Washington Post* (June 2, 1985) and the Associated Press (May 13, 1987).

14. Secretary of State George Shultz, February 5, 1984.

15. *60 Minutes*, CBS, May 26, 1996.

16. Author interview with Robert Parry, June 3, 1996.

17. Katharine Graham, *Personal History* (New York: Vintage Books, 1997), p. 617.

18. For background on his reporting for *Newsweek* about the CIA's covert funding of the Nicaraguan Catholic Church as part of efforts against the Sandinistas, see Robert Parry's *Lost History* (Arlington, Va.: The Media Consortium, 1999), pp. 135–136. The Robert Gates memoir is *From the Shadows* (New York: Simon & Schuster, 1996).

19. Author interviews with Parry, April 1997.

20. *New York Times*, November 5, 1987.

21. In a typical speech, on May 9, 1984, President Reagan put out the fabled story line: "The Sandinista rule is a Communist reign of terror. Many of those who fought alongside the Sandinistas saw their revolution betrayed; they were denied power in the new government, some were imprisoned, others exiled. Thousands who fought with the Sandinistas have taken up arms against them and are now called the contras. They are freedom fighters." Without the slightest

documentation, in a speech the next year to the American Bar Association (July 8, 1985), Reagan flatly declared "the Communist regime in Nicaragua" to be a partner in "a campaign of international terror."

22. President Ronald Reagan, June 9, 1982.

23. Associated Press, June 11, 1991.

24. *New Statesman*, March 4, 1994.

25. Ibid.

26. Author interview with John Stauber, January 6, 2004. The Congressional Human Rights Caucus held the informal hearing on October 10, 1990. The fifteen-year-old girl, identified as "Nayirah," was actually the daughter of Saud Nasir al-Sabah, Kuwait's ambassador to the United States. Stauber, coauthor with Sheldon Rampton of *Weapons of Mass Deception* (New York: Jeremy P. Tarcher, 2003), commented on the political success that Lantos continued to enjoy in a left-leaning congressional district: "Given his cheap propaganda trick on behalf of the Kuwait ruling family in 1990, and his blind allegiance to the gross Bush deceptions that sold the attack on Iraq in 2003, one wonders if his constituents will ever hold him accountable as a war propagandist."

27. President George H. W. Bush, Burlington, Vermont, October 23, 1990.

28. Mary McGrory, *Seattle Post-Intelligencer*, January 15, 1992.

29. *St. Louis Post-Dispatch*, January 9, 1992.

30. Mary McGrory, *Seattle Post-Intelligencer*, January 15, 1992.

31. *NewsHour with Jim Lehrer*, PBS, February 20, 2001.

32. See Graham, *Personal History*, especially pp. 433, 615, and 616.

Chapter 6: This Is Not at All about Oil or Corporate Profits

1. President George H. W. Bush, transcript, Federal News Service, August 15, 1990.

2. George H. W. Bush, transcript, Federal News Service, October 16, 1990.

3. George H. W. Bush, Burlington, Vermont, October 23, 1990.

4. Global arms sales figures, compiled in "Conventional Arms Transfers to Developing Nations," are released annually by the Congressional Research Service. Reporting on data for 2003, the *New York Times* (August 30, 2004) said that the study "is considered the most authoritative compilation of statistics on global sales of conventional weapons that is available to the public." In second place behind the United States was Russia, with $4.3 billion in global arms sales, about 30 percent of the U.S. total. Germany came in third, with $1.4 billion in sales.

5. Senator Warren Rudman, January 12, 1991.

6. Richard Cohen, *Washington Post*, February 25, 2003.

7. Fadel Gheit's comments appeared in the *Toronto Star*, September 19, 2004, in an article by Linda McQuaig adapted from her book *It's the Crude, Dude: War, Big Oil, and the Fight for the Planet* (Toronto: Doubleday Canada, 2004).

8. Linda McQuaig, *Toronto Star*, September 19, 2004, adapted from *It's the Crude, Dude*. McQuaig added: "The disadvantaged position of U.S. oil companies in Saddam Hussein's Iraq would have presumably been on the minds of senior oil company executives when they met secretly with Cheney and his task force

in early 2001. The administration refuses to divulge exactly who met with the task force, and continues to fight legal challenges to force disclosure. However a 2003 report by the General Accounting Office, the investigative arm of Congress, concluded that the task force relied on advice from the oil industry, whose close ties to the Bush administration are legendary. (George W. Bush received more money from the oil and gas industry in 1999 and 2000 than any other U.S. federal candidate received *over the previous decade.*)" Emphasis in original.

9. Individual personal interests often overlap with the needs of multibillion-dollar military suppliers as a huge revolving door swings between the federal government and Pentagon contractors. Citing a just-released study by the nonprofit Project on Government Oversight, the Inter Press Service reported (June 29, 2004): "The group examined the current top 20 federal government contractors from January 1997 through May 2004 and found that in fiscal year 2002, those top 20 contractors received over 40 percent of the 244 billion dollars in total contracts awarded by the federal government. The group says that it also identified 291 instances involving 224 high-ranking government officials who moved to the private sector to serve as lobbyists, board members or executives of the contractors."

10. "America's chief of public relations" was a subheadline; *New York Times*, April 30, 2004. The article's headline was "Promoter of U.S. Image Quits for Wall St. Job."

11. *Newsweek*, April 19, 1999.

12. Sylvia Poggioli, preface, *Attacks on the Press in 1998*, Committee to Protect Journalists.

13. George Orwell quoted in Michael Shelden, *Orwell: A Biography* (New York: HarperCollins, 1991), p. 367.

14. Herbert Schiller, *Culture, Inc.: The Corporate Takeover of Public Expression* (New York: Oxford University Press, 1989), p. 8.

15. *San Francisco Chronicle*, March 13, 2004.

16. Ibid.

17. For example, *USA Today* reported (June 15, 2004) that the Iraq war "has lifted sales of: gas masks from Mine Safety Appliances; bio-weapons detection kits and training from Response Biomedical; air cargo from Atlas Air; port dredging by JDC Soil Management; packaging by TriMas; body armor and vehicle protection kits from Armor Holding; telecom services and communications gear from Globalnet, CopyTele and I-Sector." But while the war boosted profits for many military contractors and some other firms, other sectors of the economy took hits. According to the same newspaper article: "The war led to sharp decreases in business and leisure travel, say air carriers, travel services, casino operators, restaurant chains and hotel owners."

18. Dennis Sunshine, Orbit International Corp., Annual Report 2003, p. 1.

19. Orbit International Corp., Form 10-KSB, Securities and Exchange Commission, for fiscal year ending December 31, 2003, p. 12.

20. Engineered Support Systems, Inc., 2003 Annual Report, p. 2 (pullout).

21. Ibid., p. 5.

22. Ibid., p. 7.

23. Northrop Grumman, 2003 Annual Report, p. 3.

24. Ibid., p. 4.

25. Engineered Support Systems, Inc., 2003 Annual Report, p. 6.

26. Chris Hedges, *What Every Person Should Know About War* (New York: Free Press, 2003), p. 5.

27. Raffi Khatchadourian, *Nation*, November 17, 2003. The article added: "Putin's 1999 vow to 'rub them out in the shithouse' was the magic combination of determination and vulgarity that his electorate, so desperate for order, wanted to hear. However, his sledgehammer approach in the rebellious province has proven disastrous. This fall's 'election' in Chechnya, designed to give the war-weary region a veneer of normalcy, was a Kremlin-orchestrated farce."

28. Khatchadourian, *Nation*, November 17, 2003.

29. Ibid.

30. Ibid. Khatchadourian wrote that "days later, as the violence became too significant to ignore, the State Department quietly expressed concern that 'problems cast doubt on the credibility of the election results.'"

Chapter 7: They Are the Aggressors, Not Us

1. Justice Robert L. Jackson, Statement on War Trials Agreement, August 12, 1945, U.S. Department of State Bulletin (The Avalon Project at Yale Law School).

2. Senator Wayne Morse, footage in documentary film *The Last Angry Man*, produced by Christopher Houser and Robert Millis (Square Deal Productions).

3. Vice President Hubert Humphrey, January 6, 1967.

4. President Lyndon Johnson, May 11, 1966.

5. Ibid., January 17, 1968.

6. Daniel C. Hallin, *The "Uncensored War": The Media and Vietnam* (Berkeley: University of California Press, 1989), p. 188.

7. Senator Bill Bradley, April 15, 1991.

8. Senator Jesse Helms, July 26, 1991.

9. Law Professors for the Rule of Law, Stanford, California (www.the-rule-of-law.com).

10. Amnesty International Secretary-General Irene Khan, May 28, 2003.

11. I. F. Stone, *Polemics and Prophecies, 1967–1970* (New York: Vintage Books, 1972), p. 88.

12. Ibid.

13. *Newsweek*, March 8, 1999.

14. Howard Dean campaign statement, November 16, 2003.

15. Howard Zinn, news release, Institute for Public Accuracy, November 25, 2003. Zinn, author of *A People's History of the United States* (New York: Harper & Row, 1980), added: "In 1962, while trying to show that there were precedents for the use of armed force against Cuba, Secretary of State Dean Rusk produced for a Senate committee a list titled 'Instances of the Use of United States Armed Forces Abroad, 1798–1945.' It listed 103 interventions between 1798 and 1895 alone."

16. Richard Norton Smith quoted in *New York Times*, April 14, 2004.

17. *New York Times*, April 23, 2004.

18. *New Republic* associate editor Ryan Lizza, *New York Times*, April 23, 2004.

19. *Time*, April 19, 2004.

20. Mike Wallace, CBS, April 12, 1967, quoted in Hallin, *The "Uncensored War,"* p. 161.

21. During the last year of his life, Martin Luther King Jr. repeatedly made the identical statement—"I never intend to adjust myself to the madness of militarism"—for example, near the close of a speech at Ohio Northern University on January 11, 1968 (text archived at Heterick Memorial Library, Ohio Northern University).

Chapter 8: If This War Is Wrong, Congress Will Stop It

1. Daniel C. Hallin, *The "Uncensored War": The Media and Vietnam* (Berkeley: University of California Press, 1989), p. 16.

2. Captain John J. Herrick quoted in Hallin, *The "Uncensored War,"* p. 17.

3. James Stockdale quoted in *Chicago Tribune*, April 27, 1990. His next words were: "Not a conspiracy, but a hysterical mix-up. I reported that, and Washington received it promptly, but we went to war anyway." See also Jim and Sybil Stockdale, *In Love and War* (New York: Harper & Row, 1984), pp. 3–36. In September 1965, Stockdale was shot down over North Vietnam; he remained a POW for 7½ years. Two decades after his release, Stockdale was the vice presidential candidate on the 1992 ticket with Ross Perot.

4. *Washington Post* news analysis quoted in Hallin, *The "Uncensored War,"* pp. 15–16. The article was by *Post* reporter Chalmers Roberts.

5. Hallin, *The "Uncensored War,"* pp. 17–18.

6. Daniel Ellsberg, *Secrets: A Memoir of Vietnam and the Pentagon Papers* (New York: Viking, 2002), p. 14.

7. Quotes from transcript of August 6, 1964, hearing in I. F. Stone, *Polemics and Prophecies, 1967–1970* (New York: Vintage Books, 1972), pp. 307–308.

8. Stanley Karnow, *Vietnam: A History* (New York: Penguin, 1987), p. 375.

9. Secretary of Defense Robert McNamara quoted in ibid.

10. Johnson quoted in Stone, *Polemics and Prophecies*, p. 308.

11. Hallin, *The "Uncensored War,"* p. 25.

12. Johnson quoted in *The Forging of the American Empire* by Sidney Lens (Sterling, Va.: Pluto Press, 2003), p. 421.

13. The deployment of American soldiers in South Vietnam peaked at 542,000 in 1968.

14. Stone, *Polemics and Prophecies*, p. 310.

15. Sydney Schanberg, *Newsday*, February 8, 1991.

16. Ellsberg, *Secrets*, p. 204.

17. Senator Wayne Morse appearance on CBS *Face the Nation*, footage in documentary film *The Last Angry Man*, produced by Christopher Houser and Robert Millis (Square Deal Productions).

18. Ellsberg, *Secrets*, p. 43.

19. Senator Warren Rudman, January 12, 1991.

20. Senator Jesse Helms, January 12, 1991. Helms also said, "Of course, there is a role for constructive criticism. But the naysayers who deny our national interest, who speak for delay when they really mean never, and who are more interested in narrow political advantage than in the national advantage—there is no room for these if the inner heart and soul of our Nation is to flourish."

21. *New York Times*, September 15, 2001.

22. Representative Barbara Lee was speaking on January 14, 2002—four months after her solitary vote against the open-ended war resolution—at a Town Hall Los Angeles luncheon. "Like everyone, I was angry," she recalled. "That did not mean that I believed that the U.S. Congress, with little evidence, little information, and almost no debate, should give the Executive Branch broad authority to potentially wage war against more than 60 nations. Our Constitution is based on fundamental principles. The separation of powers is absolutely central to our system of government. That system depends on each branch of government upholding its responsibilities and authority." (Quoted in Nancy Snow, *Information War* [New York: Seven Stories Press, 2003], pp. 118 and 120.)

23. Michael Kinsley, *Time*, April 21, 2003.

Chapter 9: If This War Is Wrong, the Media Will Tell Us

1. Martin A. Lee and Norman Solomon, *Unreliable Sources: A Guide to Detecting Bias in News Media* paperback edition (New York: Carol Publishing Group, 1991), p. xviii.

2. *Defense Daily International* (February 13, 2004) reported General Electric's total of $2.8 billion in Department of Defense prime contract awards for fiscal year 2003. GE is one of the world's top suppliers of jet engines for military aircraft.

3. Murray Waas, *Village Voice*, December 18, 1990.

4. Ben Bagdikian, *The New Media Monopoly* (Boston: Beacon Press, 2004), pp. 82–83. Two decades after Bagdikian's classic book *The Media Monopoly* first appeared in 1983, the renamed 2004 edition showed that the number of corporations in control of most U.S. media had dropped from fifty to five: Time Warner, Disney, Rupert Murdoch's News Corp., Viacom, and Bertelsmann.

5. While many companies are engaged in joint ventures with the executive branch in Washington, it's common for corporate media professionals to move from journalism to government. So it was no big deal when the ABC News program *Nightline* lost its executive producer on the day that the Gulf War ended. Dorrance Smith quit the network so he could take a job at the White House as a communications adviser to President George H. W. Bush. In 2000 he helped George W. Bush's campaign in Florida during the recount. A few years later, he was doing PR work for Uncle Sam in Iraq. "The White House originally tapped the 52-year-old Mr. Smith to go to Iraq and create a network so officials in Baghdad could communicate with officials and the press in Washington," reported the *Washington Times* (April 28, 2004). "Once that was done, he was moved over in January [2004] to the struggling IMN"—the Iraqi Media Network, running such operations as a newspaper; a radio station; and Al Iraqiya, the TV channel launched by the occupation authority. Smith was also working as senior adviser to U.S. proconsul L. Paul Bremer.

6. Daniel C. Hallin, *The "Uncensored War": The Media and Vietnam* (Berkeley: University of California Press, 1989), p. 6.

7. Ibid., p. 129.

8. Ibid., p. 8.

9. Ibid., p. 133.

10. Ibid.

11. Ibid., p. 134.

12. Michael X. Delli Carpini, "Vietnam and the Press," in *The Legacy: The Vietnam War and the American Imagination*, ed. D. Michael Shafer (Boston: Beacon Press, 1990), p. 127.

13. Reese Erlich in Norman Solomon and Reese Erlich, *Target Iraq: What the News Media Didn't Tell You* (New York: Context Books, 2003), p. 12.

14. Ibid., p. 18.

15. Thomas Friedman, *The Lexus and the Olive Tree* (New York: Farrar, Straus, & Giroux, 1999), p. 373.

16. *Washington Post*, January 24, 1990.

17. *Newsday*, December 22, 1989.

18. *Boston Globe*, December 25, 1989.

19. Malcolm Browne quoted in *Unreliable Sources* paperback edition, p. xvi.

20. Eric W. Ober quoted in *Unreliable Sources* paperback edition, p. xvi.

21. Essay by Patrick J. Sloyan written while a fellow for the Alicia Patterson Foundation, 2002.

22. Tom Brokaw, NBC, January 16, 1991; quoted in FAIR's magazine *Extra!*, Special Gulf War Issue 1991. FAIR also cited the on-air comment of CBS reporter Mark Phillips (February 14, 1991) who said, "Saddam Hussein promised a bloody war, and here was the blood."

23. Ted Koppel, ABC, January 17, 1991; quoted in *Extra!*, Special Gulf War Issue 1991.

24. Tom Brokaw, NBC, January 29, 1991; quoted in *Extra!*, Special Gulf War Issue 1991.

25. Bruce Morton, CBS, February 9, 1991; quoted in *Extra!*, Special Gulf War Issue 1991.

26. Ted Koppel, ABC, January 23, 1991; quoted in *Extra!*, Special Gulf War Issue 1991.

27. Hodding Carter, C-SPAN, February 23, 1991.

28. Michael Deaver quoted in *Unreliable Sources* paperback edition, p. xv.

29. Anthony Cordesman, *Newsday*, January 23, 1991; quoted in *Extra!*, Special Gulf War Issue 1991.

30. *Extra!*, Special Gulf War Issue 1991.

31. Dan Rather, CBS, February 27, 1991; quoted in *Orlando Sentinel*, March 3, 1991.

32. Chris Hedges, *War Is a Force That Gives Us Meaning* (New York: Anchor Books, 2003), p. 143.

33. Ibid., p. 23.

34. Ibid., p. 144.

35. Richard Holbrooke quoted in author's article, *Palm Beach Post*, May 9, 1999.

36. *New York Times*, April 25, 1999.

37. Thomas Friedman, *New York Times*, April 23, 1999.

38. *Independent*, April 24, 1999.

39. *Financial Times*, March 31, 1999. The Yugoslav government also had a stake in downplaying the carnage from the bombing, the newspaper reported:

"Serbia's state-run television, while showing ruined civilian homes, shields its viewers from bloodied corpses that might spread panic among an already highly strung population."

40. *Financial Times*, March 31, 1999.

41. Thomas Friedman, *New York Times* News Service, *Deseret News*, April 7, 1999.

42. Soon after the air war against Yugoslavia ended, the *Washington Post* (June 29, 1999) summed up an extraordinary achievement. "In the war over Kosovo, the military finally obtained its holy grail: victory without a single U.S. casualty in combat."

43. In the wake of the Columbine High School tragedy, President Clinton said that the nation's prayers went out to the victims and their loved ones. But, of course, he offered no prayers for victims and loved ones in connection with the incessant bombing of Yugoslavia. The president declared with a straight face: "We do know that we must do more to reach out to our children and teach them to express their anger and to resolve their conflicts with words, not weapons." Mainstream American journalists were far too circumspect to point out that such pieties were being uttered by a leader who was championing the deadly use of many weapons by the United States and other NATO countries. The high-school shootings occurred while NATO warplanes were in the midst of the most intense bombardment of Yugoslavia yet—with 603 "missions" reported in a 24-hour period. Civilians under those bombs were mere blips on the U.S. media screens. Such selectivity cheapens compassion and turns it into the coin of propaganda.

44. Eason Jordan, CNN, April 20, 2003.

45. Walter Rodgers, CNN, March 20, 2003.

46. Aaron Brown, CNN, March 20, 2003.

47. FAIR study, "Gulf War Coverage: The Worst Censorship Was at Home," *Extra!*, Special Gulf War Issue 1991.

48. FAIR study, "Slanted Sources in *NewsHour* and *Nightline* Kosovo Coverage," May 5, 1999.

49. Michael Dolny, memo to author, July 27, 2004. (Dolny has conducted several studies for FAIR about the visibility of major think tanks in news media.)

50. FAIR study, Steve Rendall and Tara Broughel, "Amplifying Officials, Squelching Dissent," *Extra!*, May/June 2003.

51. Ibid.

52. The leaked memo was revealed by Rick Ellis in a piece on www .allyourtv.com, February 25, 2003, the day after MSNBC officially canceled *Donahue*. Though MSNBC cited disappointing ratings, with *Donahue* lagging far behind cable competitors in the same time slot, Ellis noted that the just-canceled program "is the top-rated show on MSNBC, beating even the highly promoted *Hardball with Chris Matthews*."

53. CNN, March 24, 1999.

54. Margaret Warner, *NewsHour with Jim Lehrer*, PBS, March 31, 1999.

55. Over a period of months, starting on October 7, 2001, former generals Clark and Shepperd appeared together dozens of times on CNN during intensive bombing of Afghanistan.

56. Donald Rumsfeld, Department of Defense briefing, CNN, October 7, 2001.

57. Tom Brokaw, NBC, March 19, 2003. A year later, Bob Woodward's book *Plan of Attack* recounted a conversation on August 5, 2002, when Secretary of State Powell reportedly told President Bush, "You are going to be the proud owner of 25 million people. You will own all their hopes, aspirations and problems. You'll own it all." According to the book, Powell and his colleague Richard Armitage "called this the Pottery Barn rule: You break it, you own it." (*Plan of Attack* [New York: Simon & Schuster, 2004], p. 150) Later, when *New York Times* columnist Thomas Friedman appeared on the public radio program *Fresh Air* (June 3, 2004), he took credit for originating the "Pottery Barn rule" witticism.

58. Katie Couric, *Today*, NBC, April 3, 2003.

59. "The press policies in the war on terrorism are looking a lot like the Gulf War policies established by [George W.] Bush's father, Dick Cheney and Colin Powell," said journalism professor Jeffery A. Smith, a scholar on wartime news coverage. (*Boston Globe*, October 19, 2001)

60. Ari Fleischer quoted in *Washington Times*, October 11, 2001.

61. *New York Times*, October 11, 2001.

62. Rupert Murdoch quoted in *Guardian*, October 12, 2001.

63. *Miami Herald*, October 11, 2001.

64. Helen Thomas, *Seattle Post-Intelligencer*, October 16, 2001.

65. James Naughton quoted in *San Diego Union-Tribune*, October 19, 2001.

66. The Committee to Protect Journalists, a careful mainstream group based in New York, noted other ominous actions by the American government in autumn 2001. For instance, "the U.S. State Department contacted the Voice of America, a broadcast organization funded by the federal government, and expressed concern about the radio broadcast of an exclusive interview with Taliban leader Mullah Mohammed Omar." Later, VOA head Robert Reilly "distributed a memo barring interviews with officials from 'nations that sponsor terrorism.'" In early October, as the U.S. government geared up for extensive bombing of Afghanistan, efforts to pressure media outlets at home and abroad included Colin Powell urging the emir of Qatar to lean on the Qatar-based Al-Jazeera satellite TV network. (Committee to Protect Journalists, *Attacks on the Press in 2001*) Meanwhile, pressure on the domestic media continued. Four days after the bombing of Afghanistan started, White House spokesman Ari Fleischer urged the press not to print full texts of statements by Osama bin Laden and his cohorts. "The request is to report the news to the American people," he said. "But if you report it in its entirety, that could raise concerns that he's getting his prepackaged, pretaped message out." (*New York Times*, October 12, 2001) Newspapers were a bit less inclined than the networks to comply with such "requests," but a chill was in the air. The First Amendment shivered. "The government's attempts to pressure the media regarding the airing of bin Laden's statements are totally illegitimate," said Jane Kirtley, a professor of media ethics and law at the University of Minnesota. "Government directives like this, especially to a regulated industry like broadcast and cable, carry the force of coercion, if not the force of law." (News release, Institute for Public Accuracy, October 11, 2001)

67. *New York Times*, October 11, 2001.

68. "There have been instances," *Washington Post* publisher Katharine Graham had acknowledged during the last half of the 1970s, "in which secrets have been leaked to us which we thought were so dangerous that we went to them [U.S. officials] and told them that they had been leaked to us and did not print them. The fact is that they did get out later." (Howard Bray, *The Pillars of the Post* [New York: W. W. Norton, 1980], p. 150)

69. *New York Times,* October 10, 2001.

70. Leonard Downie Jr. quoted in *New York Times,* October 11, 2001.

71. Committee to Protect Journalists, *Attacks on the Press in 2001.*

72. *Guardian,* October 17, 2001. According to the newspaper, "the only alternative source of accurate satellite images would be the Russian Cosmos system. But Russia has not yet decided to step into the information void created by the Pentagon deal with Space Imaging."

73. Donald Rumsfeld quoted in *New York Times,* October 22, 2001.

74. Committee to Protect Journalists, *Attacks on the Press in 2001.*

75. *Time,* April 7, 2004.

76. "I am fairly certain I watched and took notes on the Vietnam coverage from somewhere between a thousand and fifteen hundred evening news broadcasts, plus some network documentaries." Hallin, *The "Uncensored War,"* p. 111.

77. Hallin, interview on *CounterSpin* radio program, November 7, 2003; *Extra!,* January/February 2004.

78. Ibid.

79. Ashleigh Banfield, speech at Kansas State University, April 24, 2003.

80. NBC management statement, April 28, 2003; quoted in *Boston Herald,* April 30, 2003.

81. Dan Rather quoted in Associated Press, May 16, 2002.

82. Rather quoted in *Guardian,* May 17, 2002.

83. CNN, April 14, 2003.

Chapter 10: Media Coverage Brings War into Our Living Rooms

1. The "Defense Department" is far from truth in labeling. But no player in Washington would suggest restoring the "War Department" name, any more than execs in charge of marketing Camels, Salems, and Marlboros would advocate rebranding them with names such as Cancer Sticks, Coffin Nails, and Killer Leaf.

2. I. F. Stone, *Polemics and Prophecies, 1967–1970* (New York: Vintage Books, 1972), pp. 57–58.

3. Michael Herr, *Dispatches* (New York: Vintage International, 1977), p. 215.

4. Daniel C. Hallin, *The "Uncensored War": The Media and Vietnam* (Berkeley: University of California Press, 1989), pp. x–xi. Those three major studies were conducted by Lawrence Lichty and George Bailey, by Oscar Patterson III, and by Hallin.

5. Edward Jay Epstein, *Between Fact and Fiction* (New York: Vintage Books, 1975), p. 210.

6. Ibid., pp. 211–212.

7. *Newsweek* quoted in ibid., p. 212.

8. Epstein, *Between Fact and Fiction*, pp. 212–213.

9. Ibid., pp. 213–214.

10. Ibid., p. 214.

11. Quotations from *Washington Post*, March 13, 1965, *New York Times*, August 5, 1965, and *New York Times*, September 5, 1965, in Howard Zinn, *Vietnam: The Logic of Withdrawal* (Cambridge, Mass.: South End Press, 2002), pp. 52–54. The August 5 and September 5 articles carried a Saigon dateline.

12. United Press International, August 3, 1965, quoted in Zinn, *Vietnam*, p. 53.

13. Susan Sontag, *Regarding the Pain of Others* (New York: Farrar, Straus, & Giroux, 2003), p. 13.

14. Floyd Kalber quoted in Epstein, *Between Fact and Fiction*, p. 215.

15. Walter Cronkite quoted in ibid.

16. Epstein, *Between Fact and Fiction*, pp. 216–217.

17. Howard K. Smith quoted in ibid., p. 217.

18. Hallin, *The "Uncensored War,"* p. 129.

19. Ibid., pp. 129–130.

20. Epstein, *Between Fact and Fiction*, p. 218.

21. Michael X. Delli Carpini, "Vietnam and the Press," in *The Legacy: The Vietnam War and the American Imagination*, ed. D. Michael Shafer (Boston: Beacon Press, 1990), p. 126.

22. Hallin, *The "Uncensored War,"* p. xi. As an overall matter, Hallin commented, "Coverage of Vietnam in a liberal 'prestige paper' like the *New York Times* was very different from coverage in a conservative paper like the *Chicago Tribune* or the *San Diego Union*, or a small local paper, which perhaps took advantage of 'hometowners' in its reportage of local boys 'in action,' prepared for the use of such papers by the Defense Department. . . . Someone who followed the war in the *New York Times* and *Newsweek* got a much more critical view than someone who followed it in the *Daily News* and *Reader's Digest*." (p. 11)

23. Walter Cronkite quoted in Hallin, *The "Uncensored War,"* p. 108.

24. Walter Cronkite quoted in Delli Carpini, "Vietnam and the Press," p. 142.

25. Delli Carpini, "Vietnam and the Press," p. 146.

26. Epstein, *Between Fact and Fiction*, p. 227.

27. Robert Northshield quoted in ibid.

28. Epstein, *Between Fact and Fiction*, p. 227.

29. Av Westin quoted in ibid., pp. 227–228.

30. Delli Carpini, "Vietnam and the Press," pp. 147–148.

31. Hallin, *The "Uncensored War,"* p. 190.

32. David Brinkley, NBC News, quoted in ibid., p. 189.

33. Walter Isaacson quoted in *Washington Post*, October 31, 2001.

34. Memo quoted in FAIR "Action Alert," November 8, 2001; also in *New Zealand Herald*, January 17, 2002.

35. Colin Powell quoted in *New York Times*, March 23, 1991.

36. Christiane Amanpour, CNN, December 18 and 19, 1998.

37. Chris Hedges, *War Is a Force That Gives Us Meaning* (New York: Anchor Books, 2003), p. 34.

38. Ibid., p. 54.

39. Ibid., pp. 83–84.

40. Donald Rumsfeld, NBC News, October 7, 2001.

41. President George W. Bush quoted in *Independent*, October 9, 2001.

42. Howard Rosenberg, *Los Angeles Times*, November 12, 2001.

43. Ibid.

44. Susan Sontag, *Regarding the Pain of Others*, p. 18.

45. Ibid., p. 29.

46. Ibid., p. 38.

47. Ibid., p. 23.

48. Ibid., p. 89.

49. Ibid., p. 67.

50. Ibid., p. 117.

51. Fred Barnes quoted in *New York Times*, March 25, 2003.

52. Rick Bragg, *I Am a Soldier, Too* (New York: Alfred A. Knopf, 2003), p. 95.

53. Sydney Schanberg, *Village Voice*, December 16, 2003.

54. www.abcnews.com, November 14, 2003.

55. On June 21, 2004, the Senate voted 54–39 to uphold the ban on news photos of flag-draped military coffins.

56. *New York Times*, June 22, 2004.

57. *Seattle Times*, April 22, 2004.

58. Charles Krauthammer, *Time*, December 8, 2003.

59. George W. Bush, April 13, 2004.

60. *Newsweek*, April 19, 2004.

61. *Washington Post*, April 25, 2004.

62. *New York Times*, December 30, 2003.

63. Chris Hedges, *Nation*, May 24, 2004. Hedges also wrote: "The only way to understand war is to see it from the perspective of the victims. . . . We prefer the myth of war, the myth of glory, honor, patriotism and heroism, abstract words that in the terror and brutality of combat are empty and meaningless, abstract words that mask the plague of war, abstract words that are obscene to those ravaged by war."

64. Forrest Sawyer, *The News with Brian Williams*, CNBC, March 21, 2003.

65. David Bloom, *The News with Brian Williams*, CNBC, March 21, 2003.

66. Ibid.

67. Ibid. Later during the invasion, on April 6, Bloom died from a pulmonary embolism.

68. John Donvan, *Nightline*, ABC, March 24, 2003.

69. Ibid.

70. David Zucchino quoted in Committee to Protect Journalists, *Attacks on the Press in 2003*, pp. 186–187.

71. *Attacks on the Press in 2003*, p. 186.

72. Ibid., p. 187.

73. AFX, April 9, 2003.

74. Herve de Ploeg quoted in Agence France Presse, April 8, 2003.

75. Victoria Clarke, Department of Defense briefing, April 8, 2003. Clarke moved on professionally after the invasion. She left the Pentagon in June 2003, becoming a regular commentator for CNN and then adding to her workload by contracting with a media conglomerate. The *Washington Post* (December 15, 2003) reported that "former Pentagon public affairs chief Victoria Clarke is signing up to be a senior adviser for communications and government affairs for cable giant Comcast Corp. The part-time job would allow Clarke to continue her gig as a CNN contributor and to volunteer with the Pentagon." When Secretary of Defense Donald Rumsfeld was getting ready for crucial testimony before congressional committees about sexual abuse and torture at the Abu Ghraib prison in Iraq, the *New York Times* reported (May 7, 2004): "To help prepare, Mr. Rumsfeld was consulting with a range of trusted outside advisers, including his former chief spokeswoman, Victoria Clarke." For Clarke, private and governmental PR work was virtually seamless. Before working at the Pentagon, she'd been an executive with Hill & Knowlton, a large PR agency that played an instrumental role at the start of the 1990s in advance promotion for the Gulf War, helping to arrange fake testimony on Capitol Hill that Iraqi troops had dumped babies out of incubators in Kuwait. For its services to the exiled royal family, the firm "was paid about $5.6 million to represent Kuwaiti exiles after Iraq's invasion." (*St. Louis Post-Dispatch*, January 9, 1992) Syndicated columnist Mary McGrory put the figure at $8 million. (*Seattle Post-Intelligencer*, January 15, 1992)

76. Colonel Rick Long quoted by Associated Press, March 19, 2004.

77. Eric Niiler, *All Things Considered*, NPR, April 7, 2004. Along with speaking about how "we" patrolled, correspondent Niiler also let listeners know that he was keeping secrets for the military: "There are command posts set up further and further into the city, and there are some other operations that are in the works, some things I can't talk about."

78. Steven Kull, news release, Institute for Public Accuracy, May 4, 2004.

79. "U.S. Public Beliefs and Attitudes About Iraq," Program on International Policy Attitudes, August 20, 2004.

Chapter 11: Opposing the War Means Siding with the Enemy

1. I. F. Stone, *Polemics and Prophecies, 1967–1970* (New York: Vintage Books, 1972), p. 75.

2. General William Westmoreland quoted in ibid., p. 76.

3. President Lyndon Johnson, speech to National Farmers Union in Minneapolis, March 18, 1968, quoted in Stone, *Polemics and Prophecies*, p. 380.

4. President Richard Nixon quoted in Stone, *Polemics and Prophecies*, pp. 380–381.

5. Stone, *Polemics and Prophecies*, p. 77. Stone added: "Self-deception is still the key to Westmoreland's presentation. Even after so many years he still refuses to recognize the popular roots of the Vietnamese rebellion. He prefers to see it as something essentially artificial and imposed, which Hanoi can turn off with some magic spigot. First we were going to end the war by bombing Hanoi, but now that we'll soon be running out of meaningful targets in the North, we are in effect promised a quick victory if only we can bomb Berkeley into submission. The

general who couldn't defeat the enemy abroad now returns to take it out on the *peaceniks* at home."

6. Letter quoted in Daniel Ellsberg, *Secrets: A Memoir of Vietnam and the Pentagon Papers* (New York: Viking, 2002), p. 312.

7. Ellsberg, *Secrets*, p. 317.

8. Ibid., pp. 317–318.

9. *Time* quoted in Martin A. Lee and Norman Solomon, *Unreliable Sources: A Guide to Detecting Bias in News Media* (New York: Carol Publishing Group, 1990), p. 252.

10. *Washington Post* quoted in ibid.

11. "The aid-and-comfort-to-the-enemy theme was standard" prior to the Vietnam War's 1968 Tet offensive, wrote Daniel Hallin. "In one NBC report [October 1965], following a story on demonstrations in Britain, Chet Huntley remarked, 'Meanwhile, Hanoi was having paroxysms of joy over the demonstrations in this country over the war in Vietnam.'" (*The "Uncensored War": The Media and Vietnam* [Berkeley: University of California Press, 1989], p. 193) Later, an enduring myth took hold about antiwar demonstrators spitting on American soldiers. "Research indicates that the story of the returning Vietnam veteran spat upon by a protester at the airport may be an urban legend," *New York Times* reporter Chris Hedges wrote in *What Every Person Should Know About War* (New York: Free Press, 2003), p. 112. "Newspaper accounts from the war era do describe spitting incidents, but the spat-upon people are anti-war protesters. However, there are credible reports of hostility and violence toward men and women in uniform. Some Vietnam veterans reported discrimination from college and graduate school admissions offices."

12. Chris Wallace, *Nightline*, ABC News, October 19, 1990. To ABC's credit, one of the guests on that *Nightline* broadcast with Westmoreland was the antiwar Vietnam veteran Ron Kovic, author of *Born on the Fourth of July*, who expressed strong opposition to the upcoming war. But the voices of Americans with antiwar views virtually disappeared from U.S. television networks during the Gulf War.

13. William Greider, *Nation*, May 3, 2004.

14. At times, the process of denouncing antiwar activists has included denigrating their sexual orientations. During the 1968 Democratic National Convention, while police beat up protesters in the streets of Chicago, the conservative icon William F. Buckley Jr. could not contain his rage. Buckley was not angry at the police (whose violence he fully supported) but at fellow ABC television commentator Gore Vidal, who had responded to Buckley's defense of the cops by calling him a "pro crypto Nazi." Buckley, the great right-wing intellectual, replied on the air: "Now listen, you queer. Stop calling me a 'pro crypto Nazi' or I'll sock you in the goddamn face." (ABC News, August 28, 1968) Soon after the trial of the Chicago Seven activists in connection with the antiwar protests outside the convention, the U.S. attorney who prosecuted them, Tom Foran, let slip a great concern when he spoke to a group of parents at Loyola High School in 1970: "We've lost our kids to the freaking fag revolution." (*Washington Post*, April 14, 1989; *Chicago Tribune*, January 3, 1999)

In May 1991, General Norman Schwarzkopf explained certain historical fine points to the public in the wake of the Gulf War. "After Vietnam," he said, "we had a cottage industry developed in Washington, D.C., consisting of a bunch of military fairies that had never been shot at in anger [and] who felt fully qualified to comment on the leadership abilities of all the leaders of the U.S. Army." (Norman Solomon, *The Power of Babble* [New York: Dell, 1992], p. 89)

Even presidents have fallen short in the manhood department. When President Clinton failed to follow the advice of journalists demanding that the Pentagon bomb Iraq in November 1998, the *New York Post* scornfully editorialized that he had not been able to "act like a man." (*New York Post*, November 16, 1998)

15. Nancy Snow, *Information War* (New York: Seven Stories Press, 2003), p. 23.

16. Rush Limbaugh quoted in *Baltimore Sun*, March 9, 2003.

17. Joe Scarborough, MSNBC, April 10, 2003.

18. Similar to "anti-American," but broader, is "anti-Western." With the Gulf War under way, Senator Joseph Biden warned on January 24, 1991: "Even after we win on the battlefield, and we will win, there is a grave danger that the latent anti-imperialistic, fundamentalist, and anti-Western hostility that exists will explode to the detriment of American interests for decades to come."

19. During a debate on CNN International in 2003, a fervent war supporter proclaimed me to be a "self-hating American."

20. Jim McDermott, *This Week*, ABC, September 29, 2002.

21. George Will, *This Week*, ABC, September 29, 2002.

22. Will, *Washington Post*, October 1, 2002.

23. *Rocky Mountain News*, October 1, 2002.

24. *Augusta Chronicle*, October 1, 2002.

25. Bill O'Reilly, *The O'Reilly Factor*, Fox News Channel, October 3, 2002.

26. Cal Thomas, *Baltimore Sun*, October 9, 2002.

27. Mara Liasson, *Special Report with Brit Hume*, Fox News Channel, October 3, 2002.

28. Paul Loeb quoted by author in *Baltimore Sun*, December 24, 2002.

29. Sean Penn, statement in news release, Institute for Public Accuracy, December 13, 2002.

30. Penn, statement at news conference at Al-Rashid Hotel in Baghdad, December 15, 2002; news release, same date, Institute for Public Accuracy.

31. Ibid.

32. Eartha Kitt quoted in *New York Times*, May 13, 1983.

33. *Chicago Daily Herald*, April 22, 2003.

34. Bruce Springsteen quoted in *Miami Herald*, April 23, 2003.

35. For a discussion of media coverage and the growth of antiwar sentiment during the Vietnam era, see Daniel C. Hallin, interview on *CounterSpin* radio program, November 7, 2003; FAIR's magazine *Extra!*, January/February 2004.

36. Hallin, *The "Uncensored War,"* pp. 10–11.

37. Ibid., p. 107.

38. Ibid., p. 200. The quoted CBS report by Cronkite aired on May 1, 1970.

39. Hallin, *The "Uncensored War,"* p. 200. Making a show of reasonableness and engagement with critics can be part of the presidential warmaking routine. So—nine days after his April 30, 1970, announcement of a joint U.S. and

South Vietnamese invasion of Cambodia—Richard Nixon got up early at the White House and went over to the Lincoln Memorial to speak to bleary-eyed young people gathering there for a large demonstration. Across the United States, hundreds of college campuses were shut down by protests. The country was undergoing sizable and angry demonstrations, with the media uproar heightened by the shooting deaths of four students at Kent State University in Ohio. Days later, two more students died during antiwar protests at Jackson State College in Mississippi. While Nixon was hostile to the demonstrators and everything they stood for, he recognized the value of photo-ops and news stories depicting his pantomime of reaching out to them.

40. Hallin, *The "Uncensored War,"* p. 208.

41. Danny Schechter, *Boston Phoenix*, September 5, 1972.

42. Barbara Ehrenreich, *Blood Rites: Origins and History of the Passions of War* (New York: Metropolitan Books, 1997), p. 239.

43. Ibid., p. 240.

44. Ibid.

Chapter 12: This Is a Necessary Battle in the War on Terrorism

1. President Lyndon Johnson quoted in I. F. Stone, *Polemics and Prophecies, 1967–1970* (New York: Vintage Books, 1972), p. 326.

2. Daniel C. Hallin, *The "Uncensored War": The Media and Vietnam* (Berkeley: University of California Press, 1989), p. 155.

3. Ibid., pp. 155–156.

4. Joan Didion, *Fixed Ideas: America Since 9.11* (New York: New York Review of Books, 2003), p. 5.

5. Ibid., pp. 5–6.

6. Ibid., p. 9.

7. Ibid., p. 30.

8. Nancy Snow, *Information War* (New York: Seven Stories Press, 2003), p. 63.

9. Chris Hedges, *War Is a Force That Gives Us Meaning* (New York: Anchor Books, 2003), p. 180.

10. Didion, *Fixed Ideas*, pp. 13–14.

11. Cokie Roberts, *The Late Show with David Letterman*, CBS, October 10, 2001.

12. On May 29, 2004, Secretary of Defense Rumsfeld told the graduating class of cadets at West Point that "despite our successes, we are closer to the beginning of this struggle with global insurgency than to its end." (Reuters, May 29, 2004)

13. Nicholas Lemann, *New Yorker*, September 9, 2002; quoted in Snow, *Information War*, p. 78.

14. William Odom, *Washington Journal*, C-SPAN, November 24, 2002.

15. Political benefits aside, a fearful environment could be commercially lucrative. A *Forbes* supplement called "Portrait of the New America: Understanding a Multicultural Marketplace," appearing in the aftermath of 9/11, ended on this note: "A decrease in overall feelings of safety since September 11 represents an opportunity for marketers of 'safety' (e.g., home security, private schools, Caller I.D., premium grade gasoline, suburbs, etc.)."

16. Didion, *Fixed Ideas*, p. 14.

17. American Compass book club ad, *Weekly Standard*, March 22, 2004.

18. Norman Mailer, "An Exchange with Norman Mailer," *New York Review of Books*, August 14, 2003.

19. The U.S. media focus on some terrorism is markedly out of proportion. In mid-May 2003, the internationally syndicated columnist Gwynne Dyer observed that the previous week had brought news reports of terrorist attacks in Chechnya, Saudi Arabia, Pakistan, Morocco, and Israel, resulting in a total of 153 deaths. He wrote: "Last week was the worst for terrorist attacks since September 11, 2001. . . . Yet there were no headlines last weekend saying '750 people dead of gunshot wounds in the U.S. since Monday' or 'Weekly traffic death toll in India tops 2,000,' and only small headlines that several thousand people had been massacred in the eastern Congolese town of Bunia." Endeavoring to put post-September 11 media fixations on terrorism in perspective, Dyer wrote: "There are several agendas running in the Bush administration, and the one on top at the moment is the hyper-ambitious Cheney-Rumsfeld project that uses the terrorist threat as a pretext for creating a global 'pax Americana' based on the unilateral use of American military power. But the project of the Islamic terrorists is still running too, and this strategy is playing straight into their hands." (*St. Louis Post-Dispatch*, May 20, 2003)

20. "When *I* use a word," Humpty Dumpty said, in rather a scornful tone, "it means just what I choose it to mean—neither more nor less."

"The question is," said Alice, "whether you *can* make words mean so many different things."

"The question is," said Humpty Dumpty, "which is to be master—that's all."

(Lewis Carroll, *Through the Looking-Glass*)

21. Hedges, *War Is a Force*, pp. 8–9.

22. Naomi Klein, Commondreams.org, September 9, 2004.

23. Tom DeLay, *Jerusalem Post*, August 1, 2003.

24. If I. F. Stone were alive today, he would no doubt be subjected to epithets such as "self-hating Jew" and "anti-Semite." Instead of trying to refute critiques of Washington-backed Israeli policies, it's much easier to equate criticism of Israel with anti-Semitism—a timeworn way of short-circuiting real debate on issues by claiming that bigotry is behind calls for adherence to basic standards of human rights. The ongoing threat of the "anti-Semitic" label helps to prevent U.S. media coverage from getting out of hand. There's no doubt that journalists understand critical words about Israel to be hazardous to careers. "Our gutlessness, our refusal to tell the truth, our fear of being slandered as 'anti-Semites'—the most loathsome of libels against any journalist—means that we are aiding and abetting terrible deeds in the Middle East," longtime foreign correspondent Robert Fisk wrote in the *Independent* (April 17, 2001). While anti-Semitism is a reality in the world—and, like all forms of racial, ethnic, and religious bigotry, should be unequivocally opposed—the effectiveness of such opposition is undermined by those who cry wolf, using charges of anti-Semitism as a weapon in a propaganda arsenal to defend Israel's policies.

25. Stone, *Polemics and Prophecies*, p. 435.

26. Ibid., pp. 435–436.

27. Ibid., p. 436.

28. John V. Whitbeck, *International Herald Tribune*, February 18, 2004.

29. Eqbal Ahmad, *Terrorism: Theirs & Ours* (New York: Seven Stories Press, 2001), p. 24. On a similar note, ten months after the Iraq invasion, Martin Luther King III said at an event in Atlanta commemorating the birth of his father: "When will the war end? We all have to be concerned about terrorism, but you will never end terrorism by terrorizing others." (Cox News Service, January 19, 2004)

Chapter 13: What the U.S. Government Needs Most Is Better PR

1. Nancy Snow, *Information War* (New York: Seven Stories Press, 2003), p. 105.

2. Colonel Kenneth McClellan quoted in *Miami Herald*, October 21, 2001.

3. For more information about the Rendon Group and proprietor John W. Rendon, see Sheldon Rampton and John Stauber, *Weapons of Mass Deception: The Uses of Propaganda in Bush's War on Iraq* (New York: Jeremy P. Tarcher, 2003), pp. 4–5, 42–43, and 49–50.

4. Donald Rumsfeld, Defense Department briefing, CNN, October 15, 2001.

5. "The myth of war is essential to justify the horrible sacrifices required in war, the destruction and the death of innocents," Chris Hedges writes. "It can be formed only by denying the reality of war, by turning the lies, the manipulation, the inhumanness of war into the heroic ideal." (*War Is a Force That Gives Us Meaning* [New York: Anchor Books, 2003], p. 26) Hedges quotes Simone Weil: "Those who believe that God himself, once he became man, could not face the harshness of destiny without a long tremor of anguish, should have understood that the only people who can give the impression of having risen to a higher plane, who seem superior to ordinary human misery, are the people who resort to the aids of illusion, exaltation, fanaticism, to conceal the harshness of destiny from their own eyes. The man who does not wear the armor of the lie cannot experience force without being touched by it to the very soul." (*War Is a Force*, p. 30)

6. Eugene Secunda, *O'Dwyer's PR Services Report*, April 1991.

7. Many liberal commentators brimmed with enthusiasm for war in Afghanistan. "I was a critic of Rumsfeld before, but there's one thing . . . that I do like about Rumsfeld," declared Thomas Friedman on October 13, 2001, during a CNBC appearance. "He's just a little bit crazy, OK? He's just a little bit crazy, and in this kind of war, they always count on being able to out-crazy us, and I'm glad we got some guy on our bench that our quarterback—who's just a little bit crazy, not totally, but you never know what that guy's going to do, and I say that's my guy." As the bombing of Afghanistan went on, Friedman's column was in a similar groove. "Let's all take a deep breath and repeat after me: Give war a chance." (*New York Times*, November 2, 2001) Three months later, Friedman was no less enthused about promoting a policy that could appear to rival the derangement of America's foes; seemingly crazy about wisps of craziness in high Washington places, he displayed a penchant for touting insanity as a helpful ingredient of U.S. foreign policy. "There is a lot about the Bush team's foreign

policy I don't like," he wrote in a column, "but their willingness to restore our deterrence, and to be as crazy as some of our enemies, is one thing they have right." (*New York Times*, February 13, 2002) Sometimes Friedman fixated on four words in particular. "My motto is very simple: *Give war a chance*," he told Diane Sawyer on *Good Morning America*. (ABC News, October 29, 2001) It was the same motto that he'd used 2½ years earlier during a Fox News interview. Different war; different enemy; different network; same solution. It was a favorite slogan in print as well. With the bombardment of Yugoslavia under way in spring 1999, Friedman had recycled "Give war a chance" from one column to another. And he suggested this approach for threatening civilians in Yugoslavia with protracted terror: "Every week you ravage Kosovo is another decade we will set your country back by pulverizing you. You want 1950? We can do 1950. You want 1389? We can do 1389 too." (*New York Times*, April 23, 1999)

8. Author interview "on background" with major at Defense Press Operations office, Pentagon, May 20, 2004.

9. *USA Today*, May 6, 2003.

10. *Los Angeles Times*, January 9, 2004.

11. *New York Times*, January 8, 2004.

12. *Washington Post*, January 7, 2004.

13. Colin Powell, State Department briefing, Federal News Service, January 8, 2004.

14. Powell speaking to the United Nations on February 5, 2003; quoted by Reuters, September 13, 2004.

15. Powell quoted by Reuters, September 13, 2004. Days after Powell's admission, a draft of the final report from the official Iraq Survey Group made news. The *Guardian* (September 18, 2004) summarized the findings this way: "The comprehensive 15-month search for weapons of mass destruction in Iraq has concluded that the only chemical or biological agents that Saddam Hussein's regime was working on before last year's invasion were small quantities of poisons, most likely for use in assassinations. A draft of the Iraq Survey Group's final report circulating in Washington found no sign of the alleged illegal stockpiles that the U.S. and Britain presented as the justification for going to war, nor did it find any evidence of efforts to reconstitute Iraq's nuclear weapons program."

16. Vice President Dick Cheney, January 22, 2004; quoted in *Independent*, June 17, 2004.

17. Cheney, June 14, 2004; quoted by Associated Press, June 16, 2004.

18. Associated Press, June 16, 2004.

19. *USA Today*, June 18, 2004. The survey was taken from January 29 to February 1, 2004.

20. *USA Today*, June 25, 2004.

21. Commanders of occupying troops often see journalists as impediments to effective military activities. After decades of occupying Palestinian territory, the Israeli army, known as the Israel Defense Forces, had earned a reputation for killing journalists (viewed by the IDF high command as unwelcome purveyors of bad publicity). Nazih Darwazeh, a cameraman with Associated Press Television News, was shot in the back of his head on the morning of April 19, 2003, while filming a stranded Israeli tank at the corner of an alley in Nablus. Two

journalists who were eyewitnesses said the shot came from an Israeli soldier under the tank. Darwazeh was wearing a fluorescent jacket marked "Press." (Committee to Protect Journalists, *Attacks on the Press in 2003*, pp. 229–230) Two weeks later, a British freelance film director and cameraman—James Miller, working on an HBO documentary in the Gaza Strip—was also shot and killed. Relatives, friends, and colleagues commissioned an in-depth professional investigation, which found that Miller and his crew "were consciously and deliberately targeted by the IDF soldiers." Miller and colleagues wore jackets and helmets marked "TV" when he was shot. (Ibid., pp. 230–231) "Over the years," the Committee to Protect Journalists said in 2004, "the army has failed to conduct thorough investigations into cases where journalists have been wounded or killed by IDF gunfire, let alone punish those responsible for the attacks. The same can be said for troops who physically attack or otherwise mistreat journalists in the field." (Ibid., p. 192)

22. Letter to Lawrence DiRita quoted in Committee to Protect Journalists, *Attacks on the Press in 2003*, p. 190.

23. Committee to Protect Journalists, *Attacks on the Press in 2003*, p. 189.

24. *Toronto Star*, April 4, 2004.

Chapter 14: The Pentagon Fights Wars as Humanely as Possible

1. Edward Jay Epstein, *Between Fact and Fiction* (New York: Vintage Books, 1975), p. 217.

2. Jacques Leslie, *The Mark: A Memoir of Vietnam* (New York: Four Walls Eight Windows, 1995), p. 44.

3. Ibid., p. 45.

4. Ron Miller quoted in Daniel C. Hallin, *The "Uncensored War": The Media and Vietnam* (Berkeley: University of California Press, 1989), p. 136.

5. Hallin, *The "Uncensored War,"* p. 136.

6. Leslie, *The Mark*, pp. 77–78. "Since no one seems to live on television, no one seems to die there," Mark Crispin Miller remarked in his book *Boxed In: The Culture of TV* (Evanston, Ill.: Northwestern University Press, 1988), p. 159.

7. Hallin, *The "Uncensored War,"* pp. 136, 137.

8. CNN, January 16, 1991; quoted in FAIR's magazine *Extra!*, Special Gulf War Issue 1991.

9. Jim Stewart, CBS, January 17, 1991.

10. Arthur Kent, NBC, January 17, 1991; quoted in *Extra!*, Special Gulf War Issue 1991.

11. Richard Blystone, CNN, January 22, 1991; quoted in *Extra!*, Special Gulf War Issue 1991.

12. "The New Science of War," *Newsweek*, February 18, 1991.

13. Tom Brokaw quoted in *Unreliable Sources* paperback edition (New York: Carol Publishing Group, 1991), p. xix.

14. *Time*, January 28, 1991.

15. Senator Phil Gramm, February 11, 1991.

16. Representative Les Aspin, June 20, 1991.

17. *USA Today*, February 13, 1998.

18. Bob Edwards, *Morning Edition*, NPR, November 26, 2001.

19. *USA Today*, November 22, 2002.

20. Ann Compton quoted in *Extra!*, Special Gulf War Issue 1991.

21. President George H. W. Bush, July 15, 1991.

22. Chris Hedges, *War Is a Force That Gives Us Meaning* (New York: Anchor Books, 2003), p. 8.

23. For example, *Larry King Live*, CNN, December 17, 1998.

24. President George W. Bush, March 17, 2003.

25. Christopher Hitchens, *A Long Short War* (New York: Plume, 2003), p. 12. The essay originally appeared on March 18, 2003.

26. *Washington Post*, March 24, 2003.

27. Transfixed with weaponry, tactical maneuvers, and grand strategies inside Iraq, media outlets rarely mentioned that shortly before the assault began, U.N. Secretary-General Kofi Annan had said that an invasion—lacking a new Security Council resolution to authorize it—would violate the U.N. charter. A year and a half after the invasion, during an interview with the BBC World Service that aired on September 15, 2004, he said: "I have indicated it was not in conformity with the U.N. charter. From our point of view and from the charter point of view it was illegal." (*Guardian*, September 16, 2004)

28. *Washington Post*, March 24, 2003.

29. *Baltimore Sun*, March 22, 2003.

30. Randeep Ramesh, ed., *The War We Could Not Stop: The Real Story of the Battle for Iraq* (London: Faber & Faber, 2003), p. 131.

31. Ibid., p. 132.

32. *New York Times*, November 17, 2003.

33. Ibid., April 30, 2004.

34. Ibid.

35. Walter Cronkite quoted in Hallin, *The "Uncensored War,"* p. 141.

36. Daniel Ellsberg, *Secrets: A Memoir of Vietnam and the Pentagon Papers* (New York: Viking, 2002), pp. 352–353.

37. Ibid., p. 353.

38. *60 Minutes*, CBS, September 30, 1990.

39. Admiral John Stufflebeem, January 25, 2002.

40. Donald Rumsfeld, *CBS Evening News*, March 8, 2002.

41. Chris Hedges, *What Every Person Should Know About War* (New York: Free Press, 2003), p. 7.

42. Barbara Ehrenreich's *Blood Rites: Origins and History of the Passions of War* (New York: Metropolitan Books, 1997) noted that "in World War I, 15 percent of the fatalities were civilians, with that proportion rising to 65 percent in World War II." The book added: "In the 'low-intensity' wars of the late 20th century—the wars of Ivory Coast, Somalia, Sudan, Liberia, East Timor, and the former Yugoslavia—civilians constitute 90 percent of the dead." (p. 227)

43. Denial about civilian deaths goes back a long way. On August 9, 1945, President Truman told the American public: "The world will note that the first atomic bomb was dropped on Hiroshima, a military base. That was because we wished in this first attack to avoid, insofar as possible, the killing of civilians." Actually, hundreds of thousands of civilians died—immediately or eventually—as a result of the atomic bombings of Hiroshima and Nagasaki.

44. *Boston Globe*, November 14, 2003.

45. *San Francisco Chronicle*, May 4, 2004.

46. *USA Today*, June 14, 2004.

47. For instance, as a matter of routine, "Names of the Dead" was the head-line that appeared in the *New York Times* on August 7, 2004, over a listing of three Marines whose deaths in Iraq had just been confirmed by the Pentagon.

48. *National Journal*, May 29, 2004, p. 1704.

49. "Mortality before and after the 2003 invasion of Iraq: cluster sample survey," *Lancet* 2004; 364: 1857–64. The study was published online October 29, 2004, and in print November 20, 2004.

50. George W. Bush, April 13, 2004. The French leader Charles de Gaulle wryly alluded to standard rhetorical evasions when he began a press conference this way: "Gentlemen, I am ready for the questions to my answers." (Leonard Roy Frank, ed., *Influencing Minds* [Portland, Ore.: Feral House, 1995], p. 98) Several decades later, in the category of truth spoken in jest, President George W. Bush referred to a common news-conference technique when he stopped himself during a reply and blurted out amid laughter from the White House press corps: "I'll ask myself a question. . . . It's an old trick." (October 11, 2001)

51. *Time*, April 19, 2004.

52. Associated Press, April 13, 2004.

53. George W. Bush, April 13, 2004.

54. Rahul Mahajan, news release, Institute for Public Accuracy, April 12, 2004.

55. Lieutenant General Bernard Trainor, *NewsHour with Jim Lehrer*, PBS, April 7, 2004.

56. *Time*, April 19, 2004.

57. Country Joe and the Fish, "I-Feel-Like-I'm-Fixin'-To-Die Rag," written in 1965 and released on a Vanguard recording in November 1967.

58. *New York Times*, April 14, 2004.

59. Ibid. Seven months later, when American troops returned to fight their way into Fallujah in mid-autumn, concerns about damage to the invaders' image were again prominent in the U.S. media. For instance, an above-the-fold news item on the front page of the *Wall Street Journal* (November 8, 2004) told readers: "The attack, expected since U.S. hesitation in the spring led to recriminations, is a bid to eradicate a nest of Iraqi and foreign fighters blamed for much of the terrorism that has enveloped the country. . . . But some worry of the blow to U.S. prestige if the civilian casualties are high."

60. Donald Rumsfeld, April 15, 2004.

61. *Guardian*, April 19, 2004.

62. *Washington Post*, April 30, 2004.

63. Ted Koppel quoted in *New York Times*, April 30, 2004.

64. Senator John McCain, May 1, 2004.

65. *San Francisco Chronicle*, May 8, 1999.

66. John Simpson, *Sunday Telegraph*, May 9, 1999.

67. "A cluster bomb can deliver from three to more than a thousand fragmentation bombs through a single mechanism," Chris Hedges wrote in *What Every Person Should Know About War* (p. 55). "The carrier missile is launched

by cannon or mortar, or as a rocket or an airplane bomb. While still in the air, the carrier releases its payload of bombs, which then separate and explode. A single cluster bomb can cover 50,000 square meters (more than two football fields square) with antipersonnel fragments. Cluster weapons provide saturation fire across a wide ground area. They are the tactical equivalent of short-range nuclear weapons."

68. "Action Alert: TV Not Concerned by Cluster Bombs, DU: 'That's Just the Way Life Is in Iraq,'" FAIR, May 6, 2003.

69. Ibid. While coverage of cluster bombs was very scant, the network evening news programs did even worse on DU reportage. "Since the beginning of the year," FAIR discovered, "the words 'depleted uranium' have not been uttered once on ABC *World News Tonight*, *CBS Evening News*, or *NBC Nightly News*, according to Nexis."

70. *National Journal*, May 29, 2004, p. 1704.

71. Ibid., p. 1705.

72. Senator John Warner, *Larry King Weekend*, CNN, October 7, 2001.

73. Jim Jennings, news release, Institute for Public Accuracy, October 8, 2001.

74. *New York Times*, October 8, 2001.

75. Jonathan Patrick quoted in *Irish Examiner*, October 10, 2001.

76. Médecins Sans Frontières, press release (Islamabad), October 8, 2001.

Chapter 15: Our Soldiers Are Heroes, Theirs Are Inhuman

1. Daniel C. Hallin, *The "Uncensored War": The Media and Vietnam* (Berkeley: University of California Press, 1989), p. 148.

2. Ibid., p. 158.

3. NBC, February 9, 1966; quoted in Hallin, *The "Uncensored War,"* p. 138.

4. CBS, February 10, 1966; quoted in Hallin, *The "Uncensored War,"* p. 138.

5. Hallin, *The "Uncensored War,"* p. 180.

6. Ibid., p. 176.

7. For discussion of how Nixon's Vietnamization approach played to broad concerns of the American public, see ibid., p. 182.

8. Jimmy Carter, March 24, 1977.

9. CNN, March 29, 2003.

10. Chris Hedges, *War Is a Force That Gives Us Meaning* (New York: Anchor Books, 2003), pp. 13–14.

11. *Washington Post*, March 25, 2003.

12. *New York Times*, March 25, 2003.

13. Associated Press, March 25, 2003.

14. Ibid.

15. *Baltimore Sun*, March 26, 2003.

16. Wade Goodwyn, *Morning Edition*, NPR, March 27, 2003.

17. Tom Brokaw, *NBC Nightly News*, April 2, 2003.

18. Kerry Sanders, *NBC Nightly News*, April 2, 2003.

19. BBC, May 18, 2003; see also *Atlanta Journal-Constitution*, May 17, 2003.

20. The assistant secretary of defense for public affairs, Victoria Clarke, responded to Robert Scheer's column that had appeared in the *Los Angeles Times* on May 20, 2003. The newspaper published her letter on May 26.

21. *Washington Post*, April 3, 2003.

22. General Vincent Brooks, *NewsHour with Jim Lehrer*, April 2, 2003.

23. BBC, May 18, 2003.

24. For background on the Pentagon's PR blitz about Jessica Lynch, see a *Guardian* article (May 15, 2003) by John Kampfner, who worked on the BBC's special report.

25. Robert Scheer, *Los Angeles Times*, May 29, 2003.

26. *Primetime Live*, ABC, November 11, 2003.

27. Rick Bragg, *I Am a Soldier, Too* (New York: Alfred A. Knopf, 2003), p. 198.

Chapter 16: America Needs the Resolve to Kick the "Vietnam Syndrome"

1. President George H. W. Bush, quoted by Howard Zinn, *Progressive* magazine, October 2002.

2. George H. W. Bush, *National Journal*, May 29, 2004, p. 1702.

3. A. J. Muste observed several decades ago: "The problem after a war is with the victor. He thinks he has just proved that war and violence pay. Who will now teach him a lesson?" (Quoted in Noam Chomsky, *The New Military Humanism* [Monroe, Maine: Common Courage Press, 1999], p. 10) It's important for leaders who have just proved that their violence can prevail to claim that war is their least favorite option, to be arrived at with great reluctance. In this way, efforts to spin a recent war are also helpful in laying the groundwork for the next one. "This nation is very reluctant to use military force," President George W. Bush said on October 28, 2003. He insisted: "Military action is the very last resort for us." A propaganda goal is to manage perceptions of the past to help maximize, in domestic political terms, the military options for the future.

4. Noam Chomsky, *Guardian* online, March 16, 2004.

5. Chris Hedges, *What Every Person Should Know About War* (New York: Free Press, 2003), p. 3. In *War Is a Force That Gives Us Meaning* (New York: Anchor Books, 2003), Hedges comments: "It is hard, maybe impossible, to fight a war if the cause is viewed as bankrupt. The sanctity of the cause is crucial to the war effort. The state spends tremendous time protecting, explaining, and promoting the cause. And some of the most important cheerleaders of the cause are the reporters." (p. 146)

6. President Richard Nixon quoted in Sidney Lens, *The Forging of the American Empire* (Sterling, Va.: Pluto Press, 2003), p. 428.

7. I. F. Stone, *Polemics and Prophecies, 1967–1970* (New York: Vintage Books, 1972), p. 139.

8. Ibid., p. 141.

9. *Wall Street Journal*, April 19, 2004.

10. General John Abizaid quoted in *Wall Street Journal*, April 19, 2004.

11. From 1969 to 1972 "American bombing . . . accelerated, three and a half million tons being dropped on Vietnam in the same three years—more than in

the five Johnson years combined." (Lens, *The Forging of the American Empire*, p. 429)

12. *Wall Street Journal*, April 19, 2004.

13. Thirteen months into the occupation, a *Wall Street Journal* news story (May 7, 2004) quoted a "Pentagon consultant," recently back from Iraq, who said: "We are not going to build a Jeffersonian democracy throughout Iraq. What we have to do is put an Iraqi face on security." The same day, a *New York Times* headline at the top of the front page said: "U.S. Forces Move on Outskirts of Najaf, Installing a Governor." The story's language was unabashed: "American forces on Thursday captured the governor's office on the outskirts of the holy city of Najaf and quickly installed a new Iraqi leader there. . . . As American troops secured the governor's office, L. Paul Bremer III, the top American administrator in Iraq, announced the appointment of the new governor, Adnan al-Zurufi, and promised the restoration of American-backed authority in Najaf." (*New York Times*, May 7, 2004)

14. William Greider, *Nation*, May 3, 2004.

15. *USA Today*, April 29, 2004.

16. Reporting on an internal U.S. Army study of the Iraq war, the *Los Angeles Times* (July 3, 2004) recounted: "As the Iraqi regime was collapsing on April 9, 2003, Marines converged on Firdos Square in central Baghdad, site of an enormous statue of Saddam Hussein. It was a Marine colonel—not joyous Iraqi civilians, as was widely assumed from the TV images—who decided to topple the statue, the Army report said. And it was a quick-thinking Army psychological operations team that made it appear to be a spontaneous Iraqi undertaking."

17. *New York Times*, April 5, 2004.

18. George Will, *Washington Post*, April 7, 2004.

19. *New York Times*, April 6, 2004.

20. Senator Chuck Hagel, April 27, 2004.

21. Quotations from Negroponte testimony, *Washington Post*, April 28, 2004, and transcription from tape.

22. During an April 25, 2004, interview on NPR's *Weekend Edition*, a former adviser to the Iraq occupation authority was pretty clear, if a bit understated, when asked about the Bush administration's concept of giving "limited sovereignty" to the Iraqi people. "The sovereign of the country is the power that has the last say," law professor Noah Feldman commented, "and you can't really have the last say in a country unless you command the army. So in a sense, you can't really claim to be sovereign if someone else runs your army."

23. George Orwell, *1984* (New York: Signet, 1981), pp. 175, 176, and 177.

24. *New York Times*, April 23, 2004.

25. Ibid.

26. From a U.S. media standpoint, the effort to gain acceptance of the self-rule label was largely successful. So, for example, six weeks after the designated transition, the front page of *USA Today* (August 12, 2004) mentioned in a matter-of-fact way that "sovereignty was returned to Iraqis on June 28."

27. "General Says He May Ask for More Troops," *New York Times*, April 24, 2004.

28. "Special National Security Estimate" quoted in Daniel C. Hallin, *The*

"Uncensored War": The Media and Vietnam (Berkeley: University of California Press, 1989), p. 60.

29. President Lyndon Johnson quoted in Hallin, *The "Uncensored War,"* p. 61.

30. General John Abizaid quoted in *New York Times*, April 24, 2004. Eleven days earlier, President Bush had held what was only his third prime-time news conference since moving into the White House, but there was nothing unusual about his rhetoric. During the session, which focused mostly on the Iraq war, he used the words "freedom" or "free" thirty-four times. Along the way, Bush sought to reinforce the common assumption that with well over a hundred thousand troops stationed in Iraq, they certainly couldn't leave now. Although it was far from his favorite format, the news conference—staged in hopes of halting a slide in popularity linked to the upspike of U.S. casualties in Iraq—did give the president an opportunity to spin out his flourishes and present his practiced lines at length. Later there was some criticism in the press, yet few journalists during the live broadcast did anything more than ask a mildly challenging question and then get out of the way as the president did his best to blow smoke. Buried in thousands of words, the contradictions were profuse. James Jennings, the president of Conscience International, had a long history of humanitarian aid work in Iraq, and his response to Bush's performance was acerbic: "Like the Mad Hatter in *Alice in Wonderland*, President Bush stood before the American people last night and tossed out numerous self-contradictory proclamations. Among them: 'We are not an imperial power,' yet the Iraq invasion was 'required by our interests.' 'We will restore sovereignty to the Iraqi people,' he said, but then again, 'We are not going to leave.' He stressed that one justification for the war was that the U.N. must mean what it says, implying that the U.N. authorized going to war, which it clearly didn't. We seek an Iraq, he said, that is 'independent and free.' He then proceeded to dictate Iraq's form of government, nature of its constitution, and elections schedule. Regarding Saddam, he said, 'He is a danger,' making one wonder if either the president thinks Saddam has escaped from prison or if he knows what the meaning of 'is' is. 'He refused to disarm,' the president intoned with a straight face, when in fact Iraq has been proved to be rather completely disarmed. 'My last choice is the use of military power,' the president said, then, 'Knowing what I know now about [Iraq's] weapons, I would still have gone into Iraq.'" (News release, Institute for Public Accuracy, April 14, 2004)

On May 4, 2004, when confirmation emerged that U.S. troop levels in Iraq would stay higher and longer in Iraq than previously stated, the news coverage was somewhat low-key. The *New York Times* reported the story the next day under the headline "U.S. Commander to Keep 135,000 Troops in Iraq Through 2005." Such headlines marked the success of efforts to portray the troop deployment decisions as implementation of military judgments rather than the results of political decisions made by elected officials subject to direct judgment from the electorate. "The commander of American forces in the Middle East, putting on hold the goal of reducing troops in Iraq, plans to keep at least 135,000 soldiers there through 2005, Pentagon and military officials said," the *Times* lead reported.

31. *Los Angeles Times*, July 18, 2003.

32. Lawrence DiRita quoted in *Los Angeles Times*, July 18, 2003.

33. Bill Keller, *New York Times*, June 14, 2003.

Chapter 17: Withdrawal Would Cripple U.S. Credibility

1. Hickenlooper-Kennan exchange quoted in Howard Zinn, *Vietnam: The Logic of Withdrawal* (Cambridge, Mass.: South End Press, 2002), p. 105.

2. *Time*, April 19, 2004.

3. Meanwhile, some who opposed the war in Iraq and questioned the occupation logic still gave much ground. "Even among harsh critics of the administration's Iraq policy, the usual view is that we have to finish the job," columnist Paul Krugman observed at the end of April 2004. "You've heard the arguments: We broke it; we bought it. We can't cut and run. We have to stay the course." Then the columnist added: "I understand the appeal of those arguments. But I'm worried about the arithmetic." The deteriorating security situation in Iraq augured badly: "we don't have remotely enough troops to turn the vicious circle around." (*New York Times*, April 30, 2004)

4. General John Abizaid quoted in *Wall Street Journal*, August 20, 2003.

5. *New York Times*, August 20, 2003.

6. Survey of editorials in major daily newspapers, *Boston Globe*, February 18, 1968.

7. *Wall Street Journal*, May 7, 2004.

8. Greg Mitchell's column noted that both the incumbent president and challenger John Kerry "seem to agree that sending more U.S. troops to Iraq might turn the tide. Most newspapers like that idea, too. Last month an *E&P* survey revealed that the vast majority of America's large newspapers favored this approach to Iraq: Stay the course." (*Editor & Publisher*, May 7, 2004)

9. Powell's statement appeared in a transcript released by the U.S. Department of State, September 12, 2003. He spoke in an interview with the French network TV2.

10. *New York Times*–CBS News nationwide poll, *New York Times*, April 29, 2004. The question was: "Do you think the United States made a mistake getting involved in the current war against Iraq, or not?" The "no opinion" responses were 6 percent in March 2003, 5 percent in April 2004.

11. *USA Today*, June 25, 2004. The same poll found: "For the first time, a majority also says that the war" in Iraq had made the United States "less safe from terrorism."

12. More than a year into the occupation, even independent presidential candidate Ralph Nader wasn't urging complete withdrawal in less than six months. It was the same length of time advocated by retired general William E. Odom, former director of the National Security Agency, whose dissident note got a hearing in a *Wall Street Journal* piece (April 28, 2004) that quoted him as saying: "We have failed. The issue is how high a price we're going to pay. . . . Less, by getting out sooner, or more, by getting out later?"

13. *New York Times*, April 28, 2004.

14. Larry Birns, news release, Institute for Public Accuracy, June 24, 2004.

15. *USA Today*, June 2, 2004.

16. *New York Times*, May 29, 2004.

17. Ibid.

18. Zinn, *Vietnam*, p. 61.

19. C. L. Sulzberger, *New York Times*, January 12, 1963; quoted in Daniel C. Hallin, *The "Uncensored War": The Media and Vietnam* (Berkeley: University of California Press, 1989), p. 37.

20. Hallin, *The "Uncensored War,"* p. 61. Through all the phases of the Vietnam War—and for that matter, during the Iraq war that began in spring 2003—a de facto rule of media thumb remained in effect along the lines of Hallin's observation that "the range of political discussion in the press is usually restricted to the policy alternatives being debated in Washington." (p. 99)

21. Senator Robert F. Kennedy quoted in Norman Solomon, *The Power of Babble* (New York: Dell, 1992), p. 76.

22. Katharine Graham, *Personal History* (New York: Vintage Books, 1997), p. 399.

23. Zinn, *Vietnam*, p. 7.

24. Terry Anderson, *Wall Street Journal*, April 14, 2004.

25. Ronald Bruce St. John, *Foreign Policy in Focus*, April 28, 2004.

26. *Newsweek*, April 19, 2004.

27. Ibid.

28. President Lyndon Johnson, speech to National Farmers Union in Minneapolis, March 18, 1968, quoted in I. F. Stone, *Polemics and Prophecies, 1967–1970* (New York: Vintage Books, 1972), p. 380.

29. *Newsweek*, April 19, 2004.

30. *Wall Street Journal*, April 21, 2004.

31. Writing for *Foreign Policy in Focus* (April 28, 2004), Ronald Bruce St. John commented: "Throughout the Vietnam War, especially in the early years, American officials deliberately misrepresented the enemy. Vietnamese nationalists were ignored with all opposition labeled Communist or with the delightfully pejorative phrase 'Viet Cong.' In Iraq, the Bush administration has once again written nationalists out of the script. Insurgents are variously labeled 'dead-enders,' 'fanatics,' 'thugs,' 'militants,' 'terrorists,' or 'outsiders,' despite growing evidence that a large percentage of the Iraqi people are opposed to the U.S. occupation. Recent intelligence reports suggest that support for the insurgents is widespread and growing."

32. George Will, *Washington Post*, April 7, 2004. Like some other pundits who'd been strongly supporting the war, George Will became increasingly agitated about its difficulties as spring 2004 unfolded. When mobilized, the Pentagon's iron fist is supposed to succeed without major ambiguity.

33. Scott McClellan, White House briefing, April 6, 2004.

34. *New York Times*, April 8, 2004.

On the same day that Rumsfeld described the struggle as "a test of will," the PBS *NewsHour* (April 7, 2004) supplied viewers with an exhaustively narrow array of perspectives on the war. The point of view was through American gun sights; the range of touted policy choices was similarly narrow. At the top of the hour, the program's host, Jim Lehrer, summarized the coverage to come: there would be an account from a *Los Angeles Times* reporter embedded with U.S. Marines in Fallujah—from the perspective of American troops—plus, in the anchor's words, "excerpts from today's briefing by Defense Secretary Rumsfeld and Joint Chiefs chairman Myers, and a look at the options with four former U.S. military officers."

That "look at the options with four former U.S. military officers" turned out to be a session about tactical trade-offs, moderated by Lehrer, who provided such questions as:

- "Is there a way for U.S. forces to quickly end this violence?"
- "Are the U.S. forces going about this whole operation in the right way?"
- ". . . the decision of the U.S. leadership that we could not sit back and let those four Americans be killed and their bodies be mutilated in such a way. We had to take action, correct?"

While battles raged in close to a dozen Iraqi cities, a retired U.S. Air Force colonel referred to the American authorities' closure of a newspaper that had served as a megaphone for the antioccupation Shiite leader Moktada al-Sadr. "The immediate problem we have to remember is we started this . . . with the aggressive policies towards Sadr that came from us, shutting down his press," Colonel Sam Gardiner said. The program's anchor spoke next.

> *Lehrer*: "The reason we shut down his press is because it was calling for violence and anti-American—"
>
> *Colonel Gardiner*: "Sure."
>
> *Lehrer*: "I just want to get that on the record."

But Lehrer's comment—ostensibly setting the record straight about what had precipitated the U.S. occupation authorities' closure of Sadr's newspaper— was in sharp contrast to the factual record, as noted in a *New York Times* news account two days earlier reporting that "the paper did not print any calls for attacks." (A different article in the same edition of the *Times* reported: "American officials said Mr. Bremer had acted because of inaccurate reporting in the paper that incited hatred for the Americans, including a February dispatch that an explosion that killed more than 50 Iraqi police recruits was not a car bomb, as occupation officials had said, but an American missile.")

On April 12, 2004, I contacted the *NewsHour* and asked whether Lehrer's statement had been based on information contrary to what was reported in the April 5 edition of the *Times*. If so, I asked for any citation that backed up his assertion. Or, if Lehrer did not have such a citation, I asked if there were plans for an on-air correction to set the factual record straight on the program. In reply to my inquiry, a *NewsHour* spokesperson cited two articles: A *Chicago Tribune* piece, dated April 5, said that "the pro-Sadr newspaper *Al Hawza* was shut down . . . for allegedly printing false information that incited violence against the coalition." And an April 6 *New York Times* piece said that the Sadr newspaper "was closed last week after American authorities accused it of printing lies that incited violence." The *NewsHour* spokesperson, Lete Childs, told me: "I hope these two articles help you understand the citations for Jim Lehrer's statement to Colonel Gardiner." But the two articles that the *NewsHour* cited only seemed to underscore the disconnect. Apparently the *NewsHour* staff hadn't been able to find a single source to back up Lehrer's on-air statement that "the reason we shut down his press is because it was calling for violence." And the *NewsHour* did not provide any explanation for why, in sharp contrast to the flat-out report in the *New York Times* that "the paper did not print any calls for attacks," Lehrer had gone on the air and claimed that it did. I reached the reporter in Baghdad who'd written the *Chicago Tribune* article, Vincent Schodolski, and asked if he was aware of any evidence that the American authorities shut down *Al Hawza* because it was "calling for violence." Schodolski replied: "I have no other citations than the reasons given by the CPA itself." My search of the official Web site for the Coalition Provisional Authority, the U.S.–led occupation authority in Iraq, turned up briefings and news releases with references to Sadr's newspaper—but no backup for what Lehrer had said on the air. At a March 30 press conference, Dan Senor of the CPA had charged that *Al Hawza* had tried to "incite violence." That was very much in keeping with what the April 5 *New York Times* reported—that while "the American authorities said false reporting, including articles that ascribed suicide bombings to Americans, could touch off violence," nevertheless "the paper did not print any calls for attacks."

At a pivotal moment in the escalation of the war, the episode was a case study of an influential TV news outlet contributing to U.S. government spin instead of scrutinizing it. The anchor of public television's main news program went out of his way to say he wanted to "get that on the record," and many of the nearly three million viewers were apt to assume that the information was accurate.

I received a response from the *NewsHour* two days after my inquiry: "*The NewsHour with Jim Lehrer* stands behind the 'Iraq: What Now?' discussion segment from April 7 and will not be making a correction." But after a flood of viewer inquiries followed an "Action Alert" put out by the media watch group FAIR (where I'm an associate), the *NewsHour* did finally make a correction. At the end of the *NewsHour*'s April 26 broadcast, Jim Lehrer read this statement on the air: "On our April 7 broadcast I made a mistake while running a discussion about Iraq. The issue was why the U.S. had closed down a particular newspaper. In an attempt to clarify what a guest had said, I stated it was because the paper had called for violence against Americans. I should have said, that was the reason given by the coalition, that those running the paper strongly deny it. I regret my mistake."

Unfortunately, Lehrer's correction—while an improvement over his initial statement—was also in need of a correction, and this time there was none. What Lehrer now claimed the Coalition Provisional Authority had alleged, it actually had stopped short of asserting. At a March 30 news conference, CPA spokesperson Dan Senor said that the *Al Hawza* newspaper "repeatedly uses rhetoric designed to incite violence against U.S. soldiers and against the Iraqi people." To Lehrer, evidently, that seemed to be the equivalent of the CPA saying that *Al Hawza* "had called for violence against Americans." The inability or unwillingness of journalist Lehrer to make the distinction was striking. Oh well . . . it was just history in the making.

35. President George W. Bush, April 13, 2004.
36. Paul Krugman, *New York Times*, April 16, 2004.

37. James Baldwin, *No Name in the Street* (New York: Dial Press, 1972), p. 188.

Afterword

1. Lyrics to "An Untitled Protest" (1968) by Country Joe McDonald, performed by Country Joe and the Fish.

2. *King Lear*, act 4, scene 1.

3. Hermann Goering made the statement to G. M. Gilbert, a psychologist who interviewed him in prison during the Nuremberg war-crimes tribunal, April 18, 1946. (G. M. Gilbert, *Nuremberg Diary* [New York: Signet, 1961], pp. 255–256)

4. Daniel Ellsberg, memo, Truth-Telling Project, April 29, 2004.

5. Daniel Ellsberg, *Secrets: A Memoir of Vietnam and the Pentagon Papers* (New York: Viking, 2002), p. 275.

6. Daniel C. Hallin, *The "Uncensored War": The Media and Vietnam* (Berkeley: University of California Press, 1989), p. vii.

7. Paul Krugman, *New York Times*, April 16, 2004.

8. Michael Herr, *Dispatches* (New York: Vintage International, 1977), p. 71.

9. Voltaire, *Collection of Letters on the Miracles*; both versions quoted in George Seldes, ed., *The Great Thoughts* (New York: Ballantine, 1996), p. 480.

Acknowledgments

This book had a long incubation period. Four decades ago, midway through my teenage years, I began to wonder about war coverage that I was reading at the breakfast table and seeing on the nightly news. Since then I've learned from countless people who took risks by asking difficult questions and struggling to provide better answers.

The staff of the media watch group Fairness & Accuracy In Reporting (FAIR) has been a vital source of information, analysis, and inspiration.

My colleagues at the Institute for Public Accuracy have shared their skills, insights, and spirits. Special thanks to Hollie Ainbinder, Sam Husseini, Cynthia Skow, Zeynep Toufe, and David Zupan.

Thanks also to James Abourezk, Medea Benjamin, Jeff Cohen, Diana Cohn, Mike Dolny, Daniel Ellsberg, Reese Erlich, Beau Friedlander, Denis Halliday, Jim Jennings, Kathy Kei, Kathy Kelly, Peggy Law, Martin Lee, Paul Loeb, Maisa Mendonca, Sean Penn, Steve Rhodes, Jennifer Warburg, and many others.

My parents, Miriam and Morris Solomon, have persevered with love and uplifting values that I will always cherish.

As usual, my literary agent, Laura Gross, was steadily encouraging and wise throughout the process that made this book a reality. Beginning with the first wisp of an idea, she cheerfully found ways to keep moving forward.

At John Wiley & Sons, senior editor Eric Nelson warmly and deftly guided this book through all its stages to completion. At critical junctures he greatly improved the manuscript and kept the book on track; his support from the outset made it possible. I also want to acknowledge the swift clarity of assistance from Wiley senior production editor John Simko and the labors of copy editor William Drennan.

Invaluable editing help came from Craig Comstock.

Of course, any flaws in the book are entirely my own doing.

From Cheryl Higgins, extensive research and discerning judgment were enormously important while I wrote this book. She dug deeply into history and exhumed many gems. And her love has sustained me beyond words or measure.

Index